Erasure and Tuscarora Resilience in Colonial North Carolina

Haudenosaunee and Indigenous Worlds
Philip P. Arnold and Scott Manning Stevens, *Series Editors*

Select Titles in Haudenosaunee and Indigenous Worlds

The Urgency of Indigenous Values
  Philip P. Arnold

———————————————

For a full list of titles in this series,
visit: https://press.syr.edu/supressbook-series
/haudenosaunee-and-indigenous-worlds/

ERASURE & TUSCARORA RESILIENCE

in Colonial North Carolina

David La Vere

Syracuse University Press

Quotes taken from historical documents in the collections of the State Archives of North Carolina and presented in this work are courtesy of the State Archives of North Carolina.

Copyright © 2024 by Syracuse University Press
Syracuse, New York 13244-5290

All Rights Reserved

First Edition 2024

24 25 26 27 28 29   6 5 4 3 2 1

∞ The paper used in this publication meets the minimum requirements
of the American National Standard for Information Sciences—Permanence of Paper
for Printed Library Materials, ANSI Z39.48-1992.

For a listing of books published and distributed by Syracuse University Press,
visit https://press.syr.edu.

ISBN: 9780815638353 (hardcover)
        9780815638360 (paperback)
        9780815657064 (e-book)

Library of Congress Cataloging in Publication Control Number:
2023043548

Manufactured in the United States of America

For Jensyn Zimmerman, Beauden Pynch, and Cooper Pynch

Contents

Maps and Illustrations

Maps

Illustrations

Acknowledgments

This book has been a long time in the making, not only from research but also from the disruptions caused by the COVID epidemic. Still, work chugged on, and through the assistance of numerous people the manuscript became a reality. First and foremost, I recognize, thank, and appreciate all the Native peoples of eastern North Carolina, those past and present, federally recognized, and state recognized and even those who are not "recognized" by any government but who know they are or are descendants of Indian peoples. I am fascinated by their societies and have tried to bring their rich history to light. I am indebted to and appreciative of them. Personal Native acquaintances, such as Arwin Smallwood (Tuscarora), Marvin "Marty" Richardson (Haliwa-Saponi), Nancy Strickland Fields (Lumbee), and Lovell Pierce (Waccamaw Siouan/Tuscarora), helped me develop better questions and provided insights about what I was studying and writing about.

The University of North Carolina Wilmington, my work home for decades, has always been encouraging about my research. Some of this help was monetary with a Moseley Award from the Department of History. Just as important were my colleagues and friends in the History Department, whom I could turn to for ideas, opinions, and support. My thanks go to Lynn Mollenauer, our department chair, who always supported my research habit. Warm regards also go to Professors Emeritus Alan Watson and Chris Fonvielle as well as to active colleagues Mark Spaulding, David Houpt, and Kris Ray. The real heroes are up in the front office with Meaghan Wright and Andrea Massey.

In the history profession itself, many people lent a hand, in particular the staff at the State Archives of North Carolina in Raleigh. I spent many a day there, and I want to give a shout-out to Gay Bradley, William Brown, Doug Brown, Katherine Crickmore, Vann Evans, Erin Fulp, Josh Hager, Lauren McCoy, Dominique Romero, Alison Thurman, and Lea Tiernan. They pointed me in the right direction and then lugged out, always with good humor, large folios and bundles of documents for me to study. Quotes taken from historical documents and presented in this work are courtesy of the State Archives of North Carolina. Many historians are also doing excellent work on colonial eastern North Carolina, some of them focusing on Native North Carolinians. Their work has informed my own and corrected my mistakes. I am much impressed with their scholarship. They include Lars Adams, Jonathan Barth, Baylus Brooks, John Byrd, Shannon Dawdy, Bradley Dixon, Stephen Feeley, Brandon Fullam, Stephanie Gamble, Pat Garrow, Lesley Graybeal, Forest Hazel, Charles Heath, Marvin Jones, Michelle LeMaster, Malinda Maynor Lowery, Kianga Lucas, Seth Mallios, Noeleen McIlvenna, Warren Milteer Jr., Christopher Oakley, Doug Patterson, Helen Rountree, Rebecca Seaman, Arwin Smallwood, and Wesley Taukchiray. Many of them I have never met in person, but I know and respect their work. I hope they will allow me to stand in their company. If I have left out anyone, please know the oversight was not intentional. Along these lines, I appreciate greatly the incisive comments and corrections the evaluators of this manuscript have provided. And thanks to David Norris for the maps.

Friends helped by putting up with the constant talk about the workings of the book. Much gratitude and friendship go to Jake Sulzbach in Houston, Kevin Sands down in Carolina Beach, Bob and Annis Ross up on Panther Point, Dan and Debbie Venegas in West Texas, Dan and Cindy Jones in Nashville, Andrew Duppstadt in Kinston, Lyn and Mick Dorman and Edie and Ted Morrison in Adrian, Michigan, and Adán Medrano in Houston.

Of course, it is family that really gives the needed support and understanding. When you are digging for that last bit of evidence, or when the words will not come, they are as supportive as ever. In all my ramblings about North Carolina history, I never once saw them roll their eyes, though I'm sure they struggled not to. Right up front come the grandchildren, who have been a great source of love and entertainment and always a welcome break from writing. Watching them grow up has given me an even greater awareness of history and change over time: Mycah and Jensyn Zimmerman and their parents, Jordyn and Mark Zimmerman; Beauden and Cooper Pynch and their parents, Charles and Annie Pynch. I also thank my sister Rhonda, sister Tracy, and sister-in-law Karen Ryan. I want to remember my parents, Dick and Ann La Vere, and my grandmother, Sara Osborne. They crop up in my thoughts constantly. Then there are my in-laws, Jack and Carol Mills, who are the greatest and welcomed me into the family with open arms, as did my sister-in-law Barb Courtney, niece Alyson, and nephew Travis and my other sister-in-law, Teresa Mills, niece Jamie, and nephew Jack. Of course, I could have done none of this without the support from my wife, Caryn. Love you, Sweetie!

Erasure and Tuscarora Resilience in Colonial North Carolina

Introduction

English overseas colonization proved a hot topic among London thinkers during the last decades of the sixteenth century. These advocates gave much thought to what the shape of English colonization should be. Though they did not put it in those terms, men such as Richard Hakluyt, a strong proponent of overseas expansion, debated whether England should develop nonsettler colonies or settler colonies. Some pushed for a small English footprint on foreign shores. An investor such as Sir Walter Raleigh or a joint-stock company such as the Virginia Company would establish a trading post, exchange goods with the Native peoples for valuable resources, then funnel these resources back to England and so create wealth for the investors, queen, and country. Others advocated for a more robust colony, one in which English men, women, and children would be transplanted to a foreign region—so comes our word *plantation*—where they would farm, fish, trade, and direct resources back to England, all while peacefully Christianizing the Native peoples and creating a bit of old England in foreign lands. No matter the type of colony, each would require good relations with the Native people as their cooperation would be essential to either colony's success. The English would not be harsh masters, they promised, not like the Spanish, who conquered and enslaved and so gave rise to the English Black Legend about Spanish atrocities in the Americas.[1]

England tried both ideas in early North Carolina, but English colonies became much more than just trading posts or small plantations, and relations with the Native peoples went far beyond just trade or spreading the Gospel. In North Carolina and elsewhere,

1

English colonizers imposed themselves on an area, claimed an already populated region for the queen, and so appropriated Native land. When the Native peoples resisted, often with violence, the English responded with violence of their own, which usually resulted in a defeat of the Native people. From that point, the English set up a top-down colonial government in which an English governor carried out English laws and turned Native peoples into tributary-paying vassals—"tributaries," as they were called by the English—and their governments into vassal states. Over the course of the British Empire, virtually all colonies underwent this process in which independent peoples and Native states were turned into tributaries, while colonies became political and economic supporters of the mother country. This could be a brutal process, and Native peoples suffered much as second-class citizens within their own country.

Some of these English colonies became nonsettler colonies, as in India, Egypt, Nigeria, and other places. Few English settlers went there to farm or wrest land from the Native peoples. Most English people in nonsettler colonies were company men, government officials, soldiers, missionaries, and their families. Native peoples continued to make up most of the population, while Native rulers and Native states became tributaries to the English or company government. Other places, such as South Africa, Australia, New Zealand, the Caribbean islands, and the thirteen American colonies, including North Carolina, became settler colonies. Settler colonies utilized the same colonization process as nonsettler ones but also experienced a massive flood of English or non-Native immigration.

Native peoples experienced war, conquest, tributary status, the imposition of English government and culture in both nonsettler and settler colonies. However, it was the influx of the non-Native population that added a new dynamic and complexity to the colony's relationship with the Native peoples. Settlers brought their own concepts of what society should be and how land should be used, and they differed mightily from the native vision. The English wanted land, and it came at the expense of the Indians in the American colonies. In North Carolina by the early 1700s, Indian peoples along the Coastal

Plain, such as the Iroquoian-speaking Tuscaroras, Meherrins, Cores, Neuse, and White Oak River Indians as well as the Algonquian-speaking Chowans, Hatteras, Yeopims, Pamlicos, and Machapungas, found themselves hemmed in, unable to hunt and farm as they always had, often losing their hunting quarters and most productive lands to British newcomers. Land conflicts caused some of the most violent colonial wars, which in turn created Indian tributaries, meaning defeated Native nations were now aligned with the colony and forced to pay a nominal tribute to show their subservient status. To resolve the land issues between the English and Indians and preserve some means of support for those Native peoples, victorious colonial governments usually assigned their tributaries to a bounded reserve of land. Outside of the reserve, all remaining lands belonged to the English monarch or, in the case of North Carolina, to the Lords Proprietors, who planned to sell the lands for profit. For the colonial governments, a happy result of the colonization process would have been compliant and peaceful Native tributaries living on their own small bits of land, causing no troubles, but serving as military allies who would guard the colony's settlements, trade clients, and potential workers. However, the coming of European settlers and enslaved Africans to eastern North Carolina created a whole new set of challenges for the Native Carolinians, including military defeat and conquest.

The Tuscarora War of 1711–15 turned most Indians of eastern North Carolina into English tributaries. By 1715, the Tuscaroras, Cores, Chowans, Meherrins, Hatteras, Yeopims, Machapungas, and other North Carolina Indians had been militarily defeated or sufficiently threatened to accept the tributary status forced upon them. They took up residence in assigned land reserves ranging in size from a few hundred acres to more than 40,000 acres. Here they could live life as they chose with little interference from colonial authorities as long as they caused no mischief. Now the colonization process began in earnest with all its intended and unintended consequences. Tributary Indian leaders would have to be approved by the North Carolina governor, who would also handle their diplomatic affairs. Violence against the colony and settlers was forbidden; complaints would be brought to the government and adjudicated according to English law. As a sign of their vassal status, each eastern North Carolina Indian nation would have to pay an annual symbolic tribute of a few deer hides, arrowheads, or peppercorns.

England's Indian tributaries and their place within the thirteen colonies and British Empire have come under the gaze of historians. For some, tributary status and land reserves were colonial attempts to protect Indians from the influx of settlers around them and the abuses aimed at Indians. Historian Wesley Frank Craven stated as much, believing that the English colonists made "sincere and persistent efforts . . . to deal humanely and fairly with the Indian."[2] Others have seen tributary status as an attempt to fleece the Indians while making them do the bidding of colonial interests as allies, trade clients, and workers. Or was tributary status just war of a passive nature, with the colonies not so much seeing the tributaries as allies but merely as a potentially hostile people who needed to be kept under control?[3] I would argue that after the Tuscarora War the North Carolina government saw tributary status and land reserves as a way to control possible enemies but also to protect them from avaricious and abusive settlers. This approach stemmed not so much from a paternal desire to protect the Indians but from the fear that injustice toward them would spark another bloody conflict worse than the Tuscarora War. However, once that fear faded over time, Native tributaries found their status diminished and their complaints taken less seriously by the colonial government.

Another theme historians have examined is just how much autonomy and freedom these Indian tributaries possessed. On one hand, colonial governments demanded symbolic tribute, commanded obedience, could enclose tributaries on reserves, and oversaw the election of Indian leaders, while tributary Indians had to accept English dominance. Tributary Indians were under the thumb of the colonial government, at least in theory and to a degree. However, tributaries possessed certain rights and privileges, and they understood they were a part of the British Empire and saw their relationship more in diplomatic than vassalage terms. Indian leaders often addressed colonial officials as "Brother," a sign of equality. In North Carolina, tributaries such as the Tuscaroras learned their rights and exercised them, often petitioning the colonial governor and the Governor's Council for protection, support, and redress.[4]

As tributaries and subjects of the king, they were guaranteed bounded lands; self-government within limits; rights to peacefully trade, hunt, and farm; a hearing of their grievances by the governor himself or by the Governor's Council; and protection from the deceptions and assaults of White settlers. Native leaders demanded the colonial government adhere to all these rights. Some colonial tributary kings became formidable politicians and diplomats who learned how to manipulate the English, such as Cockacoeske, "queen of the Pamunkey" in Virginia during the 1670s, and King Hagler of the Catawbas in South Carolina in the 1750s.[5] The first three decades after the Tuscarora War saw the rise of a particularly accomplished North Carolina Indian tributary chief in King Tom Blount of the Tuscaroras, who knew how to work the tributary system to his people's favor.

It was King Blount, as leader of the far larger Tuscaroras, who became the most influential tributary chief in North Carolina and more than proved himself the political equal of colonial governors, military commanders, White settlers, Seneca diplomats, and Indian rivals. A wily politician and deft diplomat, King Blount possessed a firm grasp of North Carolina colonial politics and used that to protect his Tuscaroras and fend off intrusions onto his people's "sovereignty"—as much as a tributary could be sovereign, that is. He constantly defended the integrity of the Tuscarora Indian Woods reserve in Bertie County, all while providing a stable and protective leadership for his people.

However, tributary leaders could not protect their people from the consequences of the colonization process that dramatically changed their world. Indian tributaries desperately tried to maintain traditional ways. As long as they lived, Blount and his captains led raids against old enemies such as the Occaneechis, Saponis, and Catawbas. Nevertheless, their rights were narrowed, and they were circumscribed in where they could go, limited in their legal rights even as subjects of the English monarch, and exposed to a plethora of English customs, goods, laws, and settler culture. New forms of government had to be navigated; new manufactured goods had to be incorporated. New forms of work came about, as did new relationships with their White and Black neighbors, all while illness, alcohol, violence, and colonial policies took their toll. Some Indians abandoned their reserves to live as individuals within the colony; some left North Carolina altogether, most of them heading north to join the Iroquois Haudenosaunee in the colony of New York; others hid out and laid low in the Carolina swamps; while some drifted away and incorporated themselves into settler society, sometimes as White, sometimes as Black, depending on the shade of their skin. As the eighteenth century progressed, and as King Blount and other kings passed from the scene, lesser leaders could keep the resistance going only so long. Declining Indian populations amid surging settler and slave numbers overwhelmed the tributary Indians. Worse, the Indian land reserves caught the eye of settlers and land speculators.

Even before the Tuscarora War, some Indians, seeing their traditional lands flooded by settlers, asked the colonial government for a bounded reserve to protect what lands they had left. For the English, the reserves were ways to provide Indians with lands separate from those available for settlers as well as means to regulate Indian interactions with settlers to ensure security to the colony. Reserves would make for an "orderly frontier" as they would be placed in strategic locations so that the tributaries would serve as guardians against hostile Indians raiding into the settlements.[6] Surveyed with defined and recorded boundaries, these lands constituted Indian homelands and centers of their community. The reserves also made the Indian nations large landowners in a region where land ownership was important. It gave them leverage with the colonial authorities and settlers. Although the colonial government intended for the reserves to regulate contacts among Indians, settlers, and the enslaved, various interactions did take place, and each people influenced their neighbors.

Under the skilled political abilities of a leader such as King Tom Blount, a reserve became an Indian country of its own where Indians could force some accommodation. Historian Richard White's masterpiece *The Middle Ground* (1991) shows how the Indians of the Great Lakes and the French in Canada compromised, with the French adapting to some Indian customs and Indians adapting to some French ones, and so created a "middle ground" of understanding and profitable economic ties.[7] Historian Kathleen DuVal found that the Indian peoples of the Arkansas River Valley were powerful enough to not have to compromise with the Spanish or French and so could force those Europeans to dance to their tune.[8] King Blount, as the leader of the Tuscaroras, the most populous Indian peoples in eastern North Carolina and with the largest reserve, could sometimes do both. A tributary by nature had to compromise with the colonial government and create a middle ground of understanding. But so did North Carolina officials have to compromise with Blount. The constant fear of another war or that, if pushed, Blount might ally with the Iroquois Haudenosaunee and make war on the colony ensured that colonial authorities gave him and his people justice or at least the benefit of the doubt. Blount became the master of using colonial fears to his people's benefit.

The reserves served as physical areas where Indians could farm, hunt, and live as they wanted, somewhat protected from surrounding settlers. For many Indians, the reserves took on the sacredness of a land where the bones of their ancestors were buried and familiar spirits walked. It was the last bit of sovereign ground where they could be Tuscaroras, Chowans, or Machapungas. The lands also provided a means, often controversial among Indians themselves, to raise money for a people who found themselves falling into poverty. By the mid-eighteenth century, North Carolina tributaries found their lands under assault from settlers, squatters, and legal chicanery. In other instances, Indian nations leased or sold portions of their reserve. North Carolina was not a singular example as most Native peoples across what would become the United States had to fight hard to protect their lands and often could not. Nevertheless, these reserves were Indian country, and in North Carolina they became closely associated with a Native identity. Indians lived on Indian reserves.

This is an important point as on their reserves Indians formed a government that was recognized by the colony and settlers. The colonial government saw them as Indians, a nation—tributaries to be sure, but with certain rights. As the historian Winthrop Jordan points out, "Indians could retain the quality of nationality, a quality which Englishmen admired in themselves and respected in other peoples. Under contrasting circumstances in America, the Negro nations tended to become Negro people."[9] This relationship between land and identity raised the important question: What would happen when Indians did not have their land reserves or a recognized government anymore? Without Indian lands, then Native peoples did not have a government. Without lands and government, then, as North Carolina and its White settlers saw it, Indians were now more like the Africans in the colonies, at best free People of Color and not really Indians at all. Erasure. It is here that we see the Native people of North Carolina and the American South as a whole enduring a colonization experience of erasure often different from that of Indians in other regions. What made it so was that alongside that influx of English settlers was an equally large flood of enslaved Africans at a time when Indian population numbers were falling.

It is unclear how many Indian people inhabited North Carolina in the 1500s, when Indians and Europeans made first contact. Giovanni da Verrazzano saw crowds of Native peoples in 1524. Sixty years later, in the 1580s, English explorers along the Albemarle and Pamlico Sounds reported scores of densely populated towns, often with hundreds of residents. Even the Piedmont and the mountains possessed large Indian populations. The demographer Henry Dobyns calculates that the Coastal Plain from Florida to Massachusetts might have housed 2.2 million Native people at about 1500.[10] Just the thin strip of North Carolina coast alone held thousands. The inland Tuscaroras at 1500 may have boasted as many as 25,000, while the Cherokees in the mountain at this time numbered even more, possibly 30,000 people, in general estimates.[11]

However, almost from the very first meeting with Europeans, Native peoples began to die off from illness as well as from colonial actions and policies. Conversely, both the European settler population and the enslaved African population in North Carolina grew exponentially. By 1730, the White population of North Carolina was about 35,000, the African population at 6,000, and the Indian population in eastern North Carolina more or less around 2,000. As White settlers and enslaved Africans surrounded the Indian reserves, Indians made relationships with both Europeans and Africans, sometimes intimate, sexual relationships. Out of these connections were born biracial and bicultural children, and the concept of "race" became ever more significant in North Carolina. As skin color became increasingly important, with White supremacy and Black African slavery growing ever more extensive, it was not long before the Indians' White neighbors began seeing them more generally as "People of Color" than specifically as Indians, especially if these Indians did not possess an Indian land reserve and had a skin color darker rather than lighter.[12] Labeling Native peoples as "Black" or "People of Color" and so "erasing" them as Indians made it easier to ignore their needs and became a way for the colony and state to wash its hands of any Indian problem. Once the eastern Indians had been turned into People of Color, the state could now concentrate on establishing Black chattel slavery and White supremacy.

With the US census of 1800, the state of North Carolina listed a total population of 476,103. Of these, 337,764 were White men, women, and children, while 133,296 were enslaved African or African Carolinian men, women, and children. The census did not list Indians. Nevertheless, Tuscaroras remained in Bertie County. Certainly, some of the enslaved African Carolinians possessed Indian "blood" or even considered themselves Indians or of Indian descent. Maybe some of the White men, women, and children did, too. The census also listed North Carolina as having 7,043 "all other free persons." This meant free People of Color, non-White people who were not enslaved. Their White neighbors would probably view them as African Americans or as Black people or "Negroes."[13] For eastern North Carolina, it was in this "all other free persons" category where we might find our Native peoples.

It was the coming of African slavery to North Carolina and the accompanying rise of White supremacy during the eighteenth century that brought about the attempted erasure and "disappearance" of eastern North Carolina Indians because they eventually came to be seen not as Indians but as People of Color. Indian relations with Africans and African Americans, both enslaved and free, have been fodder for historians. Some historians have seen an antagonistic relationship, with Indians trying to keep their distance from enslaved Africans, whom they saw treated badly by the White English. Sometimes the English deliberately used Indians and enslaved Africans to attack each other and so keep them divided. Since Indians usually experienced Africans alongside the English, many of them saw Africans as invaders, too. By the early nineteenth century, some Indians, such as the Cherokees, Creek, Choctaws, and others, owned enslaved Black people of their own. These divisions continued after the Civil War and into modern times.[14] Other researchers have seen a friendlier or at least a more nuanced relationship in which Indians accepted Africans on a case-by-case basis. Sometimes they provided havens for runaway slaves, and sometimes they might return them for a reward. Sometimes Indians and Africans engaged in trade with each other, and sometimes they did not.[15]

Whatever relationship they might have had, during the eighteenth century a triracial society developed in eastern North Carolina as Indians, English, and Africans interacted and intermixed. But over the course of the century, as Indians seemingly disappeared, and as European and African numbers increased, North Carolina became a two-"race" society in which White Americans held supremacy over Black Africans and African Americans. By the nineteenth century, antebellum North Carolina saw the Old North State in only Black and White terms: either one was a White person and thus "superior," or one was a Black person, either slave or free, but considered an "inferior" with few rights a White person must respect. The notorious "One Drop Rule" came into play in the South, meaning that if a person had any African ancestry—one drop of "Black blood" in them—then no matter their outward appearance, they were considered "Black" and therefore a Person of Color. By 1800, many Indians in eastern North Carolina had an African ancestor or kinsperson, but many also had White ancestors and kin. In the Old South, however, "African blood" trumped "English blood," and so any African ancestor made one "Black" or a "Person of Color."[16]

Everything became based on outward appearance. Darker skin and non-European features got one labeled as a Person of Color. In this Black and White world there was no room for Indians, and now landless Indians found themselves labeled as People of Color or, as the census called them, "all other free persons." So according to the state of North Carolina, by the early 1800s there were no Indians living in eastern North Carolina, only White people, slaves, and People of Color. For the purposes of the state, all the descendants of those Indians seen by Giovanni da Verrazzano on the North Carolina Coastal Plain in 1524—the Tuscaroras, Chowans, Meherrins, Hatteras, Cores, Machapungas, Pamlicos, Roanokes, and many others—were now gone: dead or moved away, "extinct." For state officials, just as for colonial officials before them, Indians were a political and racial group. Once their government disbanded and they sold off the last of their lands, then they were not Indians anymore, especially if they looked more African than what a White person believed an Indian should look like. It was this ability to turn eastern North Carolina Indians into People of Color that made their experience somewhat unique and different from that of Indian peoples in, for example, the American West. It was also the most significant unintended consequence of the colonization process. As far as North Carolina society and law were concerned, landlessness, distant parentage, and skin color erased them as Indians and turned them into People of Color and thus subject to all the laws and abuses directed toward non-White peoples. In this racial sleight of hand, the "People of Color" label was forced upon them by White authorities.[17]

Here lies the basis of this book's thesis. By 1715, once-independent Native peoples in colonial eastern North Carolina had been turned into colonial tributaries. Although Indians had to accept their tributary status and their land reserve, they used a vigorous passive resistance to maintain their traditional ways and rights as much as they could. However, over the course of the eighteenth century, land loss, illness, alcoholism, violence, poverty, settler harassment, and colonial policies proved fatal, and eastern North Carolina Indian populations declined precipitously. As their numbers dwindled and the population of English settlers and enslaved Africans expanded, eastern North Carolina Indians often sought out marriages or intimate relations with other Indian peoples as well as with Black and White people and produced bicultural children with varying shades of skin color. As Indians lost their lands, and as North Carolina became a slave society that divided itself into White and Black, the North Carolina government and its White inhabitants now labeled these Indians as People of Color with few rights. Indians of eastern North Carolina were essentially erased from the sight and thoughts of their English and later American neighbors and from the colonial records.

Indians sharply disagreed with this racial assignment, and many of these "other free persons" insisted they were Indians, descendants of once powerful, independent peoples, not just nameless People of Color. To them, Indianness did not rest on a political organization, a central government, a certain culture, or even the color of their skin but rather on family and kinship, a connection to place, and their shared history: "Kin were real people, others were something less."[18] By 1800, Indian reserves across eastern North Carolina winked out of existence, yet Indian peoples still lived in these areas, and so enclaves of Indians remained across the eastern part of the state. In Bertie County, in the area of the former Tuscarora Indian Woods reserve, though extinguished by the early 1800s, there remained people legally labeled as People of Color but who still considered themselves Tuscarora. Similar enclaves could be found where the Chowans,

Meherrins, Hatteras, Machapungas, Saponis, Occaneechis, Wacca-maws, and others had lived. Down in the swamps around Drowning Creek in southeastern North Carolina, later named the Lumber River, in what became Robeson, Hoke, Scotland, and Cumberland Counties, Indian refugees from war-shattered nations, such as the Cheraws from South Carolina, the Tuscaroras from North Carolina, and even the Nansemonds from Virginia, began re-creating Indian communities and insisting that their neighbors and the state of North Carolina recognize their Indian identity. As they saw it, one was an Indian because one was kin to these peoples and families who knew they were Indian; they viewed themselves as Indian and were connected to these particular Indian places, whether Bertie County, Hertford County, or Drowning Creek in Robeson County.[19]

The amazing story is that despite the best efforts of the colonization process, Southern slavery, and White supremacy to erase them, Indian peoples remained in eastern North Carolina and in the twentieth and twenty-first centuries were again recognized as Indians and Indian tribes by the state government. Many consider themselves Tuscaroras. That Indians still live in North Carolina in the twenty-first century says much of Native peoples' resilience and shows that the colonization process, tributary status, and White supremacy, though lethal in many respects, were not the mighty pulverizing machines they seemed destined to be for Indians. War, conquest, tributary status, illness, and societal disruption were bad enough. But erasing Indians from North Carolina by labeling them as People of Color while forcing them to navigate a Southern slave society based on skin color generated a complex Indian experience.

Historian Daniel Usner Jr. reminds us that the familiar nineteenth-century antebellum South of big plantation houses surrounded by enslaved African Americans toiling in the fields was not the original South. There was a different South before that: the colonial South in which Indians played a pivotal role.[20] That is not to say there were not enslaved Black people and plantations in eighteenth-century North Carolina. There were, and it was a time of growth for African slavery and the plantation economy, both of which took a toll on the tributary Indians. But eighteenth-century North Carolina was the time of the Indian and the colonization process. From the very first, colonial America revolved around turning Indians into tributaries. Indian wars, Indian trade, Indian slavery, Indian lands, Indian justice and injustice occupied much of the time, minds, and records of colonial America, certainly in North Carolina. For the colonies, breaking the power of the Indians, making them into tributaries subject to colonial law, and gradually separating them from their lands became paramount objectives. In North Carolina by the end of the eighteenth century, the objectives had become reality and then some. When the last bit of Tuscarora lands was sold off in 1828, we might say the colonial period in North Carolina came to an end.

Now, for White North Carolinians, Indians with no lands were mere People of Color who more logically fit in with the burgeoning slave South. The state did not have to concern itself with Indians but with slavery and White supremacy and all the consequences those institutions brought. People who considered themselves Indians but were not viewed as such now had to navigate the slave South and then after the Civil War the Jim Crow South, all while insisting on their Indian identity. From independent Indian peoples to tributary vassals to People of Color back to Indians is the story of the Indian peoples of eastern North Carolina.[21]

1

Of Vassal States
and the Colonization Process

Since the role of British colonization was to turn Native peoples into subservient tributaries and vassal states, then we must uncover the thought process of the Europeans, who believed it was their right, even their destiny, to wrest these lands from the Native peoples. Part of their justification was their belief in their own superiority and that non-White and non-Christian peoples were inferior. England put these beliefs and its colonization process into action in North Carolina.

From the deck of his small ship, Giovanni da Verrazzano marveled at the many campfires twinkling up and down the North Carolina coast. Employed by France to explore the coast of what would later be called North America, Verrazzano and his ships spent much of the spring of 1524 off the shore of what would become North Carolina. He wrote of low-lying sandy banks covered with forests and inhabited by multitudes of friendly people who welcomed him warmly. Here at this initial contact between the local Indians and Europeans, skin color already played a role, for, as Verrazzano noted, the Indians were "dark in color, not unlike the Ethiopians," and they "resemble the Orientals, particularly from the farthest Sinarian [China] regions." Periodically, he and his men would send a boat ashore, and the Native people would crowd the beach, "showing great delight at seeing us and marveling at our clothes, appearance, and our whiteness."[1] It was a chilling prophecy of how concepts of "Whiteness" and eventually "Blackness" would affect the descendants of these Indians.

Nor could these Native peoples then imagine the grim future for their children's children's children that would result from this first meeting. Some may have gained an insight as Verrazzano kidnapped a young Indian boy to take back to France, tried to kidnap a girl, and found the people farther up the North Carolina coast "whiter than the previous ones."[2] Nevertheless, the Native world now found itself being pulled into the Atlantic world and subject to the European colonization process. Verrazano sailed away, taking this child captive with him, and so, other than grieving parents, he did not make a lasting impact. That would come sixty years later.

For the Native peoples of the Carolinas, the colonization process began on July 13, 1584, when two small English ships threaded their way through an inlet of North Carolina's Outer Banks and anchored in the sound behind them. Arthur Barlowe, captain of one of the barks, said that "after thanks given to God for our safe arrival thither, we manned our boats, and went to view the land next adjoining, and to take possession of the same in the right of the Queen's most excellent Majestie, a rightful Queen, and Princess of the same."[3]

Barlowe, Captain Philip Amadas, who commanded the other ship, and their sailors performed a few possession rituals, meaning they conducted a religious ceremony, read a few lines from a script in which they officially took possession of the land, pulled up some grass, kicked some dirt clods, maybe nailed up a piece of parchment or a lead plate to a tree proclaiming that this was now English country. Sir Francis Drake had done something similar on the Oregon coast a few years earlier in 1579.[4] In that instant, England claimed all of what would later be designated "North Carolina," which the English then called "Virginia." This claim was mainly to ward off the Spanish and French, but though Barlowe did not fully express it, the underlying implication here was that the Indian peoples of the region, by virtue of not being Christians, were now subjects of Queen Elizabeth and under her authority and the authority of any governor she might send to oversee her new possession. According to the English, one had to acknowledge the rights of or uphold one's word only with Christians, at least theoretically and biblically. Non-Christians such as Indians did not count. That they had a new master certainly surprised the Native peoples of the area and led to much confusion and bloodshed over the years. But this was England's first real colonization venture outside of Ireland and still a rather new idea for the English. Nevertheless, the colonization process of subjugating Indians and turning them into tributaries and eventually People of Color had been set in motion. Thomas Harriot, a veteran of England's Roanoke expeditions, believed that the Indians could be brought to "honour, obey, feare and love us."[5]

Client States and Colonies

From time immemorial, towns, tribes, and states have subjugated others and pulled them into their own political orbit. In some instances, political entities have been absorbed, united, and become part of a single expanded state, as how Saxon Wessex eventually absorbed Sussex, Northumbria, and other principalities to make England. Others might become vassal or puppet states, essentially independent governments but dominated by the stronger power, especially when it came to foreign affairs, and reliant upon it for military protection and economic support. The Roman Empire was a master of creating vassal states, with Herod the Great as king of Judea coming to mind. Vassal states were independent entities but owed allegiance to the dominant power and provided military support when demanded. All these conquered political entities often get labeled as client states. In some instances, client states became tributary states in that they might be forced to pay tribute to the controlling power. Such tribute might consist of periodic payments of significant wealth—gold, gems, raw materials, produce, even people—that essentially transferred wealth from the subordinate to the dominant power. Other times it might be a small symbolic payment of little monetary value, maybe a few animal skins, a few arrowheads, or peppercorns given not for economic gain but to reinforce the vassal status and its subordinate relationship.

Subjugating other peoples was nothing new to Europeans of the 1580s. What was new, relatively speaking, was the idea of a nation claiming lands outside of Europe and extending its authority over the people of that region. Marco Polo had never claimed China for Venice. Other early European explorers had never tried to claim land for any country. One might argue that the Crusades marked a European effort to colonize the Middle East, but these short-lived European states were not an effort by a single European nation. Portugal's conquest of Ceuta, across the Straits of Gibraltar, in 1415 marked a national overseas expansion, as did its attempt to reach India by water. The Spanish monarchs may have had this in mind with Christopher Columbus, who epitomized this idea of national overseas colonization. As the European powers now contemplated expansion, they imagined that legal jurisdiction over these foreign territories could come through several means: "papal donation, first discovery, sustained possession, voluntary self-subjection by the natives, and armed conquest successfully maintained."[6]

In 1492, Columbus, sponsored by Spain, hoped to reach the lands belonging to the great khan of China. Hitting the Bahamas, he could not understand why he was not seeing the great cities that Marco Polo described. Though the Spanish monarchs Ferdinand and Isabella gave him diplomatic letters for the khan should he find him, they also charged the explorer with discovering new lands for Spain. Any Native inhabitants he might encounter were now to be considered subjects of the kingdoms of Castile and Aragon and, as non-Christians, targets for enslavement or conversion or both. As Spanish conquistadors followed Columbus to the Western Hemisphere and encountered its Native peoples, they wondered if the "Indians," as they referred to them, were rational beings or barbarians, whether they were inherently free beings or could be justly enslaved.[7]

Spanish scholars also debated whether Spain's claim to the western lands was legal. Most felt it was not but that Spain could not give up the lands it had acquired even if they had been acquired illegally. That would cause chaos, Spanish thinkers said. It was an argument made over the centuries by Europeans and Americans alike. As the

Spanish saw it, any lands not inhabited by Christians were fairly open to being discovered, claimed, controlled, and exploited. The inhabitants of these discovered lands might have a right of occupancy, but Spain had legal title to the land, and the people were now subjects of Spain.[8]

For the next hundred years, England watched Spain help itself to the riches of the Americas. It stood by while Spain wrung wealth from Western Hemisphere Indian nations, mines, and plantations, all while it sent its own expeditions across the North American Southeast, even building short-lived and long-lost settlements in North Carolina. As England pondered its own entry onto the international stage, it took its cue from Spain. Trying to get in on the pillaging of the Americas, in 1496 King Henry VII of England gave John Cabot and his sons the right to "find whatsoever isles, countries, regions or provinces of the heathen and infidels whatsoever they be," instructing them that they "may subdue, occupy and possess all such towns, cities and isles of them found . . . getting unto us the rule, title and jurisdiction of the same villages, towns, castles, & firm land so found."[9] Cabot was limited to pillaging and capturing the country of non-Christians, thus making Spanish and Portuguese possessions off limits. Nothing came of Cabot's voyages, but they set an English precedent.

Eighty years later, in the 1570s, Martin Frobisher explored Baffin Island in present-day Canada and "took possession of the country . . . that by our Christian study and endeavor, those barbarous people trained up in Paganism, and infidelity, might be reduced to the knowledge of the true religion."[10] Humphrey Gilbert received license "to discover, find, search out, and view such remote heathen and barbarous lands, countries and territories not actually possessed of any Christian prince or people, as to him, his heirs & assignes."[11] Regarding the "Christian prince," although Spain might claim Florida, England did not recognize Spain's claim as far north as what would be North Carolina and Virginia. So Barlowe's ceremony on that beach in July 1584, as he saw it, was a normal, legal counter to Spain's presence.

England's colonization efforts in America were based not just on Spanish precedent but also on its own experiences in Ireland. Though England had invaded Ireland in the 1100s, by the thirteenth century, as the historian R. F. Foster points out, "the purpose of English involvement in Ireland was beginning to change from acquiring lordship over men to colonizing land. . . . The sudden acquisition of large areas of underpopulated agricultural land in Ireland meant wealth for those who could develop its full potential." Now Englishmen on the make headed to Ireland for what they hoped were easy riches, and so Ireland became a settler colony. In a portent of future relations with Native American peoples, in 1366 England enacted the Statute of Kilkenny, which prohibited intermarriage between English and the Natives of Ireland, outlawed the speaking of Gaelic, and forbade English settlers from wearing Irish clothes or adopting Irish customs.[12] The English mind was quickly moving to see foreign subjects and their societies as inferior and themselves and Anglo culture as superior. Later, when skin color came into play, it would be even easier to rationalize this distinction.

One of the solutions the English devised to secure Ireland was plantations, sections of the country given to English lords, who would populate their area with Protestant English settlers. One of the largest holders was Sir Walter Raleigh, who would fund the expeditions to North Carolina's Roanoke Island in the 1580s. Making plantations meant taking Irish lands, which further alienated the Irish people and created more violence. So English soldiers found themselves slogging across the island, putting down rebellions, often engaging in the outright murder of men, women, and children. In these campaigns against the Irish, the English learned lessons on how to deal with rebellious Native people.[13] So when Barlowe and Amadas sailed into the North Carolina sounds and claimed it all for England, they had plenty of precedent and a firm idea how the colonization process was to work out and what Native peoples should expect.

Nevertheless, at Roanoke, England was trying to establish an overseas presence that might or might not turn out like Ireland. A problem was that English thinkers on overseas colonization had only a murky idea of what that presence should be. Should it be a small trading station in which a few English merchants lived full-time, profitably exchanging metal tools and cloth with the Indians and funneling back hides, sassafras, pearls, precious metals, lumber, and whatnot to English companies? Some envisioned a military base in the mid-Atlantic, mainly as a harbor for English privateers to replenish and refit and then swoop down on Spanish ships in the Caribbean. Patriotic English promoters such as Richard Hakluyt pushed the idea of a full-blown permanent settler colony. With Raleigh's Roanoke ventures in mind, Hakluyt saw a colony as a way to expand England's possessions while giving King Philip II of Spain a black eye. In Carolina, Hakluyt imagined England would reap valuable resources, such as olive oil and sugar, all while adding to the queen's wealth. Colonies would be places to send unemployed English men and women, where they would be set to work in producing raw materials. This would spur the English economy, with mother-country workers manufacturing finished goods that would enrich both the mother country and the colony. Nothing was said of an economy based on slavery.[14]

As for Indians, Hakluyt believed Spanish cruelty would make them allies of the English, who could now peacefully convert them to Protestant Christianity. As for Indian claims to the land, Hakluyt reminded his readers that the queen of England's title to all the lands from Florida to the Arctic Circle "is more lawfull and righte then [sic] the Spaniardes or any other Christian Princes." Nevertheless, he and others urged peace, understanding, and justice toward the Indians and developed rules for interacting with them. No Englishman should enter an Indian's house without being invited and was strictly prohibited from striking or misusing an Indian. That mistreatment could result in the violator being beat twenty times with a cudgel in the presence of the Indian. If that was not enough, then an Englishman's bad behavior could be punished with imprisonment or even enslavement. These rules might have been the ideal, but they were rarely enforced.[15]

Roanoke Island, 1580s

When Captains Barlowe and Amadas and their two barks sailed into the North Carolina sounds that July in 1584 and claimed it all for Queen Elizabeth, they stumbled into an Algonquian world of often antagonistic towns and chiefdoms vying for power and ascendency. Even at this early date, these Englishmen had an idea of what they expected to find in Indians from reading about the earlier English, French, and Spanish explorations. A sort of split image was developing. On one hand, Indians were beasts, possibly cannibals, sexually active, ruled by their passions, and open to treachery—essentially the "Evil Savage" image that was making the rounds of colonizing nations. On the other, Indians might be friendly, helpful, generous, hospitable, open to amicable relations and so might possess a sense of nobility. The English at Roanoke hoped for friendly relations but always suspected, even expected, Indian treachery. For them, a smiling, friendly Indian could be masking a traitor waiting for the right time to stab them in the back.[16]

Barlowe and Amadas soon encountered Granganimeo, the chief, or *weroance*, of Roanoke town on Roanoke Island at the mouth of Albemarle Sound and just inside the Outer Banks barrier islands. Roanoke was one of the towns that constituted the chiefdom led by Granganimeo's older brother, Wingina. Other towns in Wingina's chiefdom included Dasemkepeuc on the mainland across from Roanoke Island, a few other towns to the southwest, and probably Croatoan south on Hatteras Island. Granganimeo invited Barlowe and Amadas to set up their base of operations on Roanoke Island. Over the next six weeks, the English traded with the Roanokes but also learned the political lay of the land.

Stretching along the north bank of Albemarle Sound sat a string of five or six towns belonging to the Weapemeoc chiefdom and led by their *weroance*, Okisko. By the late 1600s, they would be known as the Yeopims. West of the Weapemeocs on the Chowan River were the Choanoacs, eighteen densely populated towns led by the *weroance* Menatonon and considered the most powerful chiefdom in the area. At the head of Albemarle Sound lived the Moratocs, who also spoke Algonquian. West of them on the Roanoke River sat the Mandoags, who spoke a different language than the Algonquians. Some historians believe they were the Tuscaroras; others think they were Siouan speakers, such as the Enos. Nevertheless, this area west of the sounds would become Tuscarora country. Down on the north shore of Pamlico Sound sat other towns, such as Secotan and Aquascogoc. They belonged to the "Lord of Sequotan," who many believe was Wingina. All these towns had bad relations with Pomeioke, which sat a little farther west and gave us the name "Pamlico." Farther south, the Neusiocs lived at the mouth of the Neuse River, but they also spoke a different language, and their towns were off-shoot Tuscarora towns. Up north in Virginia proper was the rising Algonquian Powhatan chiefdom, which would challenge Capt. John Smith and Jamestown in 1607. There was also a thin strip of Iroquoian speakers—Meherrins, Nottoways, and Susquehannahs—running north across Virginia, Maryland, and Pennsylvania all the way to the Five Nations of the Iroquois in New York. West of the Meherrins and Tuscaroras was a huge horseshoe of Siouan speakers running from the Virginia Monocans near the fall line southwest to the Occaneechis on the Roanoke River and the Saponis on the Eno River, across the Carolina Piedmont, where Sissipahaw, Keyauwees, and others lived, across what would be South Carolina, and on around to the coast. Far south on the lower Cape Fear River were Siouan-speaking Indians, whom the English labeled "Cape Fear Indians," as well as the roaming Woccons and Waccamaws.[17]

These larger chiefdoms, governed by a paramount *weroance* such as Wingina or Menatonon, comprised several towns, each of them governed by its own town *weroance*, as Wingina's brother Granganimeo did at Roanoke. A paramount chief such as Wingina, Okisko, or Menatonon, through inheritance, negotiation, cunning, or war, subjugated other towns and pulled them under his authority. As the Roanoke explorer Thomas Harriot pointed out in 1588, "In some places of the Countrey, one onely towne belongeth to the government of a Wiroans or chief Lorde, in other some two or three,

1. Theodor De Bry's engraving of John White's painting of an Algonquian Indian chief, c. 1580s. Although North Carolina Native leaders may have looked like this at their first meeting with the English, they soon adopted English clothing and weapons. Courtesy of the State Archives of North Carolina, Raleigh.

in some sixe, eight, and more, the greatest Wiroans that yet we had dealing with, had but eighteene townes in his government."[18] If these chiefdoms were anything like the Powhatan ones that John Smith encountered in Virginia twenty years later, then they also utilized a system of vassalage and tribute. Some of this tribute was food—bushels of corn, tuckahoe, venison, bear's oil, and such; after all, it took a great deal of food for the *weroance* to entertain foreign visitors and feed needy subjects. Other tribute would consist of luxury goods or prestige goods, things that possessed spiritual power, such as copper ornaments, shell beads, pearls, and any exotic stone or mineral. The *weroance* might keep them as proof of his authority or to reward warriors, family members, and worthy subjects. Sixteenth-century paintings of Roanoke Indian royalty show them wearing copper gorgets and beaded bracelets.[19]

Indian commoners recognized that *weroances* such as Wingina, who ruled several towns, and his brother Granganimeo, who governed Roanoke, possessed a higher status than they did. Even Barlowe saw that, commenting that "the King is greatly obeyed, and his brothers, and children reverenced."[20] When Granganimeo and Barlowe met for the first time on the beach, the *weroance* brought a retinue of forty men, who spread mats on the sand for him and four principal men to sit on, while the others remained standing behind him. Barlowe gave gifts of English goods to Granganimeo but created a diplomatic faux pas when he also gave gifts to the four Indian principal men. Granganimeo stopped him, took the gifts, and put them "into his owne basket, making signes and tokens, that all things ought to be delivered unto him, and the rest were but his servants, and followers."[21]

Like Verrazzano, Barlowe also commented upon Indians' skin color, which he described as "yellowish." Skin color fascinated Europeans, but in the sixteenth and early seventeenth centuries their attention to it had not yet hardened into biological concepts of "race," where skin color and certain physical features determined a person's intellect, ability, and even moral character.

Barlowe found Roanoke town consisted of nine houses surrounded by a log palisade. Granganimeo's house was larger than the other eight and divided into five rooms, one of them a room to receive foreign visitors. When some celebrating hunters inadvertently startled Barlowe's party, making them go for their weapons, the *weroance*'s wife assured them they were safe and "caused some of her men to runne out, and take away their [the hunters'] bowes, and arrowes, and breake them, and withal beate the poore fellowes out of the gate againe."[22] Each person knew where they stood in this social hierarchy where kinship and place were of utmost importance. If you asked a man or woman who they were, they would probably tell you of their family and clan and even sported tattoos that let others know what town they called home and whom they called *weroance*.[23] The point is that eastern North Carolina Indians understood the concepts of vassalage and tribute. They were also aware of skin color and were just as curious of European Whiteness as Verrazzano and Barlowe were of Indian darkness. Still, if Indian children with auburn- and chestnut-colored hair were any indication, skin color did not stop sexual relations from taking place between the two peoples.

For Granganimeo and his older brother Wingina, the arrival of the two English ships seemed like a blessing from the gods. Not that the Indians saw the English as gods, but the things they brought were not only exotic and full of spiritual power but also useful in daily life. Granganimeo quickly showed a "great liking of our armour, a sworde, and divers other things, which we had: and offered to laye a great boxe of pearle in gage for them: but we refused it for this time."[24] The weapons had the potential to be game changers. Wingina was actually the junior player among the regional chiefdoms. Menatonon of the Choanoacs governed more towns, and Wingina was in an active war with the Pomeioke chiefdom to the southwest. In fact, he had been severely wounded in battle and was even then during Barlowe's visit laid up at a town six days from Roanoke.[25] The weapons as well as the exotic goods, beads, tin plates, knives, and copper the English brought, controlled by Wingina and put into the trade networks, could bring wealth, influence, and power. All he had to do was control the English.

For six weeks, the Algonquians exchanged skins, shells, and copper for Barlowe's manufactured goods. It was a happy time of getting to know each other and enjoying each other's hospitality. The Roanokes were enchanted with their new friends who brought so many strange and wondrous things to them. Wingina thrilled to the idea that his new allies might help him expand his chiefdom. When the English sailed for home in September, they took with them two Indians: Wanchese and Manteo. Each would come to have very different opinions of the English.[26]

Wingina's hope for continued friendly trade and powerful alliances was not to be. The next year Raleigh decided to go Irish on the

Indians and set up a garrison on Roanoke Island under the command of a military governor, Col. Ralph Lane. The expedition of 1585 consisted of about a hundred men, half of them army veterans of the Irish wars, the other half gentlemen, craftsmen, and metal experts. Col. Lane and his soldiers were touchy, suspicious men who had learned in Ireland how to deal with subjects who resisted the queen's governor. They also returned Manteo and Wanchese, the two Native men who had gone to England with Barlowe the previous year. Wanchese, upon his return, immediately deserted the English and became one of their most spirited enemies. Manteo remained loyal to the English and served as interpreter and cultural broker and warned the English of Indians plans.

Lane's mission was to establish a base from which English privateers could harass Spanish ships in the Caribbean, explore the area for riches, and, they hoped, discover a water passage to Asia. For the next year, 1585–86, England's Roanoke colony became a battle of wills between Lane, who saw the land as belonging to Raleigh and England, and Wingina, who refused to accept that he and his people were English vassals. As Lane saw the situation, the Roanokes were just like the Irish. It would be easier on them if they accepted that they were subjects of the queen and tenants of Raleigh, obey his orders, and feed his men. Resistance would not be tolerated. In the meantime, the English brought sickness along with their tin plates and blue beads, which began to kill coastal Indians in huge numbers. Alternately awed by and terrified of the English, Roanoke society ruptured, with a pro-English faction advocating accommodation to these powerful beings who could kill enemies and friends from afar and an anti-English faction who felt getting rid of Lane and his men was best for Roanoke survival.[27]

After the deaths of his father and his brother Granganimeo, both of whom had been strong supporters of the English, Wingina, who had previously walked a middle ground, now went over to the opposition. He developed a plan to get rid of Lane and his men. Wingina announced that he had changed his name to "Pemisapan," which translated as "Wolf Who Watches from a Distance," indicating a change in his policy toward the English if Lane had been savvy enough to understand it.[28] Pemisapan now informed the governor that Menatonon on the Chowan River was plotting against the English and encouraged Lane to head up the Albemarle Sound to investigate. Lane took the bait. Pemisapan then sent word to Menatonon that Lane was coming to attack him and hoped the Choanoacs would ambush Lane and rid this cancer from Roanoke society. Lane and a detachment of soldiers went upriver, surprised the Choanoacs, captured Menatonon and his son Skiko, and found out it was all a ruse by Pemisapan. At least that is what Lane believed. With Skiko in chains to be held as a hostage at Roanoke, Lane now got England's first Indian tributary when King Menatonon, under duress in hopes of freeing his son, paid fealty to Lane and the English. Lane soon had a second tributary as Menatonon, who dominated the Weapemeocs, ordered their king, Okisko, "to yield himself servant, and homage, to the great Weroanza of England, after her to Sir Walter Raleigh." Again, Okisko acted under duress.[29] Lane, his soldiers, and Skiko's return to Roanoke shocked Pemisapan. His plan had blown up in his face. Lane and his men were not lying dead somewhere on the Chowan River but had seemingly returned from the grave and given life to the pro-English faction. His maneuvering had also driven his rivals, Menatonon and Okisko, into the arms of the English.[30]

Now Pemisapan decided to starve out Lane. The Roanokes abandoned Roanoke Island for the mainland and refused to provide food for the English. In Lane's opinion, this was rebellion. He believed Pemisapan was preparing to murder him, so he struck first. In the early morning of June 1, 1586, Lane made a surprise attack on Pemisapan at Dasemkepeuc across the sound from Roanoke. There he gunned down the *weroance*, and then one of his men beheaded Pemisapan. This violent act horrified and angered the Roanokes, who considered it an unpardonable crime. Now they withdrew farther inland, leaving the hungry English to fend for themselves. With no resupply ship in sight, Lane and his men, along with Manteo, abandoned Roanoke and sailed back to England in mid-June, when Sir Francis Drake's fleet happened by. Roanoke was proving to be as tough to break as Ireland.[31]

Raleigh had learned some lessons. The waters around Roanoke were too shallow and the Indians too hostile. Now he decided to abandon the island and the Irish garrison concept. He would instead try the plantation model, going from a nonsettler colony to a settler colony. The next year, 1587, Raleigh dispatched another expedition, this time to deep-water Chesapeake Bay north of Roanoke. Instead of soldiers, the expedition was to consist of 117 men, women, and children under the leadership of Gov. John White, a picture painter who had accompanied the Lane expedition the previous year. Instead of making it to the Chesapeake, the colony found itself stranded on dangerous Roanoke Island, where Indian anger over the assassination of Pemisapan had not subsided. Within days, Indian warriors under Wanchese killed an Englishman caught out alone. Gov. White retaliated by attacking the town of Dasemkepeuc, where Pemisapan had been killed, but instead of killing Roanokes, White mistakenly killed some of the only friends the English had on the coast, the Croatoans, who were taking the corn from the abandoned Dasemkepeuc fields. They were Manteo's people.

Manteo had evacuated Roanoke with Lane's men in 1586 and now returned with White in 1587. Although Manteo grieved over the killing of some of his kinsmen in the dustup, he blamed it on the Croatoans for not meeting with White earlier when demanded. Then White made a truly astounding pronouncement on August 13. "Our Savage Manteo, by the commandment of Sir Walter Ralegh, was christened in Roanoke, and called Lord thereof, and of Dasamongueponke, in reward for his faithfull service."[32] What did that mean exactly for Manteo to become a Church of England Christian and lord of Roanoke and Dasemkepeuc, where Pemisapan had been murdered and White had mistakenly attacked the Croatoans? Interestingly, no one demanded that Manteo give up his Indian name and take a Christian English name.[33] Nevertheless, if Raleigh had conceived this plan while still in England, and apparently he had, then it indicated that White's colony had planned all along to visit Roanoke on their way to Chesapeake Bay and drop off Lord Manteo, who would rule lower Virginia as a puppet state in Raleigh's stead. For Manteo, being named "lord of Roanoke" was an empty gesture as he was now a feudal lord with no vassals, ignored and even hated by the Roanokes. They followed Wanchese. It said more of Raleigh, who appointed this Indian lord over his Virginia holdings. He did not see Manteo as inherently inferior but rather as "civilized" and able to handle the demands and prerogatives of being an "English" lord of Roanoke.[34] Maybe Raleigh saw him like a loyal Irish lord. And Manteo's skin color did not deter Raleigh or reflect negatively on Manteo, who seemed to prove the idea of "race" as being cultural and not biological. As Raleigh probably saw the situation, Manteo was becoming ever more English. There was also a sly logic to the decision for Raleigh. Now he would have two "colonies" in Virginia: Roanoke under Manteo and Chesapeake Bay under John White. By making Manteo lord of Roanoke, he gave England a claim of permanence to North Carolina. Barlowe had claimed the land for England, so despite the failures of the Roanoke expeditions an English lord still ruled in Carolina and made it off limits to all other powers. Lord Manteo of Roanoke and Dasemkepeuc ensured that England's claim to the Carolinas would stand the test of time and European law.

Manteo's colony would not last three years. Unable to get to Chesapeake Bay, knowing they were in the wrong destination and a dangerous one, the English colonists prevailed upon Gov. White to go back to England for assistance. When he returned to Roanoke three years later, in 1590, Manteo, the colony, and all its people had disappeared, never to be seen again by the English. And so the "Lost Colony" became part of North Carolina history and lore.[35] But England always remembered its claim to North Carolina.

Creating Carolina

The Indians along the Albemarle Sound had fought off the Roanoke expeditions and subjugated or incorporated the Lost Colony. Nevertheless, it is hard to estimate the long-term impact of the expeditions

on the region's Indians. Certainly, the deaths from illness and violence lowered population numbers in the region and took out people
essential to the running of a village. But whatever malady hit the
Roanokes and their neighbors burned itself out at some point. The
assassination of Pemisapan and the collapse of the "Lost Colony"
must have set off power struggles among the region's towns and
chiefdoms. We must wonder what happened to Lord Manteo and the
English-hater Wanchese. They had to have been friends at one time
but now were polar opposites, in a way lords of the same land. Enemies may have taken advantage of the confusion to attack. In 1608
and 1609, John Smith in Jamestown sent expeditions to the Choanoacs on the Chowan River at the head of Albemarle Sound. Twenty
years earlier, Menatonon's Choanoacs had been the strongest power
in the region, with eighteen towns able to put hundreds of warriors
into the field. Now the English reported the Choanoacs to be much
diminished and a shadow of what they once had been, whether from
illness or warfare or both, we are not sure. In the early 1700s, the
Hatteras, descendants of the Croatoans, told John Lawson that their
forefathers were White people who could read from books and traveled in sailing ships. Lawson believed this connected them to the
Lost Colony through intermarriage. But it does not seem that the
Roanoke expeditions played any appreciable role in England's future
colonization efforts. They did give England what the English considered a firm European claim to the land and a model by which Indian
peoples became vassals of the English monarch.[36]

One thing the expeditions did was provide the first visual record of the Indian peoples and their places in eastern North Carolina
during the 1580s. John White painted images of Algonquian men,
women, children, towns, activities, and local animals. Most of these
paintings are now in the British Museum. Many of them were later
copied as engravings by Theodor de Bry. White's paintings and de
Bry's engravings are some of the first realistic images of American
Indians and provide a visual description of that time: how the Indians looked, how they dressed, the jewelry and tattoos they sported,
what they did, what their towns looked like, and the animals that

2. Theodor De Bry's engraving of John White's painting of the village of Secota, c. 1580s. Secota was located on the northside of Pamlico Sound. Most Native villages on the North Carolina Coastal Plain looked somewhat like this until after the Tuscarora War ended in 1715. The defeated Indians were made into colonial tributaries and placed on land reserves. Courtesy of the State Archives of North Carolina, Raleigh.

inhabited their world.[37] They showed bustling towns of mat-covered longhouses, with some towns surrounded by a log palisade. Feuding was common among the chiefdoms of this region. The residents lived among burgeoning cornfields and sounds full of fish. These tattooed men and women sporting copper necklaces were Queen Elizabeth's new Indian subjects.

When the Lost Colony vanished into the North Carolina wilderness, there also disappeared for a while any significant English contact with the Indians of eastern North Carolina. For the Native peoples, the Roanoke voyages became just a painful memory or, as for the Hatteras, memories of distant kinfolk. But England did not forget. Native Carolinians would begin to encounter Englishmen with increasing frequency. A couple of Jamestown searches were made along the Chowan River, and a few shipwrecked sailors washed up on the beaches, but no large-scale meetings took place. Then in the 1650s, traders out of Virginia began following the Great Trading Path south into North Carolina and the Piedmont. In September 1653, a hide trader related to Gov. Francis Yardley of Virginia said he had purchased Roanoke Island for £200 sterling from the chief of the island, whom his people called the "Great Commander." The exchange showed Indians' willingness to sell their lands. This was a dangerous precedent, and it is unclear if the Great Commander fully understood the ramifications of his sale. Did he consider it a sale or just the lease of user rights? Nevertheless, the English saw such transactions as a transfer of land. Now the Great Commander's lands became smaller, and he would never get them back. Was he even selling his own lands, or did some other Indians claim the island? Besides Roanoke Island, the trader said he "paid for three great rivers" and "took possession of the country, in the name, and on behalf of the commonwealth of England."[38] He seemed to overlook that Barlowe and Amadas had already taken possession back in 1584 and that Lord Manteo had ruled there in 1587.

In 1654, there were only a few Englishmen and seemingly unlimited acres of land, so the Great Commander might have felt he got the better of the deal. Soon more Englishmen were on the way, though. In 1655, the trader Nathaniel Batts, considered North Carolina's first English settler, built a small house between the Roanoke River and Salmon Creek in present-day Bertie County to encourage the deer hide trade with the nearby Tuscaroras; Chowans, whom Barlowe had called Choanoacs; the Yeopims, the name now given to the Weapemeocs; and other Indians north and west of Albemarle Sound. They provided deerskins in exchange for English manufactured goods.[39] On the heels of Batts came disaffected and landless settlers from Virginia, who drifted south through the Great Dismal Swamp and settled along the north shore of Albemarle Sound. On March 1, 1661, settler George Durant purchased from Kilcacenen, "King of the Yeopim Indians," a tract of land where the Perquimans River met the Albemarle Sound. The record of this sale of Indian land is one of the earliest documents in the North Carolina colonial records.[40] Soon there were plenty more.

In 1663 came a serious challenge to the Native peoples of the region. In that year, King Charles II, restored to the English throne after the Cromwell years, created the colony of Carolina, which included all the land from Virginia's present-day southern border down to the current Georgia–Florida border. Charles gave this huge colony to the eight Lords Proprietors, wealthy and influential men who had helped him reclaim the throne. Their names are not necessarily important to our story, and those in this position would change out over the next six decades as they died or sold out and were replaced.

The Carolina Lords Proprietors would remain in England but govern the colony within English law and wring as much wealth from it as they could. Yet they were also forward-thinking men, and in the spirit of the times they hired the philosopher John Locke, famous for his notions of the natural rights of life, liberty, and property, to draw up the Fundamental Constitutions, which would provide the governing structure of the Carolina colony. However, much of what was written in the Fundamental Constitutions in 1669 never came to pass in Carolina. It described a colonial aristocracy of landgraves and casiques, with the colony divided into signories, baronies, precincts, colonies, and manors, but these divisions never caught on. It also set up a governmental structure in which there would be a governor appointed by the Proprietors as well as a Governor's Council of appointed influential men to advise the governor and serve as an upper legislative house. There would be a parliament, sometimes called the Common's Chamber and later called the Assembly or Legislature, of men elected by the freeholders of the colony. A man had to own at least 500 acres of land to run for the Assembly.[41]

Locke tried to cover almost everything. Article 86 said that the age of a person born in Carolina would not be reckoned from the day of birth but from the day the birth was entered into the precinct registry. No marriage would be acknowledged as legal until it was also recorded in the registry. As for immigrants to the colony, all they had to do was appear before a precinct register and affirm and subscribe to the Fundamental Constitutions, and they would be considered naturalized citizens. African slavery was an accepted fact. Locke insisted that even if an enslaved person were a Christian, it had no effect on their being held in bondage. Not only that, Article 110 stipulated that "every freeman of Carolina, shall have absolute power and authority over his negro slaves, of what opinion or religion soever." African or Black slavery was to be a legal reality in Carolina.[42]

Locke did not say much about the Indians who were living in Carolina and had called it home for hundreds if not thousands of years. He urged the freeholders to treat them with respect and tolerance. Article 97 admitted that "the natives of that place, who will be concerned in our plantation, are utterly strangers to Christianity, whose idolatry, ignorance or mistake, gives us no right to expel or use them ill."[43] The only other point Locke made about Indians concerned their land. Article 112 said that no person "shall hold or claim any land in Carolina, by purchase or gift, or otherwise, from the natives or any other whatsoever; but merely from and under the Lords Proprietors, upon pain of forfeiture of all his estate, moveable or immoveable, and perpetual banishment."[44] This rule would be extremely hard to enforce. Nevertheless, since the Proprietors now owned millions of acres of land, the surest way for them to make money was to sell land to settlers, have the settlers pay quitrents, a land tax that went to the Proprietors, and then tax their produce. So the Proprietors encouraged settlement in Carolina.

Settlement still required some legal hoop-jumping for the English and their relationship to the Native peoples and their land. As the English saw the Indians, they were already tributaries by the claims and vassalage done on Roanoke Island, so in that respect the Lords Proprietors and the English monarch had authority over them. At this early date, the Indians of eastern North Carolina certainly thought differently. Nevertheless, the Proprietors claimed authority over all the lands in the Carolinas and essentially allowed the Indians to occupy them. As the Proprietors saw it, these Indians had given up large tracts of land in exchange for a legal title to a smaller area, a land reserve. To acknowledge their subservient status to the Carolina government, Indians would pay a small tribute. The Proprietors instructed their governors in the Albemarle to provide a "true account of what tribute or payment are rendered . . . from any of the Indians and upon what account such tribute or payment is demanded or prove due."[45] This instruction set up a legal problem when it came to appropriating Indian lands because English society was set up to respect the private ownership of land, and the land had been occupied by the Indians before the coming of the English. Men such as the Proprietors rationalized that they were not so much taking Indian land as that Indians were surrendering it in exchange for the English introducing them to Christianity, English culture, and material goods.[46]

With the making of Indians into tributaries and taking of their lands now rationalized, settlement of the Carolinas moved quickly. However, the southern part of Carolina proved much more prosperous than the northern. Blessed with a deep-water anchorage, the city of Charles Town, later Charleston, was founded in 1670 at the confluence of the Ashley and Cooper Rivers with the Atlantic Ocean. Soon South Carolina boomed with rice and indigo planters, deerskin traders, and merchants buying enslaved Indians and importing enslaved Africans. The Lords Proprietors loved South Carolina and put the colonial capital there. Up north along the Albemarle, shallow waters and soggy ground hampered economic activity, and so North Carolina was usually ignored by the Proprietors. There was no deep-water port in North Carolina, and no ship heavier than fifty tons could make it through the Outer Bank inlets, limiting how much hardware and trade goods came into the colony and how much produce and deerskins could be exported. So while South Carolina boomed, North Carolina busted.[47] For the Indians of the northern region, that failure proved beneficial, at least at first.

2

Resistance and Conquest
in North Carolina

The North Carolina colonial government soon attempted to make the regional Indians into compliant tributaries. Sometimes the process worked smoothly, sometimes not. As English settlers crowded Indian lands and abused their inhabitants, many Native peoples of eastern North Carolina resisted with violence, but this often resulted in the loss of their lands, their sovereignty, and their lives.

Up to the north, Virginia also boomed and so influenced events in North Carolina. Where Roanoke had failed and English interest in North Carolina lagged, Jamestown, despite a horrific death rate in its early years, survived, prospered into Virginia, and expanded, always at the expense of Virginia's own Native peoples. Devastating Indian wars in 1622 and again in 1644 caused much destruction and death on both sides, but the English could replace their dead, while the Indians could not. Every war ended with the Indians fewer in population and holding less land. Tobacco wealth brought increasing numbers of English men and women to Virginia, who came in hopes of cashing in. Some died, some grew wealthy, and others found themselves priced out of land and opportunity and so looked south to Carolina.

Contrary Settlers

Difficult to get to, isolated, cursed with swampy land and shallow waters, North Carolina's Albemarle region proved unattractive to men wanting to strike it rich quickly. However, it was a draw to small farmers who could not afford Virginia land prices. Debtors, outlaws, pirates, Quakers, levelers, loners, people on the run from creditors or the authorities, husbands abandoning wives or wives escaping husbands—all found a haven in eastern North Carolina. Authority was light, and officials few. Since these early settlers came out of Virginia, North Carolina experienced settlement from north to south rather than east to west, as most English colonies did. Soon a rather raucous and freewheeling society developed in the Albemarle. As the historian Jonathan Barth describes the region, "Albemarle residents ranging from poor Whites to free and enslaved Blacks engaged in sport, dancing, entertainment, horse racing, cockfighting, drinking, and gambling, with taverns serving as the focal point in their local communities."[1] Here free Black people could vote and serve in the militia, while cohabitation and marriage between the two peoples was not unusual. Black and White, slave and free, might work together, smuggle together, party together, live together, and make intimate relations. Here was an early democracy's lack of regard for "race" and the social hierarchy that scared other colonial governments. Even relations with the Yeopims, Chowans, and other Indians north of the Albemarle seemed amiable. Nevertheless, this could be a dangerous time for Native peoples as this kind of lawless society also meant there were few legal protections for them. These unconventional North Carolina settlers had little use for Proprietor rules and taxes and were not afraid to take matters into their own hands. In 1677, in sympathy with the antigovernment Bacon's Rebellion then taking place in Virginia, Culpeper's Rebellion forcibly removed Acting Governor and Collector of Duties Thomas Miller, who dared enforce the British Navigation Acts. This antiauthoritarian society in North Carolina worried Virginia officials, who referred to the Albemarle as "Rogues Harbor" or the "Sinke of America." They feared this lawlessness might infect their own settlers or, worse, their own slaves. Nevertheless, North Carolina grew slowly, and by the 1680s settlement had moved south of the Albemarle. Soon it was on the Pamlico River, and by 1702 English settlers were clearing lands near the mouth of the Neuse and Trent Rivers.[2]

While Bacon's Rebellion in Virginia spurred sympathetic move-
ments in North Carolina, it upset Virginia's own Indian vassal-state
system, which rippled down into North Carolina. Bacon's Rebellion
became one of the first revolutions against government authority
in North America. It started with a mistaken attack on Virginia's
friendly Susquehannahs. The Iroquoian Susquehannahs were allies
of the Virginia colony as well as important trade clients and protective buffers. This mistaken attack could have been smoothed over
by Gov. William Berkeley, who supported the Susquehannahs, but
now hundreds of landless Virginia settlers led by Nathaniel Bacon
challenged Berkeley and his friendship with the Indians. Why should
any Indians have lands that could instead go to landless settlers? they
asked.[3] Bacon's army of former indentured servants again attacked
the confused Susquehannahs, most of whom eventually withdrew
to Pennsylvania and put themselves under the protection of the Five
Nations of the Iroquois. Bacon's men then attacked other Virginia
Indian allies, including the Algonquian Pamunkeys, the Siouan Occaneechis, and the Iroquoian Meherrins. However, when Bacon died
of typhus in October 1676, Gov. Berkeley and his Loyalists went on
the offensive, stamping out the rebellion and pushing Bacon's parti-
sans farther west and south into the Carolinas.[4]

Bacon's Rebellion roiled Indian relations in Virginia. Treaties
had been violated as friendly Indians had been attacked, killed, or
driven from their lands. With the rebellion over, Virginia had to re-
establish relations with its Native allies. Now, as Virginia saw it,
the remaining Indians would become official vassals and tributaries
of the colony and king. Virginia officials persuaded the Pamunkeys,
Saponis, Meherrins, and others to sign the Treaty of Middle Plantation in 1677, with more nations signing in 1680. This treaty officially made them vassals of the king and tributaries of Virginia and
spelled out the roles for the tributaries and their overlords. Indians
would be protected by the Virginia government and guaranteed specific lands of their own, and their hunting and fishing rights would
be assured. They would continue to be trade partners with Virginia,
but Virginia only. In turn, they would serve as buffers against foreign

Indian intrusions and auxiliaries when Virginia called upon them for military service. They were to pay three arrows as tribute and twenty beaver skins as a quitrent for their lands. Now as tributaries, these Indians were dependent on the colonial government. After conquest, this was the next step in the colonization process. North Carolina officials would use the Treaty of Middle Plantation as a blueprint for future treaties with their own tributaries.[5]

The end of Bacon's Rebellion in Virginia influenced fledgling North Carolina in several ways. First, it sent not only antiauthoritarian but also anti-Indian Bacon supporters into North Carolina, where they were welcomed by the rather contrarian settlers already living there. Second, it delivered plantation agriculture and African slavery to North Carolina as entrepreneurs arrived who hoped to find a way to wealth amid the colony's shallow waters. These men took a dim view of Carolina's rambunctious society and instead hoped to bring stability and the rule of law and therefore prosperity to the poor colony. Together, these two groups brought a third influence—a new, harsher policy toward the Indians of eastern North Carolina. Bacon supporters always believed that Indian lands should be distributed to English settlers. Elites newly arriving to North Carolina would be rather sympathetic to that argument. They felt one of the best ways to bring stability to the colony was to turn the Indians into compliant tributaries and so open up excess land. Indians should submit themselves to the colonial government, accept their role as tributaries and allies, limit themselves to a surveyed and bounded land reserve that would be assigned to them, trade only with the colony, and pretty much do as they were told. Indians, who saw themselves as free people, had their own ideas on their status, so resistance was guaranteed. Another influence in the region would be a general increase in the English and African populations, which would put stress on Indian land and alter Native populations and societies.

While these anti-Indian, anti-authoritarian Virginians migrated to North Carolina, they were counterbalanced by an equal influx of Proprietor supporters who hoped to prosper in this watery land. Barth calls them the "Chowan Clique," and they were the new colonial elites—men who wanted stability, law and order, as well as a plantation economy with a slave-labor force that would ensure their wealth and prosperity. They supported the Lord Proprietors, from whom land grants and positions flowed. They expected they would occupy the colony's appointed positions on the Governor's Council, judgeships, and governmental posts, and so they encouraged North Carolina to take its place within the British Empire. They hoped to get wealthy growing tobacco, producing tar and naval stores, acquiring deerskins, raising corn, hogs, and cattle, and then exporting these products from Virginia ports or through coastal New England traders who could make their way through the sounds or in shallow-draft sloops and brigantines of their own that let them trade directly with Barbados and other North American colonies. They especially hoped to gain control of valuable lands and then resell them to later-arriving settlers at a much higher price. They looked askance at Quakers, scofflaws, antiauthoritarian settlers, and Indians who might upset this goal. Their attitude certainly put them in opposition to the lower-class "rogues" and Quaker radicals in abundance in the colony. As the new colonial elites saw the situation, laws needed to be made and followed, slavery encouraged, trade established, and the only interracial relations allowed should be through African and Indian slavery and subservience. Indians needed to be made into tributaries, violently if need be, their lands limited and bounded and any excess sold to White planters and farmers. Indians should serve as trade clients, workers, a line of defense against foreign enemies, and military auxiliaries. Like children of the day, they should be seen, but only rarely, and not heard.[6]

Bacon's men on the run south and the coming of the Chowan Clique were leading a wave of immigration into North Carolina. Because of the shallow waters of North Carolina, most immigrants debarked in Virginia's Chesapeake Bay ports and then walked south to the Albemarle Sound or walked to the Chowan River and then boated down it to the Albemarle Sound. In 1679, there were about 1,400 White and Black people, free and enslaved, in North Carolina, but that number topped 10,000 by 1700; 15,120 by 1710; and

21,270 by 1720. In 1712, there were 800 Africans, most of them enslaved, and by 1720 this group had grown to about 3,000. Indians in the North Carolina Coastal Plain in 1710 numbered roughly 5,000.[7] The writing for the Indians was on the wall if they could see it. Although they were still the most numerous people during the last decades of the seventeenth century, by 1700 they were being outpaced by the colony's White and Black populations, and the trend was gaining steam.

As settlement moved south of the Albemarle in the 1680s and afterward, it skirted east of Tuscarora territory, and so these most powerful of all Indians of the Coastal Plain had little contact with settlers or colonial officials. However, the small nations—such as the Meherrins, Chowans, Yeopims, Hatteras, Pamlicos, Machapungas, Cores, Neuse, and White Oak River Indians—were all in the path of the settlers, who soon surrounded their lands like a noose. By the late 1600s, these nations, many of them rather small, maybe a few hundred people or less, consisted of a single town or maybe two, with outlying farms. The Tuscaroras, the largest nation in the region, had as many as fifteen or twenty towns. There apparently was not much warfare among these eastern North Carolina Indians at the turn of eighteenth century, though feuding between Iroquoian speakers such as the Tuscaroras, Meherrins, and Cores and Algonquian speakers such as the Pamlicos and Machapungas would not have been unusual. Some towns surrounded themselves with log palisades. When raids happened, they were more than likely directed toward Indians in either Virginia or South Carolina. We know leaders visited other leaders on the Coastal Plain, and it would not be unusual for people of one town to visit people of another town. All were beginning to suffer land loss and abuse at the hands of incoming settlers, so they were beginning to understand they had much in common.

These Native peoples complained of their loss and the abuses they suffered at the hands of settlers. Colonial officials mostly ignored them. More seriously, when ignored by the colonial government, these same Indians took their complaints to Tuscarora chiefs Tom Blount on the Tar River and King Hancock on Contentnea Creek, a

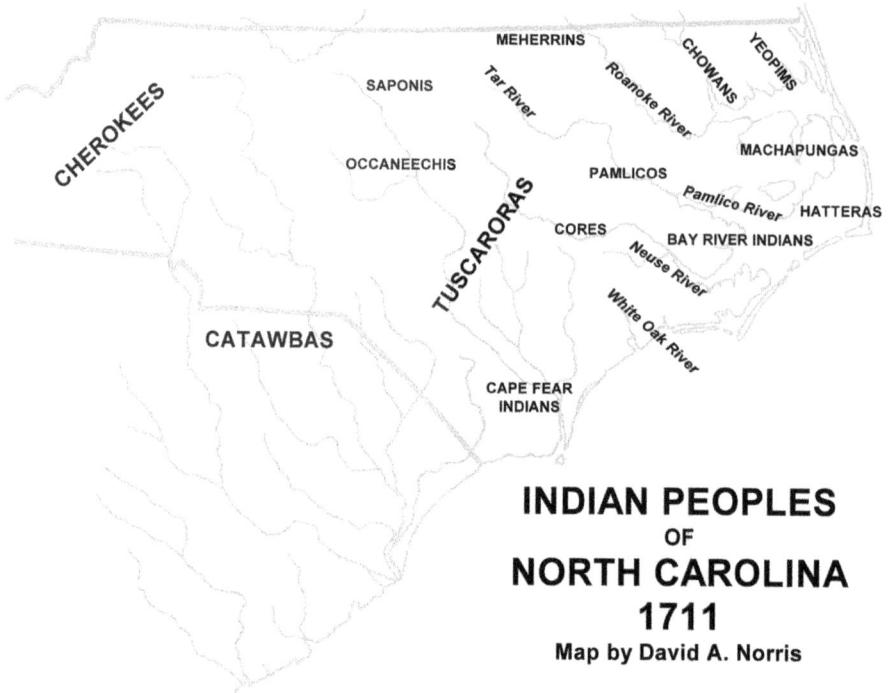

INDIAN PEOPLES
OF
NORTH CAROLINA
1711
Map by David A. Norris

tributary of the Neuse River. To achieve the Proprietor men's vision of plantation agriculture, subsistence farming, and slave labor for North Carolina, these Indians would have to be brought into tributary status, and their lands opened. Incoming settlers, even antiauthoritarian ones, wanting their own chance at good land, supported any measure that would subdue Indians and transfer Indian lands to them. The first Indians to feel the effects of this new North Carolina and the colonization process were the Chowans, living north of the Albemarle and west near the Chowan River.

New Tributaries

In November 1676 up in Virginia, Gov. Berkeley's Loyalists attacked Bacon's followers in Nansemond County and drove many into the North Carolina Albemarle. Here they were welcomed by the region's settlers, who held many of the same antigovernment beliefs. About the same time, a breakaway band of Susquehannahs moved south into Meherrin territory on Virginia's Tarara Creek. The Meherrins assisted these Susquehannahs, and then, attacked by the Senecas, they all moved farther south onto Bennett's Creek in present-day Gates County, North Carolina, which was the home of several hundred Chowans, descendants of the *weroance* Menatonon's Choanoacs. The Chowans provided refuge for the Susquehannahs and Meherrins at Meherrin Neck, which was at the confluence of the Meherrin River and the Chowan River. Bacon's men in North Carolina and their new Albemarle allies now accused the Meherrins of being Susquehannahs and refused to allow their old enemies to live so close to the North Carolina settlements. Albemarle settlers decided to attack. Unfortunately, the North Carolinians mistakenly attacked the peaceful Chowans. North Carolina suddenly had its first Indian war on its hands since the 1580s as angry Chowans, seeking revenge, raided nearby farms and plantations. In 1677, the newly appointed governor, Thomas Miller, organized a small militia force and defeated the Chowans at their town of Katoking. The Chowans made peace and became North Carolina's first tributary Indians, or one might say they reestablished the tributary status King Menatonon had made with Col. Ralph Lane back in 1586. They were immediately restricted to lands east of the Chowan River, and in 1685 the North Carolina colony assigned the Chowans a 12-by-12-mile land reserve—144 square miles—on Bennett's Creek.[8] The assigning of bounded reserves was the sure mark of a tributary, though being a tributary probably meant different things to the Chowans than it did for the colony. For the Chowans initially, tributary status may have been seen more as a promise of friendship in return for recognizing their right to lands. At least their reserve had come out of lands they had always considered theirs. They were not foreigners or strangers but now part of the English body politic, living on lands they always considered their own and protected by English law.[9]

Unfortunately for the Chowans, their lands sat north of Albemarle Sound, which was quickly filling up with immigrants coming out of Virginia. For the next several decades, the Chowans complained about settlers squatting on their lands, while nearby settlers complained of Chowans killing their hogs in the woods, hunting deer on their property, and claiming lands outside the reserve boundaries. Making matters worse, the Chowan population began to drop. During England's Roanoke expeditions, the Chowans probably numbered around 2,500, possibly more. By 1676, they had declined to about 500. Their numbers continued to shrink, so much that by 1704 the North Carolina colonial government, citing the Chowans' small population, reduced their reserve to 6-by-6 miles, or 36 square miles. Within five years, they had declined to about 60 men, women, and children under the leadership of King John Hoyter—all victims of war, rum, sickness, poisonings, land loss, and colonial pressures that upset Chowan society. This was the situation all eastern North Carolina Indians faced.[10]

Bacon's Rebellion pushed several other Indian nations into North Carolina. The Occaneechis escaped into the North Carolina Piedmont, settling for a while along the Eno River near present-day Hillsborough. The move was a long fall for the Occaneechis, who up through the early 1600s had been the major trade power in the region. At that time, they had lived in a town on an island where the Dan and Staunton Rivers came together to form the Roanoke River and guarded the Great Trading Path as it went south. Occaneechi Island became a great Indian trade market where shells and pearls from the coast might be traded for copper, stone, and newly introduced European manufactured goods. Some historians believe that survivors of the Lost Colony showed up here as captives. Even after the founding of Jamestown and the establishment of Indian trade there, the Occaneechis prospered as English goods flowed into their town. But English traders soon took their business to other Indians, and the Occaneechis lost their dominance. By the 1660s, they had abandoned their island home and moved east toward the source of the goods they hungered for. They formed a town near present-day Lynchburg, Virginia, but even then tried to preserve their trade dominance by roughing up English traders who dared deal with their Indian neighbors. Bacon's Rebellion shattered the Occaneechis' power and drove them into North Carolina. John Lawson visited their Eno River town in 1701 and described it as a pitiful place of small, smoky huts, with a swamp running through it and little food to offer. It would not be long before the Occaneechis would be on the move again.[11]

For the Saponis, a Siouan people allied with the Occaneechis, their young king, Mastegonoe, and his chief man, Tachapaoke, had signed the Treaty of Middle Plantation, making them tributaries of Virginia. Unfortunately, they were not a very populous people, which made them targets of the Iroquoian Senecas, Meherrins, and Tuscaroras. For security, the Saponis developed a strategy of periodically moving their villages and surrounding them with log palisades. By the 1670s, they lived near the Occaneechis not far from present-day Lynchburg, Virginia. Though the Saponis survived Bacon's Rebellion, they had second thoughts after signing the Treaty of Middle Plantation and soon abandoned Virginia. They briefly moved to the old Occaneechi Island town but then abandoned it, too. They would return to Virginia for a while but then leave that colony and head south into North Carolina.[12]

The Meherrins, led by "Chief Man" Ununtequero and "Next Chief Man" Harehannah, also signed the Middle Plantation Treaty and so made themselves tributaries of colonial Virginia.[13] They were an Iroquoian people and part of the Iroquoian finger stretching south out of New York down to North Carolina that included the Five Nations of the Iroquois as well as the Susquehannahs, Nottoways, Meherrins, Tuscaroras, Cores, Neuse, and White Oak River Indians. When Virginia traders met them in the 1650s, about 500 Meherrins lived on the Meherrin River and soon became firm trade clients and allies of Virginia. But Bacon's men attacked them in 1676, forcing some Meherrins and Susquehannahs south to North Carolina, which resulted in the Chowan War. Nevertheless, in 1680 Virginia, having made peace with other victims of Bacon's attacks, now called upon the Meherrins. So the Meherrins signed the Middle Plantation Treaty. Despite Virginia's guarantees of land and protection and probably pushed a little by Seneca raids, they developed second thoughts and again moved south into their old North Carolina haunts.

Like the other smaller nations, the Meherrins were a mobile people, settling in one place briefly and then resettling elsewhere, sometimes factioning into two villages, then later reuniting. During the 1680s, the Meherrins had settled on Bennett's Creek in North Carolina and then moved back and forth on either side of the Chowan River. By the 1700s, most were settled at the mouth of the Meherrin River, where it flowed into the west side of the Chowan River at Meherrin Neck. Even then, some Meherrins settled east of the Chowan River and south of the Meherrin River.[14]

The Meherrins' move south complicated relations with the North Carolina colony as they settled on lands that North Carolina had already assigned to settlers. Muddying the waters even more was the question of the Meherrins' tributary status. The Middle Plantation Treaty officially made them tributaries of Virginia. But now they lived on North Carolina soil, soil that North Carolina said the Meherrins were not entitled to because they were migrants to the colony and not original Native inhabitants. The Meherrins countered, saying they were on lands given to them by the Virginia governor. With the actual boundary between Virginia and North Carolina then in dispute, they believed they were in the right. North Carolina disagreed, saying the Meherrins were on lands that had once belonged to the Chowans but now belonged to the colony by virtue of its conquest of the Chowans in 1677. When North Carolina pressed the Meherrins over their claims, the Meherrins appealed to Virginia, and Virginia heartily supported them as it wanted the Meherrins as buffers guarding its more southerly settlements. It did not take long before North Carolina settlers accused the Meherrins of killing their cattle and hogs, burning their timber, looting their houses, and just being insolent. The Meherrins angered the colonial government all the more when they refused to pay tribute to North Carolina, insisting they were still tributaries to Virginia. Again, Virginia asserted that the Meherrins were indeed their tributaries, not North Carolina's.[15]

By the early 1700s, the North Carolina government accepted that the Meherrins lived in the colony but set stipulations. Because the Meherrins had become "an intolerable annoyance to her Majesty's subjects, committing repeated injurys upon their stocks and making frequent affrays upon their persons," they were to remove themselves to Meherrin Neck, west of the Chowan River and north of the Meherrin River. As North Carolina saw it, no Indian peoples should "possess the mouth of a navigable river." They should also give up claims to being Virginia tributaries and acknowledge tributary status to North Carolina. The Meherrins, bolstered by their support from Virginia, ignored North Carolina and expanded their settlements south onto lands belonging to settler Lewis Williams on Wiccacon Creek. There were also rumors of Meherrin warriors roaming the woods and assaulting settlers. North Carolina's patience wore thin. In August 1706, the North Carolina Governor's Council ordered the Meherrins to move their villages west of the Chowan and north of the Meherrin immediately. With crops in the field and the winter hunt upcoming, the Meherrins asked to move at the end of next spring. The council thought about it and gave a final date for their removal: March 30, 1707.[16]

When that date came and went, but the Meherrins had done nothing, North Carolina's anger boiled over. Thomas Pollock, the richest man in the colony, a land speculator, and a member of the Governor's Council, had his eyes on lands near Wiccacon Creek, where the Meherrins now sat. Pollock took matters into his own hands. During the summer of 1707, he led sixty North Carolina militiamen to drive the Meherrins off "his" land. Pollock's army invaded Meherrin country, took thirty-six Meherrin men prisoners, locked them without water in a house for two sweltering days, destroyed much of the Meherrin town, and threatened to destroy their corn crop if they did not leave these lands. The terrified Meherrins left but appealed to the Virginia government for protection. This incident caused a serious diplomatic dustup.[17]

Pollock's actions outraged the Virginia Governor's Council, which sent a scathing letter informing North Carolina that the Meherrins "are not to be considered as a nation of savages on whom the government of Carolina have power to revenge injurys by force of armes but as her Majestys subjects who are as much under protection as any of her subjects of Virginia." Virginia's Meherrin tributaries were on their own land, and North Carolina had no reason to invade them. If the Meherrins had done wrong, then North Carolina should have contacted Virginia for redress.[18]

Virginia's anger and strong support of the Meherrins threw North Carolina off balance and gave the Indians a reprieve. Meherrin settlement again spilled south of the Meherrin River, but North Carolina left them alone. The colony instead did what had been recommended: it complained to Virginia that the Meherrins were creating new towns and claiming a 3-mile boundary about them and asked for redress. Virginia shrugged off North Carolina's complaints, saying it was the settlers' own fault for squatting on legal Meherrin lands.[19] This tense standoff continued.

South of the Chowans and Meherrins and running east from the Chowan River on the north side of Albemarle Sound to the coast sat the Yeopims. They were the Algonquian descendants of the Weapemeocs, who had become vassals to Col. Ralph Lane in 1586. The Yeopims inhabited such towns as Jaupim, the origin of the name "Yeopim," Paspatank, and Poteskeet. Because early English settlement of North Carolina took place north of Albemarle Sound, it was certain that the Yeopims, just like the Meherrins and Chowans, would be crowded by settlers and eventually be forced into tributary status. In October 1697, the colonial government assigned the Yeopims a small 4-square-mile tract on North River in Camden and Currituck Counties. Then in October 1704, the colony increased the size of the Yeopim reserve to 10,240 acres, or 16 square miles.[20]

By 1700, North Carolina had two firm Native tributaries in the Chowans and Yeopims and a semitributary in the Meherrins. Despite their status, these Indian nations had complaints that simmered over the next few years.

Coastal Indians under Pressure

The situation between settlers and Indians simmered in other parts of eastern North Carolina as well. The population of British North

Carolina continued to grow and spread south, hugging the Coastal Plain. By 1711, settlers could be found from the Albemarle Sound down past the Neuse River to the mouth of the White Oak River. As settlement expanded, Indians along the Coastal Plain and barrier islands, such as the Machapungas, Pamlicos, Hatteras, Neuse, and Cores, found themselves losing lands and becoming hemmed in. They lost their hunting quarters; their cornfields were eaten by settler cattle and hogs; and if they hunted these animals or ventured too far into the settlements, they might be beaten by settlers, possibly murdered. Indians were not necessarily submissive or subservient and were willing to brawl when provoked. They complained of settler abuses, but the colonial government usually ignored them. We have no evidence of Indian delegations being welcomed by colonial authorities to discuss Indian problems before the Tuscarora War of 1711–15. When ignored, these coastal Indians took their complaints to the Tuscaroras, in particular King Hancock and King Tom Blount, to whom they detailed the insults settlers heaped upon them.

The Machapungas, also known as the Mattamuskeets, were Algonquian peoples who lived on the rather large peninsula formed by the Albemarle Sound to the north and the Pamlico Sound to the south. They were the descendants of Wingina's Secota peoples, whom the English had met during their Roanoke expeditions. By the early 1700s, the Machapungas had four towns: Machapunga and Mattamuskeet near Lake Mattamuskeet, Bay River and Raudauquaquank on the Pungo River.[21] They were linguistically related to the Chowans, Yeopims, and Hatteras of the Albemarle. Back in Lost Colony times, Indian towns had populated the peninsula, such as Secota, Dasemkepeuc, Aquascogoc, Pomeioke, and others, but now, after decades of sickness, violence, and abuse, the survivors had coalesced into the Machapungas, who claimed lands around Lake Mattamuskeet from the coast to about where Washington, North Carolina, sits today. Much of this land, especially around Lake Mattamuskeet, was salt marsh and forests. The English called it a "desert." Here, however, the Machapungas thrived, hunting deer, bear, and other small game, taking fish and shellfish, and planting corn on raised patches of ground. They seemed to have a long-standing feud with the Cores to the south.[22]

Then in the first years of the 1700s, settlers moved onto nearby lands. It did not take long before they began complaining about the Machapungas being "unpardonably insolent both in their speeches and actions" and that it was the government's "Christian duty to see us defended from these barbarous heathen."[23] In 1705, the town of Bath, the first incorporated town in North Carolina, was founded on the north bank of the Pamlico River and on lands the Machapungas thought of as theirs. The town brought more settlers, and soon the colony's surveyor general, John Lawson, was busy marking off Machapunga lands for English settlement.[24]

The Machapungas at Bay River, whom the English often saw as the separate Bay River or Bear River Indians, were closely allied with the Tuscaroras on Contentnea Creek, so closely that nearby settlers accused the Tuscaroras of manipulating Bay River politics. In September 1699, the colony negotiated a treaty with the Bay River Indians by which they became tributaries of North Carolina—or at least North Carolina thought so. As such, they were to put themselves under English law, rescue shipwreck victims who washed ashore near them, and not fight the English or their Indian allies. Each July the Bay River king and his head men were to appear before the General Court and pay a "pair of skins as a tribute to the English government."[25]

Things went downhill quickly. In 1701, settler Thomas Amy accused five Bay River Indian men of threatening his life by putting the barrel of a cocked musket against his breast. The Bay Rivers said Amy brought it upon himself by giving the Indians three pots of rum, despite being warned that it would make them rude. They threatened no one, the Bay Rivers explained, but when Amy mentioned enslaving Indians, they jumped from the canoes in fright, and several of Amy's guns toppled into the water. Three years later, settler William Powell accused Bay River leader King Louther and a band of Bay Rivers of looting his cabin, taking all his ammunition, and frightening his wife and children. Powell confronted King Louther, and Louther struck him with a bow. Powell reported that when he said he would complain to the governor, King Louther said Powell "might kiss his arse," then called Powell a "sonn of a bitch," and claimed they would return during a light moon to burn his house and take his corn. This threat scared the nearby settlers, making them believe the Machapungas and Tuscaroras were plotting a war against them. The Bay River Indians believed the same about the settlers. Certainly, King Louther complained to the Tuscaroras about all this.[26]

Not far from the Machapungas sat another Algonquian-speaking people called the Pamlicos. They were the descendants of the Pomeiokes, who had lived on the peninsula during the Roanoke expedition and had battled the *weroance* Wingina. The Pamlicos lived in a village on an island in the Pamlico River and had been hit hard by smallpox in 1696. By 1709, they could field only fifteen warriors, and their entire population comprised only about sixty men, women, and children, possibly fewer. We are not sure what island the Pamlicos lived on and whether it was nearer the coast or farther upriver near present-day Washington, North Carolina. Nevertheless, they remained close friends with the Machapungas. They, too, complained about the settlers, and the settlers complained about them. In February 1708, Robert Kingman, a captain of a sloop on the Pamlico River, heard that the Pamlicos were planning to attack his boat and "cut their throats."[27] Seems it was just a rumor.

The Hatteras were an Algonquian-speaking people who lived on the "sand banks," which was the eighteenth-century name for that long strip of offshore islands called the Outer Banks. The Hatteras were the descendants of the Roanokes and Croatans and lived on the triangular Hatteras Island, which juts far into the Atlantic, making it a natural stop for sailors cruising the coast. John Lawson believed these people had adopted the Lost Colony because so many Hatteras had gray eyes and an oral tradition that their ancestors were White people who could read books and sail ships. In reality, those gray eyes may have come from mariners, who often stopped at Hatteras

Island. Ever since the Roanoke expeditions in the 1580s, fishermen, whalers, dolphin renderers, and ships needing repairs stopped on Hatteras Island. Early on, the island's Native peoples established cooperative relations with these European sailors, often working for them, assisting them, and being intimate with them. Two Hatteras towns came about: one at Cape Creek, which showed close interaction with Europeans and may have been a bicultural town, and the other on Kings Point, which seemed more traditional. The Hatteras, because of their isolation, had little interaction with North Carolina officials and settlers but more interaction with passing Europeans than most other Coastal Plain Indians. By the first decade of the 1700s, the colony counted the Hatteras as having only sixteen warriors and between forty-five and sixty people. Although it appeared that some Hatteras seemed eager to adopt English ways, another faction was not so enthusiastic.[28]

South of the Neuse River sat one of the more mysterious Indian peoples, the Cores, who gave their name to Core Sound and Core Banks. The name "Core" rarely shows up before the early 1700s, but several other names starting with C do. For example, Gov. John Archdale in 1696 said the "Coranyees" lived on Core Sound and had been devastated by illness and warfare. The North Carolina government recognized there were two groups: the Cores and the Nynees.[29] The trader William Gale mentioned the Cores, Corennines, and Connamocksock and indicated that he had good trade with all the Indians in the area except for the Cores, Corennines, and Tuscaroras.[30] John Lawson, who knew the Indians better than most Englishmen in North Carolina, did not mention the Cores or Corennines at all in his book *A New Voyage to Carolina* (1709) but wrote that the "Connamox" lived in two towns, Coranine and Raruta, and could put twenty-five warriors into the field, giving them a population of about a hundred or so.[31] With all this confusion, for better or worse, historians have generally lumped all these peoples together as the Cores living at the town of Coranine on the barrier islands at Cape Lookout and the town of Raruta on the mainland southeast of the mouth of the Neuse River. One reason they do so is that by 1711 all these other names disappeared from the records, and only the name "Core" remained, often spelled "Cor." The Cores were an Iroquoian people and seemingly Tuscarora villages that had moved down the Neuse River toward the coast. They remained firmly attached to the Tuscarora towns up the Neuse River and on Contentnea Creek.[32]

Lawson's information on the Cores was already outdated by the time he published his book. English settlement had begun to crowd the Cores. When they resisted, the settlers complained to the governor that the Cores were insolent, attacking boats on Core Sound and committing a host of robberies and injuries. The Cores insisted they did no such thing. Nevertheless, in 1703 North Carolina declared war on the Cores, authorizing the raising of troops and impressing ships into the cause. It was not a major war, and there are no details of a battle or violence, but maybe the threat alone pushed the Cores from their lands. Now the town of Coranine moved off Cape Lookout to the mainland and took up lands along the White Oak River north of present-day Jacksonville. The English soon referred to these Coranines as the "White Oak River Indians" or sometimes the "Wetock Indians." The other Core town, Raruta, moved up the Neuse River near the confluence of Contentnea Creek and became known as Core Town. It was located just a few miles from King Hancock's Tuscarora town of Catechna, so Core Town leaders certainly told him of the insults and abuses they received from the settlers.[33]

Up the Neuse River from the old Core haunts sat the Neuse. Lawson said they had two towns: Chattooka and Rouconk. We are not sure where Rouconk was, but Chattooka sat on the peninsula where the Neuse and Trent Rivers came together. Led by King Taylor, these Iroquoian peoples could field fifteen warriors with a population of about sixty men, women, and children. The Neuse, who gave their name to the river, were also closely related to the nearby Tuscaroras. Unfortunately for Chattooka, the point of land it sat on was valuable real estate. In 1709, Baron Christophe de Graffenried, with the backing of the Lords Proprietors, settled about 300 Germans and Swiss along the lower Neuse, Trent, and White Oak Rivers. De Graffenried wanted the peninsula for his colony's capital and negotiated a deal with King Taylor, who now moved Chattooka up the Neuse toward Core Town. Where it once sat arose de Graffenried's town of New Bern, the second town founded in North Carolina. Unfortunately, the Neuse were not far enough away to escape settler abuses. When one of King Taylor's men spoke against selling their land, de Graffenried's business partner, Louis Michel, viciously beat the man. A Swiss carpenter visiting Chattooka smashed the town's double-headed effigy statue, which happened to be painted black and red, the same colors adopted by his hometown, Bern, Switzerland. King Taylor complained. De Graffenried felt no real harm was done but promised it would not happen again. It can be certain the Tuscaroras heard about these incidents, too.[34]

There were many other Indian peoples in the area, of course, but most of them fell beyond the reach of the North Carolina government. Out on the Piedmont and the upper Cape Fear River, besides the Occaneechis and Saponis, also lived such Siouan peoples as the Catawbas, Enos, Shakoris, Keyauwees, and Sissipahaws. On the lower Cape Fear River lived the Woccons, Waccamaws, and Cape Fear Indians. Far out in the western mountains lived the Cherokees, but they had little interaction with the North Carolina government at this time. Except for the Occaneechis and Saponis, who remained firmly tied to Virginia, these other Piedmont and lower Cape Fear peoples gravitated toward South Carolina, and many became tributaries of that colony. So the White Oak River was about as far south as North Carolina settlement extended in 1711. The westward boundary of settlement was a little more nebulous but essentially was a direct line south from the Chowan River to the mouth of the White Oak River. Just west of this line sat the huge Tuscarora nation, with its heavily populated towns along Contentnea Creek, the Tar River, and Roanoke River and in several swamps and creeks connected to them. North Carolina settlement during this time went from north to south, so the Tuscaroras proper had not yet been too affected by land loss and abuse, but they certainly heard about them from the Indians to their east.

Tuscarora Troubles

The Tuscaroras were by far the largest Indian nation in eastern North Carolina, with a population of about 8,000 by the 1690s.[35] They were the farthest south of the Iroquoian finger stretching down from the Great Lakes. In fact, centuries earlier they had lived among the Iroquois nations in New York before migrating south and so kept in close contact with the Senecas and other members of the Five Nations of the Iroquois Haudenosaunee. This split from their New York kinfolk seemed to leave a strong imprint on the Tuscarora mind. From it, they took the lesson that in times of crisis it was acceptable to leave behind the area of troubles even if that meant splitting away from one's own kinfolk. They recognized that different agendas, different strategies, and different factions were not only a reality but necessary for the Tuscarora people to survive. This lesson would help them survive the English.[36]

By the late 1600s, Tuscarora villages of rectangular, oval-roofed longhouses dotted the uplands overlooking the waterways of the region. In going up Contentnea Creek, a tributary of the Neuse, a traveler would find the Tuscarora towns of Catechna, Caunookehoe, Innennits, Neoheroka, Kenta, and Torhunta. To the north, far up the Tar River, sat the town of Toisnot, near present-day Wilson. Downriver on the Tar-Pamlico sat Ucohnerunt, just east of present-day Greenville, Nakay near present-day Washington, and Nonawharitsa farther down the Pamlico toward the coast. Northernmost along the Roanoke River, a tributary of the Albemarle Sound, a traveler would find the towns of Taski and Cheeweo on the south side of the river. There were villages at present-day Jordan's Landing on the Roanoke River, one on the Cashie River, and others, but we do not know what the Tuscaroras called them. Tuscarora villages had also moved down the Pamlico and Neuse Rivers toward the seacoast. English settlers referred to these Iroquoian speakers and their towns by various names, such as "Core," "Neuse," and "White Oak River Indians," but they all were really of Tuscarora heritage and spoke

Iroquoian. By the late 1600s, there were between fifteen and twenty good-size Tuscarora villages and a multitude of smaller hamlets and farms scattered from Contentnea Creek, the Neuse River, and White Oak River north to the Roanoke River.[37]

Each Tuscarora town was independent, autonomous, and governed by a town chief and a council of war captains, diplomats, and respected older warriors. When the town was confronted by any important issue concerning war, peace, diplomacy, trade, hunting, or the like, then the chief and the council discussed it thoroughly and exhaustively. Every person attending the council got to speak without interruption. While consensus was a goal, it could not always be reached. In that case, a decision might be delayed until consensus could be reached. If the chief was respected enough, he might push through his own ideas, or, conversely, he might just go with what the majority thought. The council acted as a brake on any rash action the chief might take, and he could not speak for the town until the council gave its assent. But there were other constituencies the chief had to take into consideration. Women had influence and could make their approval or disapproval known through their clans and clan elders as well as through their husbands and sons. Another important group the chief had to be aware of was the young warriors. Because the council consisted mainly of older men, it tended to be more conservative, more deliberate. The young warriors, their masculinity and aggressiveness at a peak, tended to be more volatile and rash. The town chief had little coercive power to make them do what he wanted or to stop them from raiding, so the young warriors could push the village in directions the chief and council may not have wanted to go. It took much persuasion to keep them in line.[38]

Then there were factions within the town and nation—people and groups who had different ideas about what town policy should be and competing visions for the Tuscarora future. In modern times, a faction is negatively perceived as being unnecessarily contentious and self-serving. However, in Tuscarora society factions were mainly policy disagreements, though personalities certainly played a role. Each faction had different ideas about what should be done. This was not necessarily bad because rather than the entire town or nation follow a single strategy that might lead to destruction for all, alternative strategies provided insurance that at least some of the people would survive. The trick was knowing which strategy and which faction had the better prospect for success. Bred into the Tuscarora national character was a willingness to divide and follow alternative policies. It could be seen in Tuscarora history as centuries ago they had been willing to migrate away from the Iroquois people's unstable governments in New York and finally make their way to North Carolina. So for every Tuscarora chief, there was a rival or several of them who thought they knew better.[39]

The town council's insistence that every major decision be hashed out meant that every Tuscarora town or village was free to go its own way, follow its own diplomacy, form alliances or leave them, make war or peace as it saw fit. The Tuscaroras were a nation by language, culture, clans, history, and place, but no overarching Tuscarora government held all the towns together. There was no supreme Tuscarora authority, no one Tuscarora chief who could command all Tuscaroras or Tuscarora towns. Unlike the Iroquois League of the Longhouse in New York, or Haudenosaunee, no Tuscarora confederacy united the towns, nor was there any central town where Tuscarora representatives met to discuss policy, as the Haudenosaunee did at Onondaga. Some men, such as King Hancock or King Blount, might be considered spokesmen for several affiliated towns, but such men, like all town chiefs, possessed little actual authority. Chiefs served as counselors among their people and as mediators between towns or with the English. But the chief could not make a decision or agreement on his own. It had to come out of each town's council discussions. This system frustrated English officials, who wanted to deal with someone in charge who could make immediate binding decisions for all Tuscaroras. They called town chiefs "kings," imagining they had far more power and authority than they actually possessed.[40]

Certainly, Tuscarora towns could unite, make alliances, or follow similar paths. If several towns found that their interests converged, then there was nothing stopping them from acting in concert. Here is where an able and persuasive town chief might lift himself up to something more like a paramount chief of several towns. A successful chief, one whose predictions came true and who wisely advanced his people's interests, might have other town chiefs and councils look to him for advice. His words held weight, and Tuscaroras gravitated toward him. Other Indian peoples might look to his leadership as well. Nevertheless, the town councils had the last word, though a persuasive chief with many followers might convince them to go with his plan. Then again, failure and setbacks could just as easily lose him his following and influence.

By 1711 and despite the tradition of autonomous towns, two powerful leaders had come to dominate Tuscarora politics: King Hancock at Catechna, who drew in the towns along Contentnea Creek and the Neuse River in the south, and King Tom Blount, who had the ear of the more northerly towns along the Tar-Pamlico and Roanoke Rivers. Blount and Hancock had somewhat differing visions for the Tuscarora future. Much of that future involved questions of how to deal with the English, who by the late 1600s and early 1700s were settling near the Tuscaroras and taking lands that had belonged to allied villages. The most serious incursion, at least for King Hancock's Contentnea Creek Tuscaroras, came in 1710 when Baron Christophe de Graffenried settled his 300 German and Swiss colonists at the mouth of the Neuse River and on territory that had long been considered Tuscarora territory. There were also issues over the deerskin trade, the Indian slave trade, and abuse by settlers that infuriated the Tuscaroras and all Indians of eastern North Carolina.

By 1711, English manufactured goods such as firearms, gunpowder, metal tools, glass beads, cloth, and clothing were facts of life in just about every Indian home. They were acquired mainly through the deer hide trade. Every winter, whole Indian communities left their main town and went to their hunting quarters, where they took as many deer and bear as they could. The meat was eaten or preserved, and the hides were cured by the women. The tanning process could be back-breaking, knee-crushing labor as it required women to work bent over on their knees. Hands ached as they spent hours scraping the meat and hair off the hide, kneading in a concoction of deer brains and corn to make it supple, stretching it over a frame, then drying it over a smoky fire. It could take a week to fully process a single deer hide. Multiply that by the scores of hides a family needed to make it through a year, and one can imagine the hard work women did. Some hides were used by women to make clothing and utensils, but most were exchanged with English traders for manufactured goods. This made the Indians dependent on the English for these necessities, and so threatening to cut off trade was a way for the colonial government to control the Indians and get them to toe the line.[41]

Trade brought familiarity as traders learned Tuscarora phrases to smooth their way. "Wouwockaninniwock": "The Englishman is thirsty." "Utta-ana-wox": "Have you got anything to eat?" "Waust-hanocha": "I will sell you goods very cheap." "Tnotsauraauweek": "Let it alone!" New words entered the Tuscarora vocabulary: *Nickreuroh*, or "Englishman"; *ooonaquod*, "rum"; *oukn*, "gunpowder"; *auknoc*, "gun"; *ocques*, "buckskins."[42]

It was among these foreign traders that the Tuscaroras and other Indians of the Carolinas met their first Africans and realized how the English divided the peoples of the world by skin color. It did not take them long to realize that among the English white skin was supreme, while Black people and Red people were treated as lesser beings. Carolina Indians were receiving their first lessons in racism and White supremacy.[43] For the Tuscaroras, these trading relationships were mainly with Virginia traders, not North Carolina ones. The North Carolina government had little interaction with the Indians just to its west.

Another problem with the trade was that it brought in alcohol, which disrupted Indian society. Drunkenness, brawls, accidents, and violence became common. "Nothing has been so fatal to them as their ungovernable passion for rum," William Byrd of Virginia noted, "with which, I am sorry to say it, they have been but too liberally supply'd by the English that live near them."[44] As early as 1696, Gov.

John Archdale said that rum was a major cause of the extermination of Indian peoples. John Lawson, like Archdale and Byrd, agreed, believing that rum was the great destroyer of Indian nations.[45]

Not all North Carolina Indians drank alcohol, which was easily available from Virginia and South Carolina traders. Probably most did not. Some could drink a little and leave it alone. But some individuals, just as in all societies across the world, became alcoholics. For them, alcohol became addictive, and with it arrived all the problems that came with drunkenness—broken families, injured people, economic loss, and damaged relationships. Exactly why did Indians drink? There may have been a spiritual aspect of an alcoholic high, or maybe it was just fun or a way to fight boredom or depression. Yet exactly why some Indians became alcoholics is also a mystery. To this day, there are debates about whether alcoholism is a behavioral or genetic disorder. Indians do not have a genetic disposition toward alcohol any greater than any other ethnicity or people. They were not a people biologically geared toward becoming alcoholics. But on an individual level, many Indians did drink, get drunk, become alcoholics, and cause family and social upheaval. How many Indians died from alcoholism or its peripheral damage cannot be known, but it was causing problems for eastern North Carolina Indian societies.[46]

For some Englishmen, deerskins were not enough, and they turned to enslaving Indians. Up in New England, during King Philip's War of the 1670s, Puritans enslaved captured Wampanoag warriors and their families and sold them out of the colony.[47] Early on, Virginia had been involved in taking Indian slaves. In 1691, a Tuscarora captive could be purchased for a quantity of black wampum worth about £60 sterling. In that year, Virginia colonist Daniel Pugh kidnapped four Tuscarora men and sold them to planters in Barbados.[48] South Carolina took the Indian slave trade to new heights. Soon after the founding of Charles Town in 1670, merchants, seeing profit in supplying slaves to Barbados sugar plantations, unleashed their own Indian allies—the Westos, Savannahs, Yamasees, and the many Siouan-speakers living within that colony—to capture other Indians. Long lines of captured Indians, mainly women and children, were soon being marched back to Charles Town for a life of slavery in Barbados, the South Carolina rice and indigo fields, or the Virginia tobacco plantations. Even North Carolinian settlers captured or purchased Indian slaves to gain headright lands and for labor on their farms. Enslaved Indians were cheaper than enslaved Africans.[49] By 1715, more than 32,000 Indian captives, maybe many more, had been exported through South Carolina. It is unknown how many Indians from eastern North Carolina wound up in the Charles Town slave pens, but the trade often occupied the minds of eastern North Carolina Indians. In Barbados, the enslaved lived a short, hard life of overwork and sickness. Although those bound for other American colonies might or might not live longer than those in Barbados, they were still enslaved and usually wound up working as domestic servants or field hands.[50]

A final indignity of the Indian slave trade was the disease it spread across the American Southeast. Once Europeans arrived in the Americas, Indians began dying off in huge numbers. Thomas Harriot, on England's Roanoke Island expedition of 1585, reported that soon after they left, the Indian inhabitants in every town the English visited began to die rapidly, "in some towns about twenty, in some forty, in some sixty & in one six score, which in truth was very many in respect of their numbers."[51] Epidemic disease had arrived in North Carolina, but the slave trade made matters worse when disease-ridden captives spread their germs as they were marched across the Southeast. Survivors of shattered villages crowded into nearby towns, and soon sanitation diseases such as typhus and cholera struck. In 1696, at the height of the Indian slave trade, the Great Smallpox Epidemic hit the Southeast and killed tens of thousands. Gov. John Archdale told of a "pestilential fever among the Carolinians that hath swept away many towns," with God "thinning the Indians to make room for the English."[52] As the slave raids shattered Indian towns and nations, they also destroyed the last vestiges of the old Mississippian chiefdoms and, along with the diseases they spread, created what historians have called a "shatter zone" of instability in the Indian Southeast. The Indians of North Carolina fell into this shatter zone of war, disease, hunger, culture loss, village disruption, and population decline. The Tuscaroras lost thousands to slave raids and disease.[53]

The Indian slave trade sowed chaos across Indian North Carolina. The early eighteenth century was a time of pestilence, grief, and anger for many Native peoples. Population numbers declined. Reliable figures for North Carolina Indians are hard to come by, and the numbers are extremely variable. Virginia officials in 1685 believed the Tuscaroras numbered about 8,000 people, with several thousand other Indians in North Carolina's upper Coastal Plain, for a total of about 10,000.[54] Others have said that in 1660 there were as many as 30,000 Indians on North Carolina's upper Coastal Plain.[55] But the numbers were in a free fall. In 1600, the Chowans were believed to have a population of 1,500, but by 1700 it had dropped to just 60. The Weapemeocs also had 1,500 in 1600, but now the Yeopims could count only 40 in 1700. The Meherrins had 700 in 1,600 but less than 100 in 1700. The Tuscaroras had declined to about 5,000 people, with maybe 1,400 warriors. In all, by 1700 the Indian population of the whole North Carolina Coastal Plain had dropped to about 7,200 and continued to fall.[56] As John Lawson saw the Indians' situation, "Small-Pox and Rum have made such a destruction amongst them, that on good ground I do believe there is not the sixth Savage living within two hundred miles of all our settlements as there were fifty years ago."[57]

Ratcheting up the pressure on the Tuscaroras and other North Carolina Indians were the Senecas from New York. The Senecas were one of the nations that made up the Five Nations of the Iroquois Haudenosaunee in the colony of New York. In the east sat the Mohawks near the Hudson River; west of them were the Oneidas, Onondagas, Cayugas, and Senecas. In centuries past, these Iroquois nations often warred against each other, but the Peacemaker brought the Great Law of Peace to the Five Nations, which ended civil wars and created the Iroquois League of the Longhouse—the Haudenosaunee—which served as a powerful confederacy with a republican government. The Great Law not only brought peace among the Five

Nations but was also to be offered to all other Indian peoples. If they accepted, they would become secondary, nonvoting members of the Haudenosaunee. If they refused, then the Five Nations were justified in waging war against them and bringing them into submission as tributaries. Their warriors would be added to Haudenosaunee strength. Beginning in the 1640s, the Five Nations, fueled first by Dutch and later English flintlocks, eventually defeated the French-allied Hurons and other Indians connected to French Québec. Although the Five Nations were normally allies of the English in New York and Pennsylvania, the Senecas, as the westernmost nation, tended to be less bound to the English and willing to follow their own diplomatic agendas. By the 1670s, Seneca war parties were moving south, hitting the Susquehannahs and other Indians in Maryland, Virginia, and the Carolinas. These raids into the Carolinas picked up steam after 1700.[58]

The Senecas became a dagger in the side of the South Carolina Indians. Almost every year, Seneca war parties traveled south along the Great Iroquois Warpath, visited the villages of their Tuscarora kinfolk in North Carolina, then used these villages as springboards to raid the Siouan peoples of the Piedmont and South Carolina. Deer hides, livestock, and captives were taken and prestige earned on these raids. Lawson had much to say on the Senecas. They were, he said, "a sort of people that range several thousands of miles, making all prey they lay their hands on. These are fear'd by all the savage nations I ever was among." He considered them the "mortal enemies to all our Indians." As he saw them, the Senecas were addicted to war and could not imagine living without it. Lawson believed that even if peace were made, the Senecas would still find a way to make war because peace was outside their element. English traders heading out to the Indian villages feared meeting up with the Senecas.[59]

Then in the summer of 1710, the Senecas caught word of the problems the Tuscaroras faced in North Carolina and saw a potential addition to the league. At Conestoga, Pennsylvania, in June 1710, three Tuscarora town chiefs met with Pennsylvania officials to discuss relocating to that colony to escape the slave raids out of

South Carolina. Here in front of everyone, the Tuscaroras detailed the problems bedeviling them. Pennsylvania officials were open to the idea of the Tuscaroras relocating there but requested North Carolina to provide a certificate of good behavior for the Tuscaroras and approve of the move. North Carolina ignored the request. The Senecas did not. They heard firsthand of Tuscarora problems and in them saw a chance to dominate a weakened nation and possibly pull it into the League of the Longhouse.[60] Not just the English had eyes on making North Carolina Indians into client states and tributaries.

In 1711, scores of Seneca warriors and diplomats descended on the Tuscarora towns and began meddling in Tuscarora politics. They whispered into the ears of young warriors, played on their Tuscarora pride and masculinity, shamed them for taking such abuse from the English. "The whites had imposed on them," the Senecas told the Tuscaroras, and when the White people were done using them, they would knock the Tuscaroras in the head. The Tuscaroras were "fools to slave & hunt to furnish themselves with the white people's food." Why not just kill the White people and take what they wanted? And if the Tuscaroras decided to make war on the English, then they should "not fear want of ammunition for that, [as] they [the Senecas] would come twice a year & furnish them with it."[61]

Chaos in North Carolina played into Seneca hands as the colonial government was already in the midst of a near civil war with Cary's Rebellion and so had little ability or inclination to listen to Indian complaints, much less to do anything about them. Cary's Rebellion was a political spat between a coalition of antiauthoritarian settlers, Quakers, and disenchanted Bath County men who felt they were being cut out of political power and the wealthier men from the western parts of Albemarle County. From 1708 to 1711, the North Carolina government barely functioned, and so Indians' complaints fell on deaf ears. Other than Surveyor General John Lawson, few colonial officials had any contact with the Indians of the colony. It is unknown if tribute was even collected from the Chowans and Yeopims during these years. There were rumors that some of

Thomas Cary's men visited the Tuscaroras and encouraged them to attack supporters of Edward Hyde, whom the Lords Proprietors appointed as the colony's official governor. So while the Tuscaroras and the others Indians complained and tempers rose, colonial officials seemed almost criminally ignorant about what was going on just a few miles west of the settlements.[62]

The historians Alan Simpson and Mary Simpson sum up the English view of Indians this way: "The Indian was a heathen savage, to be liked for his kindness, feared for his treachery, admired for his skills, respected for his moments of dignity, and pitied for all his inferiority to civilized Christians—a poor savage in times of peace, a diabolical savage in times of war."[63] With this view in mind, it would be difficult for the average English settler to consider his Indian neighbor as a fellow subject of the same English monarch. Indians learned their own lessons about White people. Sometimes settlers hired them as guides, hunters to provide food, pack haulers, or workers on their farms. But it was just as common for an Indian to be beaten if he showed up among the settlements. Hunting parties that stopped by settler cabins and asked for food or water were turned away more often than not. Even Lawson could admit that "we look upon them with scorn and disdain, and think them little better than beasts in human shape, though if well examined, we shall find that, for all our religion and education, we possess more moral deformities and evils than these savages do, or are acquainted withal. We reckon them slaves in comparison to us."[64]

By the end of the first decade of the 1700s, Indians across eastern North Carolina feared for their livelihoods and their lives. They were becoming strangers in their own land, and that land seemed to be shrinking. The few nations that had already become tributaries felt they were not being protected as promised, and those that were not tributaries had no interest in submitting to the English. Indians had many complaints, but no one in the North Carolina colonial government seemed to care. Conflict seemed inevitable, but the English were blissfully ignorant.

Tuscarora War

War came in September 1711, when King Hancock's Tuscaroras caught Surveyor General John Lawson and Baron Christophe de Graffenried scouting land in Tuscarora territory. After a two-day trial, Lawson was executed, de Graffenried was held captive, and King Hancock, leader of the Contentnea Creek Tuscaroras, declared war on North Carolina. Appealing to all the angry Indian peoples of the Coastal Plain, Hancock created what historians have called the Catechna Alliance, named after his own town, Catechna, which served as the center of resistance. The Alliance consisted of Catechna and the other southern Tuscarora towns along Contentnea Creek as well as the Cores, Neuse, White Oak River Indians, and the Algonquian-speaking Machapungas and Pamlicos. None of them were tributaries or client states of England, except for the Bay River Machapungas, who had put themselves under tributary status in 1699. The other members of the Alliance, if asked, would have said they were fighting to resist becoming tributaries, to avenge abuses, and to force North Carolina to rethink its Indian policy of taking their lands and abusing their people while ignoring Indian complaints.[65]

Up along Albemarle Sound and the Outer Banks, the Chowans, Meherrins, and Yeopims, who had already been declared tributaries of North Carolina, as well as the Hatteras, did not join the Catechna Alliance, did not make war on the English, and would later provide warriors to fight against the Catechna Alliance. Their loyalty to the English may have had more to do with their location surrounded by North Carolina settlers, not far from Virginia and rather distant from the towns of the Catechna Alliance. Not all Tuscaroras joined King Hancock's Alliance, either. Hancock's main rival, King Tom Blount of the Tar River town Ucohnerunt, who spoke for many towns along the Tar-Pamlico and Roanoke Rivers, refused to join the Alliance and the war. Blount and his Tuscaroras were not tributaries of the colony, but he hoped to steer a neutral course by not supporting either Hancock or the colony. His towns were just west of the English settlements of the Albemarle and not far from Virginia, so the chances of his people being attacked should he go to war were high. Blount was an impressive and pragmatic politician who seemed to realize that war with the English would not work out well. He may also have not wanted to support King Hancock, whom he saw as his main rival for Tuscarora leadership. Whatever the reasons, those towns along the Tar-Pamlico and Roanoke Rivers that looked to Blount for leadership did not go to war against the English. Here was a classic example of the Tuscarora strategy of opposing agendas: Hancock would lead his Tuscarora's war faction, Blount would lead the neutral faction.[66]

On September 22, 1711, the warriors of the Catechna Alliance attacked English, German, and Swiss settlements from the Pamlico River in the north down to the White Oak River in the south. Across three days of continuous attacks, more than 140 settler men, women, children, White and Black, free and enslaved, were killed; between 30 and 40 were taken captive; hundreds of farms, plantations, boats, and buildings were destroyed, herds of livestock run off or slaughtered. The warriors plundered what they could and headed back to their villages to await North Carolina's response. The attacks brought North Carolina to its knees, and the already dysfunctional colony could make no coherent counterattack. No Englishman trusted the tributary Indians to help, so turning to them did not seem to have been a consideration in those first few weeks after the attacks. Nor does it appear that the tributary Chowans or Meherrins volunteered their immediate assistance. Gov. Edward Hyde instead appealed to South Carolina for an expedition against the Tuscaroras.

South Carolina, heavily involved in the Indian slave trade, saw Hyde's appeal as an opportunity to take captives in a righteous war while performing a moral duty to aid fellow Christians and a neighboring English colony. In the spring of 1712, South Carolina sent an expedition led by Col. John Barnwell, composed of about 35 South Carolina officers and militia and more than 700 Indian allies, including the Muskhogean-speaking Yamasees as well as the Siouan-speaking Catawbas, Waterees, Cheraws, Sugerees, Waxhaws, Cape Fears, and others. But the Tuscaroras and their allies in the Alliance had decided upon a different type of warfare. Instead of taking on Barnwell's army in the field, they withdrew to a heavily protected fort at Catechna. Constructed along European lines with palisade walls, firing ports, flankers, and bastions, it proved a formidable piece of military engineering designed by the Indians with the assistance of Harry, a runaway enslaved African from Virginia. Indians and Africans were already finding a common ground in resistance to the English.[67]

Barnwell's army assaulted Hancock's Fort, as it came to be called, twice, in March and again in April 1712, but it proved too formidable. Taking casualties and running out of supplies, Barnwell offered a peace treaty, which the Tuscaroras accepted, though part of the deal was that they dismantle the fort and hand over Harry the slave engineer, whom Barnwell immediately hacked to pieces with his cutlass. The Tuscaroras were also to hand over King Hancock, but he was not in the fort. Another demand by Barnwell was that the Indians agree to pay tribute to North Carolina. The Indians agreed. Wanting Barnwell to destroy Indian power, not make a peace, Gov. Edward Hyde refused to accept Barnwell's treaty, and so the war continued for the English, while the Indians thought they had made peace. In May, a surprise attack on Core and Bay River Indians who had gathered to sign the peace treaty and the enslavement of hundreds of them showed the Indians that the war was still on. Now the Indians, angry at English treachery, went back on the attack.[68]

Though the Catechna Alliance had survived Barnwell's attacks, the war was turning against it. The enslavement of many of the Cores and Bay River Indians hurt Alliance manpower. Several Tuscarora towns along Contentnea Creek, with their tradition of autonomy and factionalism, deserted the Alliance and took refuge in Virginia. Then in late 1712, King Tom Blount of the upper Tuscaroras ended his policy of neutrality and went in partially on the side of the colonial government. At the onset of the war, North Carolina and Virginia had immediately banned all trade with Blount's Tuscaroras until Blount indicated he was willing to join the colony in its war against the Alliance. That fall, at the behest of North Carolina officials, Blount captured King Hancock and turned him over to colonial authorities for execution. He also unleashed his warriors against non-Tuscarora members of the Catechna Alliance, such as the Machapungas and the Pamlicos, effectively wiping out the latter. Even worse for the now leaderless Alliance, South Carolina was sending a second expedition to finish the job Barnwell could not.[69]

Led by Col. James Moore, who had experience attacking fortified positions from making slave raids into Spanish Florida, the expedition, just shy of a thousand Indian warriors, was much the same as Barnwell's the previous year, with many of the same militiamen and warriors. By March 1713, Moore's army had besieged the Indians in their fort at Neoheroka, a town higher up on Contentnea Creek. It was another European-style fort, only stronger and correcting any deficiencies exposed by Barnwell's attacks on Hancock's Fort. Moore ordered an assault, and in three days of savage fighting his men took the fort, burned to death scores of Indians who had sought refuge in underground bunkers, killed many more during the attacks in and around the fort, and enslaved hundreds, who were marched back to the Charles Town slave markets. The Catechna Alliance had been crushed. Though a few Catechna town, Core, and Machapunga holdouts remained for a while, they made peace in February 1715.[70]

With the help of South Carolina and Tuscarora king Tom Blount, colonial North Carolina had broken Indian power in the east and could now force the remaining Indians to become tributaries and the subjects of the British king.

3

A Tributary King for the Tuscaroras

With the end of the Tuscarora War and the defeat of the Catechna Alliance, the colonial North Carolina government could now implement its plan of turning the remaining Indians of eastern North Carolina into tributaries and assigning them land reserves. One way to ensure peace and compliance was to appoint Native leaders, such as King Tom Blount, to oversee the Native tributaries. However, King Blount was not a passive puppet but found ways to assert his authority and protect his people by playing on English fears.

For North Carolina, the Tuscarora War ended the old Rogues Harbor free-for-all democracy. Now governors, the Governor's Council, and the colonial courts brought the stability the Chowan Clique wanted and cemented North Carolina's place within the mercantile British Empire. Although shallow waters prevented a vigorous overseas trade, plantation agriculture and related industries took hold. Tobacco, fishing, cattle, logging, rice, tar, pitch, and naval store production, handled mainly by increasing numbers of enslaved Africans, brought the colony into the Atlantic world. By 1720, there were about 2,000 enslaved Africans in North Carolina. This number jumped to 6,000 in 1730. Among the enslaved workers were also Indians taken during the wars or bought from slave merchants.[1] Nevertheless, the colony was overwhelmingly a land of subsistence farmers. With the Tuscarora bottleneck broken, many settlers filtered out to the Piedmont and mountains, where they faced the Catawbas and Cherokees, who would eventually be subjected to the colonization process.

Despite the colony's victory over the Indians, it was a nervous time for North Carolina. Proprietor oversight was spotty until 1729, when the Lords Proprietors sold the colony to King George II, and North Carolina became a royal colony. There was also the expansion of French Louisiana just west of the Appalachian Mountains, which meant the constant threat of war with the French and their Indian allies. In 1715, the Yamasee War broke out in South Carolina when many of the same Indians who had served with Cols. Barnwell and Moore now turned their muskets on that colony. With the help of North Carolina troops, a band of King Blount's Tuscaroras, and a few Core warriors, South Carolina defeated the Yamasee alliance and brought its own Indians into tributary status. Some South Carolina Indians, such as a few Cheraw families and others, took refuge in the swamps of southeastern North Carolina, making North Carolina officials worry they might reinfect that colony's own Indians with war fever.[2]

This fear of another Indian war was very real for shell-shocked North Carolina. The Indian attacks on September 22, 1711, haunted the colony, and that day remained an official day of fasting and prayer in North Carolina for decades.[3] Though King Tom Blount had proved loyal to the English, colonial officials still distrusted him and imagined he was just biding his time, waiting for the Senecas to join him for an attack on the colony. To prevent this, colonial governors determined that now there would be a much closer relationship between the government and the colony's Native inhabitants. In this new world, the Indians would become official tributaries under the laws of the government. They would choose their own leaders, but those chosen had to be approved by the colonial governor. The Native tributaries could govern themselves according to their own ways as long as those ways did not conflict with colonial law. The colony would handle all Indian diplomacy with other colonies and other Indians. Any criminal actions between the Indians and the English would be handled by colonial authorities. Indian nations would be assigned reserves of lands with surveyed, marked boundaries, where, theoretically, they could live as they wanted without being bothered by settlers. Indian complaints would be heard and investigated, justice meted out, and measures instituted to prevent another costly

Indian war. The Tuscarora and other Indian nations in the colony were to be puppet states, trade clients, and allies, and their warriors would serve as military auxiliaries when called upon. But there would be no doubts that North Carolina would be in control.[4]

The Indian situation in eastern North Carolina was much different in 1715 than it had been in 1711. The war had shattered Indian towns and peoples. The Pamlicos, Neuse, and White Oak River Indians all disappeared from the colonial records, though individuals and families of those peoples still lived in the area or joined with other peoples. Core and Machapunga survivors retreated east to the marshes around Lake Mattamuskeet, though the name "Bay River Indians" also disappeared as a separate entity. North of the Albemarle, the Chowans, Meherrins, Yeopims, and Hatteras, who had sided with the colony, survived the war intact, though the Hatteras had been briefly displaced by Catechna Alliance attacks and had turned to the colony for assistance. The Saponis and Occaneechis sat out the war in the Piedmont or up in Virginia, though North Carolina had asked them to ally with the colony.

The Tuscaroras had been hit hard. The war had divided the nation, and the half that had gone to war had been destroyed or were refugees. Hundreds had been killed or enslaved. The lower Tuscarora towns along Contentnea Creek had been abandoned, and their survivors sought refuge with Blount's people, went farther north to Virginia, or faded into swamps to lie low and join with other refugees. Some headed to the Cheraws in the swamps of southeastern North Carolina, especially down on Drowning Creek, later known as the Lumber River. Blount still led a host of Tuscarora towns and villages that spread across the Tar and Roanoke Rivers. Though counts are sketchy, by the summer of 1715 Blount's Tuscaroras numbered around 3,000 men, women, and children. Several hundred more were in Virginia or taking refuge in the swamps. That meant that during the previous twenty-five years, from 1690 to 1715, the Tuscarora population had dropped by about 4,000 to 4,500 people, many killed, enslaved, or relocated elsewhere. Nevertheless, Blount's Tuscaroras remained the largest Indian nation in eastern North Carolina.[5]

The death and enslavement of so many Tuscaroras shocked Tom Blount. His own people and kinfolk, more than half the nation, destroyed, in hiding, or marched off as slaves. The Battle of the Neoheroka Fort in 1713 was one more great Indian defeat at the hands of the colonizers, certainly one of the costliest. It served as a warning of what could happen if Indians dared make war on the colony again. The English would never make peace, never give up until Indian power had been destroyed. This had to be a sobering thought to Blount and other Indian leaders.

Moore's victory at Neoheroka impressed Gov. Alexander Spotswood of Virginia, who noted that the colonel's South Carolina forces killed or enslaved more than a thousand Indians. The "blow having extremely frightened" the Indians, Spotswood advised Gov. Thomas Pollock of North Carolina "to improve it, by engaging them in a Peace."[6] Spotswood, ever the savvy diplomat, understood that the key to peace in North Carolina rested with Tuscarora leader Tom Blount. He also understood Blount's personality. "Talk high to him," Spotswood wrote to Pollock, "make him King of all those Indians under the protection of North Carolina." This approach would stir Blount's ambition and so make him faithful to the English. Make a treaty with him, Spotswood urged, and then Pollock can insist Blount deliver up all those warriors who had made war on the English. Just as important, a loyal King Blount would be an ear for the government on what was happening in Indian country. This information, Spotswood warned, was essential to preventing future attacks. Spotswood assured Pollock that once North Carolina recognized Blount as king, Virginia would recognize him as well.[7] Gov. Pollock saw this as sound advice and sent word to Blount to meet him at Pollock's Balgra plantation on the Chowan River. He planned to coronate Blount as king of the Tuscaroras.

King Tom Blount

We do not know Blount's Tuscarora name. Whatever it was, it has been lost to history. Every record that mentions him calls him "Tom

Blount" or just "Blount," sometimes spelled "Blunt." Tradition says he was born into his mother's Bear clan around 1675 in the town of Ucohnerunt on the Tar River in eastern North Carolina. Even that date is unsure. At his birth, the clan mother gave him a name. But names were changeable things, and he may have gone through many over the course of his life. At some point, he either took or accepted the name "Tom Blount." There was a Virginia trader, Tom Blount, who visited the Tuscaroras in the latter part of the 1600s. This Virginian could speak Tuscarora and often served as an interpreter. It is possible Blount took this man's name. So he is forever Blount, Tom Blount, and later King Blount.[8] This was not unusual; many North Carolina Indians were either accepting English-style first and last names, or that was how they were being named in the colonial records.

Blount was born the year before Bacon's Rebellion broke out in Virginia, and as he grew up, the English and English goods were already a fact of Native life. Virginia traders regularly visited Tuscarora towns, bringing guns, gunpowder, kettles, axes, and all sorts of goods, which the Indians paid for with deerskins. Indian warriors became expert shots with the flintlock trade muskets, and the traders, seeing profit in Indian demand, had no hesitation providing guns for the right number of deerskins. After all, guns made for better hunters. They also made them better warriors. As evident by his later prestige and rank, Blount must have been a fierce warrior in his day. By 1711, he was seen as the spokesman for many of the "upper" Tuscarora towns on the Tar-Pamlico and Roanoke Rivers. We do not know what he looked like, but John Lawson described an Indian he met as always carrying a brace of pistols in his belt, along with a cutlass and a musket.[9] That could be Tom Blount. Along the way, he learned to speak and understand the English language as well as English ways and how to deal with English people. He learned to promise and then delay, to put off as long as possible. It was one of the weapons tributary Indians had in their arsenal when it came to dealing with the colonial government.

We see Blount practicing this art of delay in the first mention of him in the colonial records. It was a lawsuit brought against him in June 1705. Tom Blount of the Tuscaroras rented a mare from William Brice, who lived along the Trent River. Blount was to use the horse for three months and then return it. If he had not returned it by the end of the three-month period, he would pay fifty doeskins as a penalty. Now it was June, the three months had come and gone, and Blount had not returned the mare or paid the fifty doeskins. Brice appealed to the North Carolina Governor's Council, which handled the colony's Indian affairs, begging it to compel Blount to make satisfaction.[10] There is no record of the council compelling Blount to pay or of him returning the mare or the doeskins. And Brice had a reputation as a shady character. But this was not a case of a naive Indian not understanding what he was agreeing to. Blount had long dealt with traders. He understood contracts and credits. In this case, he knew he could get what he wanted—both the mare and the doeskins—by delaying. It proved a good strategy.

Blount became known as a wily and perceptive politician in both the Indian and the English worlds. During the Tuscarora War, Blount led the neutral faction and had been under incredible pressure from all sides. It took a herculean effort to keep most of his warriors from joining the Catechna Alliance, especially in those heady first days of Indian victories. Blount became a beacon to those Tuscaroras who rejected war, wanted peace, and looked to him as an alternative to King Hancock and his war strategy. Despite Blount's insistence that he would not go to war against the colonies, both North Carolina and Virginia officials distrusted him and expected he would eventually throw in with the Alliance. Making it harder on him was that both colonies immediately instituted a trade ban on all Tuscaroras, and so Blount's people lost access to guns and tools at a dangerous time. Gov. Spotswood of Virginia as well as Gov. Edward Hyde and then Gov. Thomas Pollock of North Carolina demanded he go to war against the Alliance, promising so many blankets and goods for every enemy captive or scalp he brought in. They promised to lift the trade embargo if he sent his warriors to attack the Tuscarora towns along Contentnea Creek.[11]

On the one hand, Blount had no desire to go to war against the English. That was a fool's errand. He led the Tuscarora faction that stressed peace and neutrality. On the other, he did not want to do the colony's dirty work and attack his own Tuscarora kinfolk. So Blount used his long-honed strategy of promise and delay. He agreed to side with Carolina in the war, assured colonial officials that they had nothing to fear from his people along the Tar and Roanoke Rivers, but reminded them that his warriors could make no attacks unless they received caravan loads of trade goods, in particular guns, powder, and shot. And then he did nothing.

In the fall of 1712, though, Blount seemed to have a change of heart. Gov. Pollock, upset at Blount's dawdling, insisted that Blount provide twelve hostages from each Tuscarora town. Only then would he give them ammunition. If not that, Blount could show his willingness to help by capturing King Hancock.[12] Rather than deliver hostages, Blount agreed to capture the Alliance leader. Hancock had escaped from the Catechna fort before Barnwell's treaty and had been lurking around Blount's towns. Blount explained to Pollock that he would pretend friendship with Hancock, go hunting with him in the woods, and then suddenly take him captive. This decision would haunt Blount and his reputation up to this very day. Still, there was a certain Tuscarora logic to it. After the attacks on September 22, it had become Hancock's war. For the English, King Hancock was leader of the Alliance, had executed John Lawson, and had initiated the war. He was the most wanted man in three colonies. Even worse for the beleaguered king, the Catechna Alliance had abandoned him as it agreed to hand him over in the Treaty of Hancock's Fort in April 1712, though the old king was not at the fort when the treaty was made. He had become a tragic figure on the run, and unless he escaped the region, it was guaranteed that he would eventually be captured and executed. Hancock's visits to Blount's towns put Blount in a precarious position. Harboring a marked man like Hancock could invite a colonial attack. Hancock was a danger, and the town councils must have agreed with Blount. So sometime in November 1712 Blount went hunting with Hancock, took him prisoner, then handed him over to Gov. Pollock, who executed the forsaken king.[13]

A few months later, Blount could inform Gov. Pollock that he had sent his own diplomats to meet with the Five Nations of the Iroquois in Albany, New York, and could report that they would not support the Catechna Alliance's war. Blount's efforts mollified Pollock, who softened his attitude toward the Tuscarora leader and believed his word might, just might, be trusted. In contrast, Blount seemed to have little regard for Pollock—after all, North Carolina was a weak, divided colony that could not prosecute the war on its own. Unlike Virginia, North Carolina provided few trade goods to the Tuscaroras. So while the Virginia trade spigot had been turned off, Blount's people had received some goods, guns, and ammunition from the Meherrins, possibly from the Senecas, and other Virginia tributaries who still welcomed Old Dominion traders. So when Pollock gave Blount letters he wanted carried to other Tuscarora towns asking them to make peace with North Carolina, Blount never delivered them. He refused, he told his Tuscaroras, to be a letter carrier for the English.[14] This decision increased his prestige among the Tuscaroras who followed him.

Despite this declaration of independence, in June 1713, three months after Col. Moore's successful assault on the Neoheroka Fort, Blount finally unleashed his warriors against what remained of the Catechna Alliance. His men must have been pleased after having been held back for so long. Now they were able to take captives and scalps and so gain prestige and trade goods. In late June, Blount appeared before Pollock with eight Indian captives. The governor did not record which people they belonged to, but he purchased them from Blount for £10 each.[15] Settlers credited Blount's warriors with clearing the western side of the Chowan River of enemy Indians. On another occasion, his men brought thirty Indian scalps to Pollock.[16] His warriors also cleared the Pamlicos from their island.[17] Some of his warriors ventured into the Lake Mattamuskeet swamps against the Cores and Machapungas but had little luck.[18]

Future generations of eastern North Carolina Indians have often seen these attacks by Blount as well as his capture and surrender of King Hancock as evidence of Blount betraying his own people. That he would attack other Tuscaroras has put him in a bad light with some modern-day Indian people.[19] But was Blount attacking his own people? Certainly, he played the main role in King Hancock's capture and execution, but making war on his own people may not be so. We do not know the nationality of those captives and scalps Blount's delivered to Pollock. They may or may not have been Catechna Tuscaroras. As for clearing the west side of the Chowan River, it is also not clear what Indians those might be, but the Meherrins lived west of the Chowan, and Blount's Tuscaroras had always had a touchy relationship with them. The Pamlicos and the Machapungas were Algonquian peoples, not Tuscaroras. Although the Cores were a Tuscarora people, they had thrown in with the Machapungas. Yet it is also possible Blount's warriors could differentiate between Cores and Machapungas. Besides, they had little success around those Lake Mattamuskeet marshes. The key point is that King Blount found a way to fulfill his treaty obligations to the English, increase his prestige with his own people and with Gov. Pollock, give his warriors a chance to earn war honors and captives, and do all this without attacking his own Tuscarora kinfolk. Blount was showing himself to be a truly masterful politician.

Pollock came to realize that Blount's refusal to go to war alongside the Catechna Alliance had saved the colony from destruction. Now it was time to reward this ally. In spring 1713, not long after Moore's victory at Neoheroka, Pollock called for a council with all Indian nations not then at war with the colony to make an official treaty of peace and vassalage. The treaty was really between Pollock and Blount, though many Indian "kinglings" sat at the council, and all eastern North Carolina Indians were to be bound by it, including those Tuscaroras taking refuge in Virginia. Gov. Pollock, taking Spotswood's advice, rewarded Blount for "his faithfulness and good service done to us, we will make and acknowledge him king and commander in chief of all Indians on the south side of the Pamlico

River under protection of this Government and . . . we will [make] a firm and lasting peace with him and all the Indians that acknowledge him as such."[20]

However, becoming king of all Indians came with a price. Pollock listed his demands. Blount was to deliver up to twenty of Hancock's principal men involved in the execution of Lawson, the captivity of de Graffenried, and the "massacre" of the settlers in 1711. He should also hand over any other participants his people might come across. All plunder taken by the Catechna Alliance, including "captives, horses, arms, goods and cattle," must be returned. Blount and his warriors were "to pursue, kill and take as enemies the Catechnees, Matamoskits and all the Indian enemies to the English." Finally, to ensure Blount would do what he said, Pollock insisted that by May 10 or 11 Blount was to return with two hostages from each of the towns he now governed.[21] It was a tough treaty, but Blount had to be somewhat happy about how it had turned out. He was king of the Tuscaroras, with authority over all Indians in eastern North Carolina, recognized as such by the English in both North Carolina and Virginia and backed by their power. He was also now officially a tributary of the colony and a subject of Queen Anne.

For Pollock, dealing with a single Tuscarora king rather than a leader from every town made sense. Someone was bound to be the sole Tuscarora king after the war, and Blount was the logical choice, the only choice. Besides, Englishmen back then understood authority and the power a monarch wielded. Queen Anne sat on the British throne and ruled the empire. The Lords Proprietors in London owned the colony. Thomas Pollock, the governor of North Carolina, wielded power in their stead, and he had total power. Even the colony's legislature had given him the authority to run the war as he saw fit and deal with the Indians as he needed, and if an Indian committed a crime, Pollock was "fully impowered to inflict such immediate punishment on them as he shall think ye crime requires."[22] So now instead of autonomous Indian towns with powerful councils of elders, there would be an Indian king governing a people but answering to the colonial governor.

However, a single king with full authority over them was something new and disquieting for the Tuscaroras. They were a people who cherished town autonomy, with a council that had more authority than the chief and where all major decisions would have to be hashed out. Under the new English plan, Blount spoke for all Tuscaroras, all towns, villages, and hamlets, and could ignore council decisions if he chose. As king of a people who had always utilized a system of town autonomy, differing factions, and political rivalries, Blount became a polarizing figure. With town autonomy crimped, factions and rivals blossomed but could never come to fruition. The new regime did not allow for the natural rise and fall of Tuscarora factions and leaders. The English held final authority and so could support their puppet king over any other rival or faction. In the past, the Tuscaroras could get rid of a despot or someone whose plans were increasingly unsuccessful by following his rival. Now they could not. Blount was in total charge, something unheard of among the Tuscaroras.

Pollock's other treaty demands did not seem particularly onerous to Blount. Handing over wanted men, returning plunder, making war on the Alliance, and giving up hostages had been asked of him before. But he was an artful politician and knew how to promise, delay, and then do nothing. Turn over twenty of the chief men involved in the war? Certainly, if he could find them. Return plundered English goods? Definitely, but most of that plunder had been taken to South Carolina by Barnwell and Moore's victorious Indian allies. Blount had already returned a stolen horse that belonged to an English settler. Hand over hostages? Sometimes he did, sometimes he did not. His own brother had been a hostage to Spotswood in Virginia. Make war on the Alliance? He had done this in his own measured way. Even then, Blount had other cards he could play. During the treaty council, just to show his importance to the governor, Blount reported that the Seneca sachem Canaquanee had visited him with about a hundred warriors at Ucohnerunt and had urged him to join Canaquanee in destroying the English. As Canaquanee explained it, the English "only amused" Blount "with fair words to keep him from doing them mischief but when they had destroyed the rest of his nations he might be sure to be destroyed likewise." If the Tuscarora king would ally with the Senecas, then Canaquanee "would settle him out of danger of the English." In telling of his meeting with Canaquanee, Blount assured Pollock that his commitment to keeping the peace with the English had never wavered and that he had told Canaquanee "to leave them to themselves and mind his own concerns."[23] That the Senecas were appealing to Blount had to give Pollock the shivers. That fear gave Blount leverage.

More than anything, Pollock feared the powerful Senecas joining what remained of the Catechna Alliance, Blount throwing in with them, and the new alliance making war on the colony. Both Pollock and Spotswood always believed the Senecas, maybe even the entire Five Nations of the Iroquois League of the Longhouse, were just over the horizon, gathering to attack the southern colonies. That fear did not end with the Tuscarora War. Blount constantly had to reassure Pollock that he and his Tuscaroras were friends to the English and that no attack was in the making. That assurance gave Blount prestige and standing with the colonial government because he was seen as an intermediary who could persuade the dangerous Senecas not to go to war. He would be Pollock's eyes and ears on what was going on in Indian country.[24] Nevertheless, Pollock's own fears and suspicions meant he would have to tread just as carefully with Blount as Blount would with him.

Up in Virginia, Gov. Spotswood worried that Pollock's terms were too harsh and might push the Tuscarora king into the arms of those very Senecas. As he wrote Pollock, insisting that Blount turn over twenty Indian chiefs and any Indian who had raised the war club against a White person was just too much. Making such harsh demands on the heels of Moore's crushing victory at Neoheroka, where so many Tuscaroras had been killed or enslaved, could make Blount believe peace was just too costly and so take the Senecas up on their offer. North Carolina could ill afford another war, Spotswood chided. Instead, he urged, Pollock should just ask for three or four specific principal men. That way Blount could feel easy in handing them over. A gentler route might make a better peace. Spotswood, always willing to stick it to North Carolina when he could, also complained that Pollock's treaty did not make any mention of Virginia's efforts or require Blount to make peace with Spotswood's colony.[25]

The whole thing almost fell apart when a band of Col. Moore's South Carolina Indian allies captured Blount's wife, two of his children, and his sister's son. Hearing of it, Gov. Pollock leaped into action. After counseling with Col. Moore, they located Blount's family in the South Carolina Indian camp, and Pollock purchased them out of his own pocket. They were back at Blount's town within days. Capt. Maurice Moore, brother of Col. Moore, and Charles Glover, an interpreter, escorted the family home. The two Englishmen then remained at Blount's town to guard him from further attacks. Pollock officially asked Gov. Charles Craven of South Carolina to stop his colony's Indians from attacking Blount's towns.[26]

What had the makings of a tragedy became a victory for Blount. His family was returned, but even more the incident showed his importance to both Tuscarora and North Carolina fortunes. That the colonial governor acted in Blount's behalf so quickly, spent his own money to redeem the captives, and sent them back escorted by Col. Moore's own brother certainly increased Blount's prestige. It did not hurt that two colonial officials now protected his town. It would not be too difficult for a Tuscarora man or woman to imagine that Blount held these two men as hostages, though neither actually were. That the North Carolina government worked for Blount and went out if its way to appease him seemed evident a few months later when the Meherrins to the north captured two Tuscarora children. Blount complained to Pollock, explaining that the children's parents were loyal friends of the English. Again, Pollock moved quickly. He had the North Carolina Governor's Council order the Meherrins to return the two children, or "they will answer the contrary at their perrill," and if they did not, then Pollock will "take such further measures as he shall think fit to compel them thereto." Having felt Pollock's anger before, the Meherrins promptly returned the two children.[27] Blount's prestige among the Tuscaroras skyrocketed. He was a leader who got results.

It now came time to give King Blount his own realm.

A Reserve and a Migration

Since Blount had been named king of all Indians south of the Pamlico River, Pollock directed him to settle his people on lands between Onion quits-tah Creek, a tributary of the Pamlico River, and the Neuse River.[28] Unfortunately, Pollock's directive is as nebulous as many colonial texts, so we are not exactly sure where these lands were. The name "Onion quits-tah Creek" does not appear on modern maps. Nor does it show up on John Lawson's map of 1709 or Edward Moseley's map of 1733, the two best maps of early eighteenth-century North Carolina. The Tar-Pamlico River also causes a little confusion. In modern times, the Tar River, with its headwaters in Granville County, flows southeast, but when it hits present-day Washington, North Carolina, it becomes the Pamlico River and eventually empties into Pamlico Sound. However, back in Blount's time, the name "Pamlico," or some near spelling such as "Pampticough," was given to the whole river. Though there is currently a Blount's Bay and a Blount's Creek south of Washington on the Pamlico River, they do not appear to be named for King Tom Blount. Pollock would not have settled the Tuscaroras so far east because this area had long been filling up with settlers. Pollock's directive more than likely put Blount and his Tuscaroras near Ucohnerunt, Blount's original home village, and west of the line of settlement. It was to be a land reserve for Blount and his people as the Governor's Council stipulated that the Tuscarora lands were "bounded and limited."[29] So in 1714, Blount and his Tuscaroras officially moved onto their reserve. To make the relocation easier, Blount requested and received a hundred bushels of corn from the colony's public store.[30] Still, Blount's realm was a vast shrinkage of Tuscarora territory because all towns along Contentnea Creek, the Roanoke River, and the lower Pamlico and lower Neuse Rivers had been lost as well as most of their old hunting quarters. Blount's Tuscaroras were now indeed tributaries to the colony.

As such, Blount's Tuscaroras also lost their hunting rights in Virginia. All Tuscaroras entering Virginia would have to show a passport. King Blount objected and told Gov. Spotswood that "the country belonged to them before [the] English came thither; so . . . they had a better title than [the English] and ought not to be confined to such narrow limits for hunting." This complaint gives insight on how Blount, the Tuscaroras, and the other Indians of eastern North Carolina saw the land. It had been their land long before the English arrived, and even now, despite being tributaries, they believed they still had certain rights concerning it. Spotswood, however, appealed to a higher power and informed Blount that God—"Mohomny"—had taken the land from the Indians and given it to the English because the English obeyed Him, while the Indians did not. This appeal also provided an important insight into how the English saw the land and the Indians' claims to it: the English now had dominion over the land and could parcel it out because they had God's favor. Blount replied that he could not tell what Mohomny wanted them to do, so how did Spotswood know the will of Mohomny? Spotswood launched into the Christian story of how God sent his son to earth and taught them what they were supposed to do and so reasoned that this gave the English control over the land. Blount replied that he "had talked with several Governors and other English, but he really never before heard that Mohomny had a Son."[31] Because Jesus as the son of God is the basis of Christianity, Blount's lack of knowledge about him shows just how little missionary effort had been done in North Carolina. Despite his claims, Spotswood would soon find that Blount still held the trump card as Virginia traders relied heavily on the Tuscaroras to visit their trading post in southern Virginia.

However, just as Blount settled into his official lands, he faced a challenge. Old factions resurfaced, and now many Tuscaroras took the opportunity to abandon their homes in North Carolina and move north to join the Iroquois Haudenosaunee in New York. The

Senecas had long dabbled in Tuscarora politics with the hope of pulling them into the League of the Longhouse. Seneca warriors had certainly pushed the Catechna Alliance toward war, listing the abuses the English had heaped on its members, pushing for Lawson's execution, and promising ammunition and support.[32] Now in the chaos of the war's aftermath, the Senecas urged the Tuscaroras to abandon their homes down south and join them up north. Refugees in Virginia were some of the first to take the Senecas up on their offer. Gov. Spotswood reported that Seneca diplomats were among those offering assistance "upon condition of incorporating with them."[33] Down in North Carolina, many Tuscaroras living under the authority of King Blount also decided to move north.

The exodus came in 1715 just as Blount and his people settled into their home between the Pamlico and Neuse Rivers. Accurate numbers are hard to come by, but it seems that around 1,500 Tuscaroras, both individuals and entire families, left North Carolina, heading for a new home in New York. On their own and without any assistance from the colony, groups of Tuscaroras headed up the Great Iroquois Warpath, cut across the Shenandoah Valley to the Potomac River into Maryland and then Pennsylvania. They eventually hit the Susquehanna River and traveled up it to its Great Bend just north of the New York border.[34] However, not all made it to New York. Families and small groups sometimes splintered off and settled in Virginia, Maryland, and Pennsylvania. The journey was not always peaceful as both Indians and English settlers attacked some migrating Tuscaroras. A group was massacred in Carroll County, Maryland.[35] Nevertheless, the majority made their way to their Iroquois kinfolk in New York and added their warriors, women, families, and knowledge to the Haudenosaunee.

The arriving Tuscaroras gave the Iroquois a boost in confidence because they could now field 3,000 warriors.[36] When New York officials protested these new arrivals, an Iroquois sachem explained the situation this way: "The Tuscarora Indians are come to shelter themselves among the five nations. They were of us and went from us long ago and are now returned and promise to live peaceably among us, and since there is peace now everywhere we have received them. . . . We desire you to look upon the Tuscaroras that are come to live among us as our Children who shall obey your Commands & live Peaceably and orderly."[37] In 1722, these Tuscaroras would officially become the Sixth Nation of the Haudenosaunee. This would strengthen the connection between the New York Tuscaroras and Iroquois and those Tuscaroras remaining in North Carolina. The New York Tuscaroras would serve over the course of the eighteenth century as an escape valve for discontented North Carolina Tuscaroras. The joining of the North Carolina Tuscaroras to the League of the Longhouse gave them increased leverage with colonial officials but also created additional factions among North Carolina Tuscaroras.[38]

Exactly why these 1,500 Tuscaroras chose to leave North Carolina and their kinfolk at this time has never been fully explained. Was it a reaction to Tom Blount and his being named king of the Tuscarora? Certain Tuscaroras and factions disliked that he had never joined the war against the English and was responsible for the execution of King Hancock. Working against him in some instances were his close relations with the English, his ego, his kingship over a people that had never before had a king, and that he seemed to be the symbol of how far the Tuscaroras had fallen. All or any of these factors could have made a Tuscarora choose the Senecas over Blount.[39] More than likely, most of these Tuscaroras going north were survivors of the Catechna Alliance and those towns along Contentnea Creek and the lower Neuse. Others may have been like the Tuscaroras of Toisnot town farther west, who had never been part of Blount's people in the first place. With the Senecas calling to them and offering refuge, this seemed the perfect opportunity to make their move. These Tuscaroras carried their anger toward the English with them. Up in New York, they made it dangerous for English traders traveling the Mohawk River Valley. Rumors swirled that these new Tuscarora arrivals wanted to recruit Iroquois war parties to make raids on North Carolina. It was said that it took much Iroquois diplomatic skill to keep them under control.[40]

It was possible that some of Blount's own people decided to go north with the exodus. After all, even then the choice appeared stark: stay in North Carolina as tributaries under the thumb of the English, who showed no hesitation in abusing and enslaving Indian peoples when it suited them, or relocate to live among the powerful Iroquois, who had not been subjugated by the English and in fact seemed to stand up to them. But leaving would be difficult as it meant giving up their homes, the graves where their ancestors were buried, the sacred sites where spirits walked, just about everything they knew for an uncertain life as refugees among distant kinfolk who knew little about them. Nevertheless, some went. But many remained with Blount. It was hard to give up their lands and kinfolk, the place they had for centuries called home. Land and place were important to Indians and their identity. As the historian Bradley Dixon points out, "The land tied the [Native peoples] to their ancestors, and its boundaries marked off friend from foe. The land embodied a pattern of human relationships among the [Indians] as well as between them, other Indigenous people, and the colonists."[41] To many Tuscaroras, Blount seemed wise and knowing. He had kept them out of the war, protected them from the fate of King Hancock's people, and stood up for them; therefore, many remained loyal to him. About 1,500 or so Tuscaroras remained with Blount in North Carolina. Half of the North Carolina Tuscaroras went north, and the other half remained.

The exodus was traditional Tuscarora factionalism at play. Before the war, the Hancock and the Catechna Alliance faction supported war. Blount and his people remained the neutral or peace faction. There had also been a removal faction made up of those who had wanted to relocate to Pennsylvania in 1710 due to the Indian slave trade but were turned down. During the war, many of the removal faction took refuge in Virginia. But now Hancock's war faction had been destroyed, while Blount's peace faction remained, and he was now king of all Tuscaroras. Many of the removal faction now headed north to join the Iroquois or south to the woods and swamps of southeastern North Carolina. Though the Tuscaroras might now

be scattered between North Carolina and New York, the nation survived, and the Tuscarora people remained alive.[42]

Indian Woods

In April 1715, the Yamasee War in South Carolina began, and for
a while the situation looked bleak for that colony. A contingent of
Tuscarora and Core warriors led by North Carolina commanders
went to help the South Carolinians. Nevertheless, the Yamasee War
put Blount on the defensive. The Yamasees, Cheraws, Catawbas, and
other Indians at war with South Carolina had long been enemies
of the Tuscaroras. Raids and counterraids between the two peoples
had been the norm for centuries. The Indian slave trade out of South
Carolina had increased the attacks. Col. James Moore's expedition
during the Tuscarora War brought these old enemies to Blount's
doorstep, and the violence continued.[43] The chaos of the Yamasee
War unleashed further attacks. The Cheraws, trying to escape South
Carolina counterattacks, moved into the abandoned Tuscarora villages along Contentnea Creek, putting these old enemies just a few
miles from Blount's door on the Tar-Pamlico. Blount warned North
Carolina officials that he believed the Cheraws were preparing to attack settlers along the Neuse and Pamlico Rivers and his own people.
The Cheraws had already captured one of his men, he said. Blount
also passed along a rumor he had heard that the Cheraws had recently attacked and killed nine or ten Virginia traders.[44]

Some accused Blount of overstating the Cheraw threat to increase his importance with the colonial authorities.[45] But he was not
the only one worried. Gov. Charles Craven of South Carolina asked
North Carolina to send troops and Indian allies to "annoy" the
Cheraws. Gov. Charles Eden of North Carolina sent twelve militiamen and a number of Blount's warriors to investigate.[46] When Gov.
Spotswood of Virginia asked North Carolina to allow him to settle
some Cheraw families on the upper Neuse north of Tuscarora territory, both Blount and North Carolina strongly objected, and nothing
came of the plan.[47] Down on the Trent River, settlers William Brice

and William Hancock informed Gov. Eden they had been attacked by the Cheraws and offered to lead a retaliatory raid if the government would pay for it. Not wanting to fund another full-scale war, Eden had Blount send some of his warriors down to investigate and attack the Cheraws if need be. They discovered the whole thing was part of a scheme cooked up by Brice and Hancock to get the colonial government to fund their own slave raids against the Cheraws. Nothing came of the hoax, which, former governor Pollock said later, had the potential to spark an even more deadly conflict.[48]

Though North Carolina feared the Cheraws and their allies might do some mischief and even stationed companies of militiamen and Blount's warriors at crucial points, the Cheraws eventually made peace with South Carolina. By 1718, some had moved back to South Carolina, but others took refuge in the swamps of southeastern North Carolina, around Drowning Creek and its marshy tributaries, lying low and out of sight of the settlers. They would become the nucleus of a large community of Indians from many different nations that would come to inhabit that part of southeastern North Carolina.[49]

The Cheraw occupation forced Blount to reevaluate the location of his reserve. In 1717, citing attacks by the Cheraws and other South Carolina Indians, Blount asked the North Carolina government to move his reserve away from the Pamlico River and farther north to the Roanoke River, one river system away. That location would still be within traditional Tuscarora territory and the area in which most of Blount's people had lived before the war. For many, it would be a move home. The North Carolina Governor's Council noted that Blount and his Tuscaroras "have been very serviceable to this Government and still continues [sic] so to be. And as a particular mark of favor from the Government they do hereby give unto him the said Blount land lying between Mr. Jones's lower land on the northside of the Moratock [Roanoke] River to Quitmak Swamp." Officials warned Blount that his Tuscaroras should be careful not to "molest nor disturb the Inhabitants" or kill the settlers' cattle during their hunts on lands adjacent to their tract. They should also take care not to claim any lands outside their bounds on either side of the Roanoke River. The Tuscaroras made their move by Christmas 1717.[50]

"Indian Woods," as the tract came to be called, was a Tuscarora land reserve consisting of 41,113 acres, just a shade more than 64 square miles, located on the north side of the Roanoke River between Quitsnay Swamp and Deep Creek in what would become south-central Bertie County. Now the North Carolina Tuscarora nation comprised just two towns. Ooneroy, sometimes spelled "Uneray," sat directly on the north side of the Roanoke River just north of present-day Hamilton. Ooneroy may have been the town John Lawson called "Oonossoora." The other town was Resootka, which sat a few miles north of Ooneroy on a creek that emptied into the Roanoke River. It may have been the town Lawson called "Anna Ooka," but again it is unclear as Lawson never explained where these towns were located.[51]

This was now the Tuscarora's North Carolina homeland and King Blount's realm. It was a far cry from the Tuscaroras' former expanse, which had at one time included lands along Contentnea Creek and the Neuse, Pamlico, and Roanoke Rivers and stretched all the way down to the coast to the White Oak River and west to the Piedmont. Still, it was not a bad place. Their new home had plenty of river frontage and a mixture of swamps, piney woods, and good farming land. At that time, it was west of the line of English settlement but not too far west of the colonial capital soon to be named Edenton, which sat at the confluence of the Chowan River and Albemarle Sound about 40 miles away. There were still deer and bear in the woods, fish in the river, tortoises and turtles on the creeks, and land for farming. Here was the place where the shell-shocked Tuscaroras could recover from the war in which about half of their people had been killed or enslaved; a fourth had removed themselves to New York or other places; and only a fourth now remained in their Indian Woods home. Things would be different than before the war. They had a king and were under the thumb of the English. But they could at least rebuild their nation and bring back some semblance of the Tuscarora life they once knew. It would not be easy.

3. Tuscarora Indian Woods Historical Highway Marker near Windsor, North Carolina. After the Tuscarora War, the Tuscaroras, now tributaries of the colonial government, were assigned to a land reserve in Bertie County on the north side of the Roanoke River. They named it "Indian Woods." Other tributaries received reserve lands as well. Photograph by the author.

Fortunately, Indian Woods had King Tom Blount. Blount, shrewd politician that he was, understood the government's fears and used them to his advantage. He insisted the North Carolina government uphold every part of the treaty it had made with him and demanded every perquisite and right due him and his people. Blount made it a point to attend whenever one of his people was arrested by colonial authorities and brought to trial. Though Blount could speak passable English, he insisted on always having an interpreter present, usually his trusted friend William Charleton. If he felt settlers were abusing his people, then he approached the governor or the Governor's Council and asked for redress.[52] The right to petition the governor and Governor's Council was one of the most important arrows in a tributary king's quiver. With petitions, he sought redress, sometimes even the changing of laws.[53]

Sometimes Blount could edge into passive resistance. Much to the anger of nearby settlers, Blount welcomed runaway enslaved Indians to his reserve. In July 1724, Col. William Maule informed the Governor's Council that Blount was harboring an enslaved Indian at Resootka. The council ordered Blount to deliver the slave to Maule per the peace treaty of 1713. If he would not, then he should appear before the council and explain why not. Using his most successful tactic, Blount delayed and did nothing. In October 1724, John Royall accused Blount of harboring an enslaved Indian named March, whom Royall had sold to Francis Pugh. Again the council ordered Blount to appear before it and bring March with him. Again Blount delayed. It was not until almost a year later, on August 3, 1725, that Blount appeared before the council. Nothing was said about Maule's slave, but as for March, Blount said he had gone away with the Senecas. He assured the council that the next time he saw March, he would bring him to the council for judgment. Two years later, in 1727, Pugh was still accusing Blount of keeping March from him. As late as 1731, Isaac Hill accused Blount of detaining his Indian slave named George and wanted him back.[54] It seems Blount and the Senecas were creating a sort of Native Underground Railroad that moved enslaved Indians out of North Carolina and up to the New York Iroquois.

King Blount's efforts to protect his people on Indian Woods has often been overlooked. Nevertheless, he was controversial in his own day and among his own people. Half of the Tuscaroras on the reserve had abandoned Blount's leadership to move to New York. Even among those who remained he was not always held in esteem. In October 1725, Blount appeared before the Governor's Council to inform its members that "some of his people are disorderly and are throwing off their obedience to him as their Ruler." Blount asked for the government's protection and support. The council, happy with Blount's reign at Indian Woods, commanded "all the Tuscaroras to render the said Blount obedience, otherwise they will be looked upon as enemies to the government."[55] This incident seems to have resulted from Senecas meddling in Indian Wood affairs, trying to get Tuscarora warriors to join them in attacks into South Carolina. Blount apparently tried to stop this interference, which caused dissention among the warriors.

That Tuscarora warriors periodically rebelled showed the pressures put on Blount by his own people. He understood that his position as Tuscarora king was unnatural because he could not be overthrown, at least by Tuscaroras. Nevertheless, a supreme leader was a colonial reality, and Blount was under pressure from the English to keep his people under control. But Tuscarora ways ran deep, and young men wanted to raid the Catawbas for goods they could pillage and for the prestige that resulted. The Senecas instigated raids and unrest among the Tuscarora warriors, enticing them to raid into South Carolina with them or join the League of the Longhouse. The Tuscaroras who had migrated to New York in 1715 and so formed the Sixth Nation of the Iroquois exerted their own pull. Kinship ties between New York and North Carolina remained strong, and New York could be an escape path for discontented Carolina Tuscaroras. Blount had to keep all these factions under control and the English at bay as well. Fortunately, he was an able leader with a firm understanding of postwar colonial politics and diplomacy. While being a tributary to North Carolina was a bitter pill, he understood the limits of Tuscarora power and tried to work within those limits. Insisting on always having an interpreter, always attending the courts whenever one of his Tuscaroras was brought up on charges, appealing personally to the governor and petitioning the Governor's Council when issues arose with nearby settlers or other Indians, and being willing to stand up to colonial authorities when he could were all ways to protect his people and advance their interests. It was about all a tributary could do.[56]

Any doubt about Blount's willingness to support his people, help enslaved Indians, and challenge colonial authority can be seen in a most amazing meeting that took place in May 1731. William Watis, a representative of Gov. Robert Johnson of South Carolina, came to Edenton and insisted on meeting with Blount and Gov. George Burrington of North Carolina. On May 10, King Tom Blount, whom Watis misnamed "William," Captain George, eight Tuscarora principal men, and their interpreter William Charleton traveled the 40 miles from Indian Woods to Edenton. With Gov. Burrington sitting in, Watis accused the Tuscaroras of banditry in coming into the South Carolina settlements, where they killed cattle, stole enslaved Indians and horses, murdered Indian allies of South Carolina, and insulted White planters. More specifically, Watis said Blount's warriors took Mr. Mashos's enslaved Indian and killed Mr. Mashos's horses right in front of him. They stole three head of cattle and a horse from Mr. Pawley; took two more horses from Mr. Henlys on Black River; killed a cow and a calf; took a slave of Mr. Bell; and stole shirts and clothing from a laundry line. There is no use to deny it, Watis insisted; he knew it was Blount's Tuscaroras because he had followed their tracks from South Carolina across the Cape Fear River all the way here.

It was not us, Blount claimed, it was the Senecas. He had told the Senecas not to take the slaves, but they would not listen. Yes, he had promised last year not to raid into the South Carolina settlements, but South Carolina Indians had attacked his own people, killing Captain Jack and wounding another. So when some Seneca warriors visited, the Tuscaroras decided to take revenge on some Indians living on a White man's plantation in South Carolina. They attacked them and came home. That was all.

Watis got angry at what he believed was lies. Do you want war with us? Watis thundered. Attacking Indian allies and stealing property in South Carolina could be considered war.

Blount replied that they did not want war but that it was the Senecas who did these things. Besides, South Carolina Catawbas are at this very moment prowling near Indian Woods, killing North Carolina settlers' livestock and targeting Tuscaroras.

You cannot have it both ways, Watis insisted. When North Carolina settlers have their cattle killed, you blame it on South Carolina Indians. When South Carolina settlers accuse the Tuscaroras of killing their cattle, you blame it on the Senecas.

If you do not believe us, Blount said, then it was useless for us to come these 40 miles to Edenton.

I came 400 miles, Watis grumbled, and all I am hearing are lies about the Senecas. I know it was your people.

Gov. Burrington interrupted, telling Blount that the evidence was overwhelming and that he must take responsibility. The governor reminded Blount that he had admitted his people had gone into South Carolina with the Senecas.

Blount and his men conferred among themselves for a little bit. Finally, Blount replied: It was the Senecas, but we promise to never again go into the South Carolina settlements, and so we should be forgiven for the past.

That's not enough! Watis insisted. I came here to get reparations and the return of any enslaved Indians you took.

Like a prosecuting attorney, Blount now turned on Watis. Who saw us take a slave?

This question caught Watis by surprise. Now he had to admit that no one actually saw the Tuscaroras take the slave, but they were seen in the area when the slave disappeared.

Well, said Blount, if no one saw us take the slave, then it was the Senecas, and the Senecas should pay the damages.

Watis became furious, saying the Tuscaroras would be declared enemies of South Carolina, and he would call upon the Catawbas and Cherokees to make war on Blount's people.

Blount calmly replied that he knew the Catawbas and Cherokees were then at war with each other, and so he did not fear both attacking him. Also, his warriors certainly knew the road to

CHOWAN

MEHERRIN ●   ●   ● **YEOPIM**

Roanoke R.   *Chowan R.*

Albemarle Sound

TUSCARORA ●

Tar-Pamlico R.

MACHAPUNGA ●

Neuse R.

HATTERAS ●

TRIBUTARY LAND RESERVES 18th Century

Map by David A. Norris

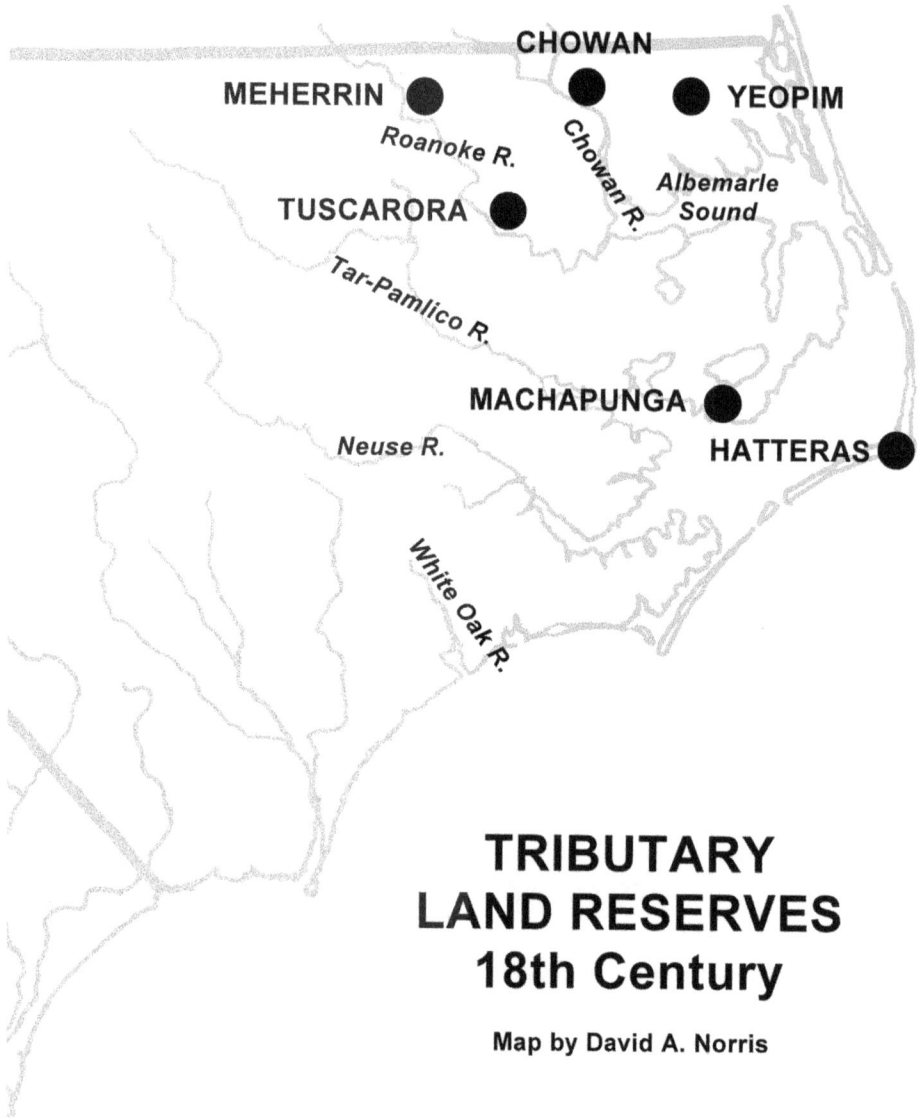

Catawba town. But if Watis wanted reparations, he should look to the Senecas.

Watis told Blount that his people would now be declared enemies of South Carolina, and he would write to the Senecas telling them of the lies Blount was leveling against them.

Gov. Burrington jumped in again and urged Blount to pay the damages. If he did not, then when the Catawbas came against the Tuscaroras, the North Carolina government would give him no assistance. Think hard on this, the governor warned.

Blount and his men went outside to confer and came back a few hours later. Blount announced that they would not pay any of the damages Watis demanded. He promised his warriors would no longer venture into South Carolina, but he could not stop the Senecas from going down there.

And that was that. Blount and his men returned to Indian Woods, and the Tuscaroras never paid any damages to South Carolina.[57] Blount was the master of tributary diplomacy. He would have to use all his skills to hold his people and Indian Woods together.

4

New Realities for the Tributaries

With the Tuscarora War over, now came the days of the reserves where the Tuscaroras and other tributaries had to face a new world. Though they tried to keep their old ways on the reserves as best they could, interaction with their White and Black neighbors forced these Native peoples to walk a new and different road.

The reserves were Indian lands with defined boundaries set down in government records and guaranteed by legislation. Indians insisted they be given written guarantees as they understood the importance the English placed on written land deeds. As detailed in the next chapter, just as the Tuscaroras received their land reserve, so did the other smaller tributaries, such as the Chowans, Yeopims, Meherrins, Machapungas, and Hatteras. These reserves ranged in size, from the Tuscaroras' 41,000 acres to the Hatteras's 200 acres. On their reserves, the Indians would face the full force of English culture.

Within the reserves, the Indians were free to re-create their traditional life, to live as they wanted, governed by a king of their own people, but only as client states under the authority of the North Carolina colonial government and by extension the Lord Proprietors and the English monarch. There was to be no doubt about this. Indians would be guaranteed these limited lands and be protected by colonial authorities. In return, they must accept English authority over them as well as the influx of settlers and slaves and the growth of English plantations and farms around them.

They were conquered nations, and every year their king and principal men were to appear before the colonial governor and pay a ceremonial tribute, often just a few arrowheads, deerskins, or peppercorns. The Feast of St. Michael the Archangel, September 29, eventually became the usual day for annual payments. This was a telling choice as the day honored the Archangel Michael, who defeated Satan during the war in heaven and cast the devil down to rule in hell. Surely the colonial authorities saw a similarity in the Tuscarora War. They had won the war over the Indians and then had cast them onto land reserves in North Carolina. The colonial government also had the right to intercede in Indian affairs whenever it saw fit. Although the Indians could elect their king, he had to be approved by the colonial government and could be deposed by the governor if need be. As tributaries, these Indian nations were to be military allies, buffers protecting the English settlements from attacks by foreign enemies, trade partners, and friends of the colony.

The assigning of Indian reserves seemed to be an honest attempt by North Carolina to provide for and protect the Indians. While some of this protection may have been directed by the Lords Proprietors or been actual Christian paternalism, the fear of another Indian war made the colony often go out of its way to provide for its tributaries, at least to a degree. The Indians could not have all the land, but they would have at least some. Reserves, which the colony felt were large enough to accommodate what seemed to be a dwindling Indian population, were carved out of traditional homelands. They were to be Indian land. That some reserves were later expanded and some created late in the colonial period and the extent the government went to protect Indian boundaries showed that the colonial government wanted Indians to have land of their own. Indians dispossessed of all their land would not be good for colonial stability. But the reserve could not protect the Indians from the poverty that made some see their lands as a cash cow.

The term *reserve* might be best to describe these Indian lands, not *reservations* in the sense that term was applied to later nineteenth-century lands allocated to Indians that one might find in Indian Territory, Arizona, the Dakotas, and elsewhere out west. Those latter-day reservations certainly contained thousands of acres of bounded lands, but there was also a permanent government presence there, including a government-appointed agent who governed the Indians, as well as collateral workers, such as a doctor and storekeeper—all living at an agency where the government disbursed money and merchandise and which served as the reservation capital. These nineteenth-century reservations were to be hothouses of civilization in which Indians would be subjected to various "civilizing" schemes in order to rapidly detribalize them and assimilate them into the American mainstream.[1] Assimilation was not the goal for the colonial reserves. As long as the tributaries did not cause problems for their neighbors or the authorities, then they could do as they pleased. Neither detribalization nor civilization was part of the colonial plan in North Carolina. While authorities and missionaries might encourage the Indians to send their children to schools, they were rarely required to do so, nor did they have to convert to Christianity. During the colonial period, little attempt was made to "civilize" them or change them from being Indians.

Their tributary status and land reserves created a strange world for the Indians. On the one hand, as tributaries they had to seek a middle ground of accommodation and compromise with the colony. They had to accept powerful puppet kings where towns had once been autonomous and councils had made decisions. Indians essentially had to adapt to the English settlers and enslaved Africans mushrooming up around them. On the other hand, the land reserves allowed the Indians to exert a control over their lives and culture.[2] There was no permanent colonial presence on Indian Woods or the other reserves. Only in emergencies or at certain times might a protective guard, the colonial surveyor, or an investigative commission be sent to the reserves and then only temporarily. Settlers did not venture onto the reserves unless they had business, and even then some feared to do so. This was Indian country. Above all, these reserves, sometimes consisting of thousands of acres of land, gave the Indians a source of wealth. These lands were highly desirable and worth good money as the remaining available lands were bought up around them. In certain counties, the Indians would be some of the largest, if not the largest, landholders. They also paid no taxes or quitrents to the colony or Lords Proprietors. So the reserves were Native sovereign land; the Indians owned them, and they gave the Indians some economic leverage with the colony, the county, and the local settlers. However, they also made Indians targets for the land-hungry. Even on their reserves these tributary Indians of eastern North Carolina found their lives changing as they tried to preserve their traditional way of life.

Cultural Accommodations

For the tributary Indians of eastern North Carolina—Tuscaroras, Meherrins, Chowans, Yeopims, Machapungas, Cores, and Hatteras—these reserves became beloved homelands, an Indian territory in themselves. These acres were their national lands guaranteed by the colony where they could be Indians. The reserves became, as King John Hoyter of the Chowans called them, "his one Netev ples."[3] The colony seemed to accept this reasoning as English law recognized Indian ownership of their Indian lands. This connection between Indians and their lands became an important marker of Indianness. Indians lived on Indian land reserves. That was one of the things that made them Indians, as the colony saw it. Indians without lands did not have working governments, so for the colony the Pamlicos, Neuse, Bay River Indians, White Oak River Indians, and others who lost their lands and governments ceased to be independent nations, ceased to be recorded as nations in the colonial records, ceased to be seen as Indians. Nevertheless, individuals from these nations, who very much considered themselves Indians and Native peoples, still lived in the colony but were usually ignored by colonial officials. Some might join with the Tuscaroras on Indian Woods or with other Indian peoples. Some might head to the New York Tuscaroras. Many of these "detribalized" Indians might lie low in the forests and swamps and create their own Indian communities, as was happening down on Drowning Creek in the southern part of North Carolina and in other enclaves in eastern North Carolina. Others lived on the margins of White society, doing menial jobs or farmwork to survive, often living among poor White people and African Peoples of Color.[4]

Blount, the other kings, and their peoples tried to re-create their traditional cultures and societies as best they could, and in many ways they did. Blount's people still spoke Tuscarora, though English was making inroads. Women still farmed, and men hunted. They worshipped as they always had. The raids and counterraids between old enemies continued, though colonial governors tried to stop these attacks between tributaries of different colonies. Well past the mid-eighteenth century, Tuscarora warriors led by war captains, such as Captain Peter, Captain George, and Captain Jack, raided into South Carolina, often hitting the Catawbas and other long-standing enemies. As we saw with William Watis's complaint, the tributaries sometimes ventured into the South Carolina settlements, where the Tuscaroras might steal or kill horses, hogs, and cattle, pilfer clothing, or liberate enslaved plantation Indians and bring them back to their North Carolina reserve. These attacks brought counterraids, and the Catawbas certainly knew their way to Indian Woods, where Blount said they often killed Tuscarora cattle or individuals caught out alone. Captain Jack and another Tuscarora warrior were killed, and some visiting Seneca warriors were wounded by South Carolina Indians at the head of New River in North Carolina.[5] That these raids and counterraids among Indian tributaries of different colonies continued after the Tuscarora War may be chalked up to the need to take revenge for past attacks, the desire for goods, and the prestige that came with brave deeds. But they were also a way of keeping traditional life alive.

Many, but certainly not all, of these attacks on the Catawbas and raids into South Carolina were instigated by New York Senecas and Tuscaroras, who continued visiting their kinfolk at Indian Woods. Blount had a complex relationship with the northerners. If they came wanting to meddle in reserve affairs or convince his Tuscaroras to move to New York, then Blount had no use for them. In August 1723, he informed the North Carolina Governor's Council that a party of "Northern Indians" was coming to Indian Woods with the "intent to seduce the young men of his nation" and "commit mischief on him and on the white people." He asked the council to send some Englishmen to Resootka to prevent this. Alarmed, the council ordered interpreter William Charleton to take six men to Resootka, lay out a fort, and man it. The colony would pay the expenses.[6] Settlers and colonial officials worried about Iroquois warriors coming into the colony with their "insolent carriage and behavior."[7] This was the kind of information the authorities had hoped Blount would provide when they made him king. It reinforced Blount's importance to the colony. It also showed a side of Blount that he would appeal to North Carolina government to shore up his position at Indian Woods. Some Tuscaroras might disagree and view him as a despot. At other times, Tuscarora warriors joined the Senecas on raids into South Carolina and Virginia, seemingly with Blount's blessings.

In April 1717, Tuscarora and Seneca warriors wholly upset Governor Spotswood's plans for Ft. Christiana in Virginia. In 1714, Spotswood hoped to create a colony-wide defense to protect Virginia settlements from "foreign" Indian raiders. With this goal in mind, he created Ft. Christiana on the south side of the Meherrin River in southern Virginia in present-day Brunswick County. Ft. Christiana would serve as a trading post run by the Virginia Indian Company where Indians from the region could exchange deer hides for guns, tools, and other goods. Spotswood hoped this post's presence would undermine illegal traders who caused problems, win friends among other Indian nations, and increase the flow of deerskins into the colony. Defensively, it was to be a barrier against "foreign" Indian attacks.[8]

In 1717, the Virginia Indian Company at the fort hosted about a hundred Catawbas, who had come to trade there. Under company rules, the Catawbas had to disarm and stow their weapons inside the fort. In the early morning of April 10, while the unarmed Catawbas slept outside the fort walls, Tuscarora and Seneca warriors struck. They killed five Catawbas, wounded many more, and took five captive. The Catawbas blamed the attack on Virginia treachery, but Gov.

Spotswood suspected that rogue traders, upset at the Virginia Indian Company's trade monopoly, had informed the Tuscaroras that the Catawbas would be there unarmed and urged an attack. The ploy worked as the Virginia Indian Company was soon disbanded, the fort was abandoned, and trade went back to being unregulated.[9]

These tributary-on-tributary attacks could be brutal. The Tuscaroras, along with their Seneca kinfolk, decimated the Catawbas, Cape Fears, Saponis, and Occaneechis. If a man had the misfortune of being taken captive, then it was almost guaranteed he would be tortured, mutilated, and slowly killed. William Byrd of Virginia wrote that the Senecas and Tuscaroras often scalped their enemies, cutting the skin at the hairline and "then clapping their feet to the poor mortal's shoulders, pull the scalp off clean, and carry it home in triumph." If they captured a war captain, he would be tortured worst of all, and they eventually would "roast him alive." At least that is what Byrd believed.[10] So for the first half of the eighteenth century, raids by Tuscaroras, Senecas, Catawbas, and others, all English tributaries, burned across North Carolina, South Carolina, and southern Virginia, with the colonial governors seemingly powerless to stop them.

If the Native peoples of eastern North Carolina could raid as they always had, they had to learn new ways when it came to dealing with the settler and slave populations growing up around them. The reserves were not prisons, and Indians could come and go as they pleased. Besides raiding old enemies, they left their reserves to go hunting and fishing, collect resources, trade, serve as military auxiliaries for the colony, visit, or do various jobs for their English neighbors. Despite past abuses and the toll taken by the Tuscarora War, Indians remained intensely curious about their English and African neighbors. Indian men and women often visited the nearby settlements. For the Tuscaroras, Chowans, Yeopims, and Meherrins, the closest settlement was the town on the east side of the Chowan River, where it ran into the Albemarle Sound. Locally known as Queen Anne's Creek, for years this town served as the capital of the North Carolina colony. In 1722, when Gov. Charles Eden died, it was incorporated as Edenton. It remained the capital of North Carolina until 1743. Indians wandering the streets of Edenton became a familiar sight. The town of New Bern on the lower Neuse River was also a popular destination for Indians.

As Indians ventured into the settlements, there must have been hundreds of peaceful, friendly interactions, greetings, conversations, assistances, and exchanges. However, such contacts rarely make it into the records. It was usually when things went wrong and the colonial government got involved that a paper trail was created of these misadventures. On August 4, 1722, John Cope, a Tuscarora from Blount's town of Resootka and noted as a Christian Indian, visited Edenton and spent much of the day getting drunk. About three in the morning, Cope fell through a window into the home of former governor Thomas Pollock. Pollock's adult son, Cullen, was asleep on the second floor when he was awakened by the sound of glass shattering. He found John Cope sitting on the floor. Cullen had two enslaved Africans carry him outside. Thomas Pollock had Cope arrested and turned over to a Special Court of Oyer and Terminar for trial. The trial was held on August 14, and King Tom Blount was ordered to attend. Cope did not deny the charge, merely stating that he was drunk. However, twelve White jurors found him not guilty and ordered him discharged from custody. It is mind-boggling that an inebriated Indian would be found not guilty of breaking into the house of a respected former governor, president of the Governor's Council, and probably the wealthiest man in North Carolina! Pollock did not appeal the decision. The reason for the verdict, it seemed, was that neither Pollock nor the government wanted to antagonize Blount and his Tuscaroras. Since no real harm had been done, Cope was returned to Blount's custody.[11] This incident reinforced Blount's reputation among Indians that he could stand up to colonial authorities and get his way.

In May 1725, one of Blount's Tuscaroras visited Bath, got drunk, and accidentally fired a gun into the home of George Moy and wounded two children inside. The children were not seriously injured, and everyone admitted that the shooting was done without malice. The Tuscarora was fined twelve buckskins and twelve doe-skins, and his gun was confiscated until he paid the fine. The money from the skins would cover the cost of the children's medical treatment. Blount apparently paid the fine, and the gun was returned.[12]

One of the main things Blount and his Tuscaroras had going for them was the colony's fear of another Indian war. The Tuscaroras were still the largest Indian nation in eastern North Carolina, and for decades after the war colonial leaders feared the Tuscaroras would ally with the Senecas and launch another devastating attack. As North Carolina saw it, abuses by settlers had started the war, so the colonial government wanted to prevent anything that might spark another. With this in mind, it often gave Blount and his Tuscaroras the benefit of the doubt. Capt. Nicholas Crisp protested that his lands along the Roanoke River had been designated as part of the Tuscarora hunting quarter, and he could not receive title to them. Crisp was under the impression that the Tuscaroras were to be settled between the Pamlico and Neuse River and that giving them any land along the Roanoke would stop English settlement in the area. The Governor's Council sympathized but said Crisp would have to make a separate arrangement with Blount for the Tuscaroras to give up that hunting quarter. Once Crisp had an official arrangement with Blount and the tract was free of Indian title, then Crisp could get his title, despite the rule that land could be purchased only from the Lords Proprietors. This case also showed that the colonial government saw the land issue in more diplomatic terms and that Blount was free to negotiate with Crisp if he wanted. Still, as a sop to Crisp and other landholders who found their lands included in the new Roanoke River Indian Woods reserve, these settlers would not have to pay taxes on them as long as the Tuscaroras lived on the lands. The land reserves gave the Indians leverage with the government and settlers.[13]

Another important asset available to the tributary kings came at their official meetings with the colonial governor when it was time to pay their tribute. These councils took place once or twice a year. Other official meetings occurred when a new governor arrived in the colony, and the Indians appeared before him to confirm their loyalty and tributary status. These official meetings were important ceremonial, diplomatic, and political occasions. John Brickell, a physician, naturalist, and writer of *The Natural History of North-Carolina* published in Dublin in 1737, described a meeting between Gov. Richard Everard and Kings Tom Blount, John Hoyter of the Chowans, and John Durant of the Yeopims at the governor's house in Edenton in 1730. It was a dazzling occasion. Each king arrived with his retinue of "Queen, Children, Physician, Captains of War and Guards," and each guard was armed with a gun, a supply of shot and powder, and a tomahawk. For such a formal meeting, the three Indian kings wore their ceremonial best clothes. Tuscarora Blount wore a suit of English broadcloth, a shirt, cravat, shoes, hat, and women's stockings with images of clocks printed on them. Yeopim Durant sported a blue livery, a waistcoat with silver lace, as well as a shirt, stockings, and shoes. Chowan Hoyter wore a red soldier's coat, waistcoat, and breeches. Brickell said that once the council was over, the men would put the clothes away until the next ceremonial meeting. They were more than just clothes, however. Indians such as Blount, Durant, and Hoyter used clothing as a way of expressing their power, authority, and even equality with the English. It also signified their attachment and commitment to the English government.[14]

At the meeting, the governor invited the three kings into his home for a dinner. The other members of the retinue drew off from the house a short distance to allow the kings and governor to counsel privately. This was a working dinner, and the kings had the governor's ear. Now they could take their petitions and concerns directly to him in person. During this meeting in 1730, Blount, Hoyter, and Durant expressed their concern about the Senecas coming into North Carolina to do mischief and wanted the governor's promise that he would assist them if they called for help. The governor assured them of his support. Brickell noted that the three kings spoke English tolerably well, but they were also "cunning in their Discourses, and you would be surprised to hear what subtile and witty Answers they made to each Question proposed to them." The dinner ended with drinks and toasts to the governor, whom the kings always called "Brother," which put them on an equal standing. The governor also sent rum to the queens and other members of the kings' retinues. The council with the governor over, Blount, Hoyter, Durant, and their retinues went into Edenton to do business with the merchants and storekeepers.[15]

Over the years, Blount had much to complain about. He accused ferry operators of discriminating against the Indians, "exacted more from them for being carried over than what was allowed by law and very often refused carrying them at all." He also complained about settlers selling rum to his people.[16] The Governor's Council tried to provide redress. For the first few decades after the Tuscarora War, the Indians actually received justice from the colony.

When settlers abused Tuscaroras, the government stepped in. In June 1722, settler Luke Measel said he was out hunting east of Indian Woods when he heard a gunshot. Investigating, he found one of Blount's Tuscaroras reloading his musket after killing a deer. Measel told the Tuscarora to leave the area and go hunt on the other side of Quitsnay Creek, meaning within the bounds of the Indian Woods reserve. The Tuscarora made some remark that angered Measel, who now wrestled the gun from the Indian and clubbed him on the head with it. While wrestling, Measel sicced his dog on the Tuscarora, and it severely bit the Indian about his knees. Blount complained, and the Governor's Council ordered Measel arrested and taken to King Blount's town of Resootka. This was done, and Measel appeared before a group of men designated as Indian commissioners. Measel admitted hitting the Indian but denied siccing his dog on him. It is unknown how the case worked out. Measel probably paid a fine.[17]

A similar incident happened just months later. The Tuscarora Sighacka Blount went hunting with his dogs east of Indian Woods, which took him among the English settlements. Sighacka eventually encountered Christopher Dudley and some other White men. Dudley asked what he was doing, and Sighacka replied that he was hunting beaver. Dudley explained that this was his land and that Sighacka should not hunt here because the Indian's dogs would attack his cattle and hogs. Sighacka replied that his dogs hunted only beaver, raccoons, and deer and would not hurt cattle or hogs. Besides, he would hunt wherever he pleased. This response angered Dudley, who snatched up a board and struck Sighacka across the head. The Indian grabbed a stick to defend himself, and the two wrestled. Dudley eventually pushed the Tuscarora against a corral and broke his arm. The settler John Gardner stepped in, told Dudley to leave the Indian alone, and kept Sighacka from advancing on Dudley. Again, King Blount complained, and the local justices of peace ordered Dudley arrested and charged with "hurting and maiming a Tuskerora Indian." Dudley was ordered not to leave the precinct without permission from the court. He was eventually brought to trial. Chief Justice Christopher Gale showed the respect given to King Blount when he determined that Dudley "violently assaulted and beaten & broke the arm of an Indian man belonging of the Tuscarora Nation, whereby many ill consequences are to be feared to the tranquility & peace of this government." Though Dudley was convicted, it is unclear what penalty he paid for his assault.[18] The Governor's Council was quick to fix any problems Blount's Tuscaroras might encounter with settlers.

However, there were some instances where Indian leaders could do nothing, as in the case of the Indian George Seneca. On July 1, 1726, Seneca, who lived in Bertie County, where Indian Woods was located, went into the settlements and arrived at the plantation of Thomas Groom, also of Bertie County. Whatever provoked Seneca is a mystery, but the court charged that Seneca, "not having the fear of God before his eyes, but mov'd by the instigation of the Devil and his own cruel fierce and savage nature," picked up an axe, which the court valued at two shillings, and struck Groom's wife, Catherine, and his two infant daughters, instantly killing all three. Seneca fled to the Meherrin reserve, but the Meherrin leaders, when they heard of the incident, turned him over to the colonial authorities. Seneca was arraigned and went on trial, with the Meherrin leaders ordered to appear. Seneca pled guilty, and the colony hanged him on the afternoon of August 26, 1726.[19]

For the Tuscaroras, Meherrins, Machapungas, Chowans, and other Indians of eastern North Carolina, life on the reserves was a time of evolution. Although they kept the old ways as best they could, they were certainly influenced directly and indirectly by the English government and the nearby settlers and slaves. Long before the Tuscarora War, Indians had picked up the use of firearms, wore English clothes, and used European shovels, axes, hoes, knives, and kettles. English names became common among them, though who knows what names family members called each other at home. But these types of things were the easiest to assimilate as Indians had always hunted, warred, farmed, and traded, and these were just new tools. Now as tributaries and facing increased contact with the English, changes in Indian life grew dramatically.

Women suffered a setback under the tributary system. They remained the mothers, caregivers, cooks, tool makers, midwives, doctors, gatherers, farmers, and wives. But they lost their political clout. In the old days, women had influence; they could start and stop wars and decide what to do with enemy captives. North Carolina Indian life was matrilineal, in which a person was born into their mother's clan, so women controlled the fields, the household, and the children. Clan matriarchs could be a force to reckon with.[20] But as population numbers dropped, clans became smaller, and eventually over time ceased to exist. This was especially so in some areas, such as along Drowning Creek in what would later become Robeson County, where many different Indian peoples who had different clans, languages, and customs came together and began creating a new Indian community.[21] This process is called "ethnogenesis," and the historian Gary Clayton Anderson says it occurred when "bands altered themselves culturally to forge unity with other groups, abandoning languages, social practices and even economic processes to meet the needs of the new order."[22]

As warfare between Indian tributaries died down in the latter part of the eighteenth century, then so did women's power to start and stop wars and deal with captives. Merchants, traders, and storekeepers dealt with men, not women. Native men found they could ignore their women's demands, and sometimes they had to. The diminishment of women's influence was most serious when it came to land sales of a nation's reserve as women constantly opposed them but could do little to stop their men from selling off the reserve.

One of the greatest changes came in the Indian economy. In the days before the English arrived, goods circulated in society through the exchange of gifts. We call it reciprocity. Food and tools were exchanged among kinfolk and one's people; one gave but also received. This was not trade or barter but rather the giving that all family members did to take care of each other. More direct trade was made with foreigners. Little reciprocity existed here because each tried to drive as hard a bargain as possible. The English offered guns, rum, tools, and cloth, and Indians offered deerskins or Indian captives. But after the Tuscarora War, the Indian slave trade ended, and the deer hide trade in eastern North Carolina began tapering off. The English found the Indian slave trade too volatile, and as the number of potential Indian slaves declined, Englishmen increasingly turned to importing enslaved Africans. As for the deer hide trade, in the past Blount's Tuscaroras and other eastern North Carolina Indians had dealt with Virginia traders. But the decline in Indian numbers in eastern North Carolina meant Virginia traders shifted their attention west to the Cherokees. By the 1730s, the Cherokees were becoming tributaries of England and being pulled into the British Empire. They started going through their own colonization process, which would result in the Anglo-Cherokee War of 1758–61.

As the eighteenth century progressed and the deer hide economy slackened among the tributary Indians when deer numbers declined, the eastern North Carolina Indians found themselves in an increasingly cash economy. The necessities of life did not now come from visiting Virginia traders but from nearby stores, storekeepers, and merchants who served settlers, slaves, free People of Color, and Indians. As early as 1700, Col. Robert Quary operated a store in Bath, where settlers and Indians traded crops, skins, naval stores, and anything profitable in exchange for manufactured goods coming in from other English colonies and the Caribbean. Pirates also provided valuable goods and tools to a colony that lacked regular access to English ports. On the east side of the Tuscarora Indian Woods reservation, Spruill's Store opened at a place called Grabtown. Here the Tuscaroras, many of whom feared going to Edenton lest they be beaten, could shop and trade in peace.[23] Walton's Store served the Chowans up near their reserve. John Brickell, who witnessed the council between the North Carolina governor and Kings Blount, Hoyter, and Durant, noted that after the council the three kings and their retinue went into Edenton "to dispose of their deer skins that were remaining, for blankets, guns, powder, shot, ball, and other necessaries they had occasion for, and especially rum, whereof they are very fond."[24] Storekeepers certainly accepted deer and other skins, but over time they came to prefer cash, in this case "proclamation money," which was a devalued North Carolina currency worth only about a third of official British pounds sterling. They also might accept any of the bits of hard foreign coinage used as currency in the American colonies. Of course, pounds sterling were best of all.

Indians needed money and goods, the settlers needed workers, and it was not long before the two found each other. In the earliest days of Carolina colonization, most Indians in the employ of Englishmen served as guides, hunters, or haulers of goods. John Lawson utilized during his travels across the Carolinas in 1701 a bevy of guides, who changed out when they went from one territory to another. Lawson spoke highly of Eno Will, who owned an enslaved Sissipahaw of his own and kept Lawson's party well fed with turkeys and other game. For Lawson, Eno Will possessed the "best and most agreeable temper that ever I met with in an Indian, being always ready to serve the English, not out of gain, but real affection." However, Will admitted that his affection for the English gained him many Indian enemies, and he feared he might be poisoned. He made Lawson promise that if he were killed, Lawson would avenge him.[25]

After the Tuscarora War, as Indians settled onto their assigned reserves, and settlers and slaves filled in the spaces around them, there was little need for Indian guides. However, the need for Indian hunters, haulers, and other workers remained. Indian fishermen, such as the Machapungas, gladly sold grilled shad to passing settlers but also passed on their boating knowledge to enslaved Africans and to their own children, who may have had an Indian, African, or English parent. Hunters sold venison and dressed skins to English neighbors and storekeepers. An Indian might spend a day hunting or fishing for an Englishmen in return for trade goods or a little cash. When commissions from both North Carolina and Virginia surveyed the border between the two colonies, the Saponi Indians served as hunters. The Virginia crew hired a Saponi named Bearskin, and he proved very successful in feeding them with venison, bear, and turkeys.[26]

As Indian lands became restricted, and it became more dangerous to travel too far into the settlements, Indians found they could do jobs for their neighbors. They had done this before the war and continued to do so after it. Settlers hired Indians to help build houses and barns. Some served as field hands during the planting and harvesting when help was needed. This is what Indian women did, but if an Indian man was involved, then this signaled a major cultural change as the fields had always been the domain of women. Indians also worked as haulers of water, hewers of wood, and paddlers of periaugers. Many did whatever job a settler wanted or needed, sometimes as day laborers, sometimes as slaves.[27]

Though the Indian slave trade pretty much ended after 1720, enslaved Indians in North Carolina remained a fact for decades. This close contact with White and Black people might bring Indians into all sorts of misadventures. At about one o'clock on the morning of September 14, 1718, the Currituck merchant John Bell, Bell's son, and an unnamed Indian were sitting in Bell's periauger at John Chester's Landing on the Pamlico River between Bath and the coast. Unfortunately for them, Edward Thatch, sometimes spelled "Teach," but universally known as "Blackbeard the Pirate," and a few crewmen came cruising down the Pamlico at the same time in their own periauger. Blackbeard spotted Bell's boat and commandeered it while holding Bell, his son, and the Indian at gunpoint. The pirate plundered the merchant of more than £66 worth of goods, including fifty-eight yards of crepe, a box of pipes, a half-barrel of brandy, a silver chalice, and several other items. We must imagine that the Indian was a hired servant and not enslaved as Blackbeard may have plundered him as well.[28]

King Hoyter and the Chowans also picked up the workings of both English law and the cash economy. Willowby, a Chowan, sold an enslaved Indian to the settler James Sitterson, who lived on Core Banks. For whatever reason, Sitterson never paid Willowby and avoided the Indian's demands. Now, in April 1720, King Hoyter went to the North Carolina Governor's Council and explained the situation. The governor ordered Sitterson to pay Willowby what he owed.[29] In March 1723, King Hoyter sued the estate of John Sale for £11 sterling, which Hoyter said Sale owed him. It is unclear how the Englishman became indebted to the Indian John Hoyter, whether through a loan or for services Hoyter provided, but the court had no hesitation ruling in the king's favor.[30]

Although the tributary kings might still mediate some issues among their people, now when property disputes between Indians arose, they began to turn to the English courts. In 1736, the Chowan Thomas Durbin sued the Chowan John Robbins in Chowan County Court for £8, 10 shillings, over a promissory note. The case dragged on for years, and we do not know the final outcome. But as the historian Michelle LeMaster points out, the Chowans "appear to have adopted the English concept of debt as a legal contract involving monetary sums." Cash money was quickly becoming the Indian currency as well.[31]

Indian tools and crafts also found a demand among merchandise-deprived North Carolina settlers. The Tuscaroras had a reputation as weavers and beaders, and these skills earned them nicknames such as the "Shirt Wearers." Such skills probably came in handy later as some Indians took up sewing for their White neighbors. Indian Robert Abrams borrowed money from a local settler to buy needles, thread, and fabric so he could become a tailor. Tuscaroras were also known for their wooden bowls and ladles. These items had formerly been traded with other Indians, such as the Saponis and Occaneechis in the Piedmont, but now some found their way into settler homes.

John Lawson discovered that Indians had a knack for carving wooden gunstocks, canoes, and other items. He found that Indians who had been enslaved by the colonists learned "handicraft-trades very well and speedily."[32] Indian pottery and household utensils more than likely showed up in settler homes as well. Tuscarora enemies, the Catawbas, became famous for making pots and other items and sold them to nearby settlers. Tuscarora women probably did the same.[33]

Indians also experienced revolutionary changes just by their proximity to the English and Africans. At some point, the curved longhouse went out of style, and Indians built log cabins and houses that looked more like the homes of their English neighbors. Forced to live on a bounded reserve, Indian families needed more permanent houses that could last years rather than a season or two. Farming and gardening remained important, and the Indians planted orchards and fenced their lands. Some, like Long Tom of the Machapungas, tried growing rice. The Tuscaroras living near the Roanoke River installed pipes to drain swamps and open more arable land on Indian Woods. A gallows was set up in the event a Tuscarora had to be punished according to English laws. Horses became commonplace, and eastern North Carolina Indians began riding even short distances, distances that they would easily have walked in earlier times. William Byrd noted that the Saponis rode awkwardly, and the women rode astride the saddle, which embarrassed them, and so they refused to clamber atop their horses in the presence of Englishmen.[34] Indians adopted not just horses but also cattle and pigs. Settlers allowed theirs to roam the woods, but Indians could not afford to. So Indian men and women became keepers of livestock.[35]

Christianity and Education

Christianity also spread among the reserves, albeit slowly and not from any persistent colonial efforts. From the very first days of the Roanoke expeditions in the 1580s, Englishmen had been fascinated by the Indians' religious practices. Thomas Harriot, in his classic "A

Briefe and True Report," wrote of Roanoke deities, temples, prayers, offerings, handling of the dead, and even an Indian afterlife of good and bad places rather similar to his own concepts of heaven and hell.[36] George Fox, considered the founder of Quakerism, traveled through North Carolina in 1672 and found Indians to have a moral conscience, to know right from wrong, and so to be possessed by the "Light and Spirit of God."[37] John Lawson agreed, having found them to be "great observers of Moral Rules, and the Law of Nature; indeed, a worthy Foundation to build Christianity upon."[38] Bearskin, the Saponi hunter, told William Byrd much the same thing: there was a "Master God" who set the world in motion, loves good people, and will have the bad knocked in the head.[39] Not all agreed with this assessment of Indians' spirituality and morality. Baron de Graffenried believed the Indians were strongly influenced by Satan and could do demonic things, such as call up the wind on calm days.[40] Indians in turn showed a measure of curiosity about Christianity. Harriot reported that the Roanokes and their neighbors, after being hit with sickness, took a keen interest in the Bible. Many would be "glad to touche it, to embrace it, to kisse it, to holde it to their breastes and heades, and stroke over all their body with it; to shew their hungrie desire of that knowledge which was spoken of."[41] It really was not the knowledge of Christianity the Roanokes wanted but protection from the sickness and violence the English had brought with them.

One of the reasons King Charles II had originally chartered the Carolina colony in 1663 was to spread Protestant Christianity to the Native peoples. However, missionary work and Indian conversion went slowly. When George Fox preached to some North Carolina Indians, he said they received him kindly and acknowledged what he said to be true. But there was no great rush among them to convert. Early colonial governor John Archdale admitted there was little conversion taking place. He suggested missionaries be trained in the chemistry of herbs and minerals and through this gain favor with the Indians. That way and through trade, he said, would work better toward converting the Indians than making war on them.[42]

In the early 1700s, the Society for the Propagation of the Gospel in Foreign Parts sent Anglican missionaries to the colony. Most preached to isolated North Carolina settler communities and baptized their children, but enslaved Africans and Indians also received a smattering of attention. Yet the Society for the Propagation of the Gospel did not seem to have any profound effect on the Native peoples. Colonial North Carolina never did see the rise of Christian Indian preachers that was found in Puritan New England. Some Englishmen even discouraged Indian conversion. In 1716, Ebenezer Tucker found himself ousted from his St. Andrews Parish congregation when he offered the Holy Sacrament to an enslaved Indian who had never been baptized or instructed in church ways. Rev. Thomas Newnam traveled through northeastern North Carolina in 1722 and believed there were only 300 Indians left in that area. Although they were "quiet and peaceable," he despaired of ever seeing any converted. In 1726, Rev. Thomas Baylye reported that over the previous three years he had baptized as many as 400 children and numerous Black people, but only three adult Indians. A decade later, Rev. John Garzia said he had baptized almost 2,300 settler men and women across North Carolina, but only eleven Black individuals and one Indian.[43]

In 1741, the famed evangelist George Whitefield remained skeptical of reports that scores of Indians had been converted during a revival at some unnamed plantation in North Carolina. What plantation? Whitefield wondered. And even if the Indians did convert, he did not believe it meant much. They might be able to recite the Lord's Prayer and Ten Commandments in "the Vulgar tongue" and might have been baptized, but Whitefield said he must question that they actually believed in Christ.[44] Moravian bishop August Spangenberg might have agreed. In 1752, Spangenberg toured Indian Woods and noted that no effort had yet been made to Christianize the Tuscaroras.[45] As late as the 1760s, Rev. Alexander Stewart reported that in Beaufort County he baptized fifty-two White people and seventeen Black infants and gave the sacraments to 102 people. In contrast, he baptized only two Machapunga boys in Beaufort County and none in Hyde County.[46]

According to Stewart, the Machapunga Indians he encountered did not know much about Christianity; still, he felt it was best to baptize them anyway. He did find a "northern Indian" living among the Machapungas who had been reared as a Christian and who promised to instruct them in Christian principles.[47] In 1763, Rev. Stewart was back in Beaufort County, and he reported the Indians attended church and "behaved with decency, seemed desirous of instruction & offered themselves and their children to me for baptism." He baptized six adult Indians, six boys, four girls, and five infants as well as sixty-four White children, one White adult, eleven Black adults, and eleven Black infants. Stewart was so impressed that he had himself appointed as the superintendent of schools in that part of the province and set up a school to teach four Indian boys, four Indian girls, and two African American boys "to read & to work."[48]

By the end of the eighteenth century, most remaining Indians in North Carolina would probably have considered themselves Christian or at least understood the basic tenets of Protestant Christianity as well as their White neighbors did. This Christianization probably did not come about by any serious evangelism effort by White missionaries but more from mere contact between Indians and their neighbors. As enslaved Africans did, North Carolina Indians probably took aspects of Christianity and mixed it with their own traditional religious beliefs. This did not mean that Indian religious beliefs entirely disappeared. Just because an Indian family went to church on Sunday did not mean they quit dancing or holding ceremonies during the week. Unfortunately, as Indian numbers and land holdings declined, their White neighbors took less and less interest in them. So traditional beliefs among the eastern North Carolina Indians became a part of their oral tradition while remaining a mystery to their White and Black neighbors.

The education of Indians went hand in hand with Christianity. Many Indians understood the advantage of learning to speak English. Eno Will asked Lawson to take his fourteen-year-old son Jack and teach him to read and write.[49] Gov. Alexander Spotswood of Virginia was a big proponent of education for Indians. Even before the Tuscarora War, he insisted that Virginia's tributary Indians send the children of the king and his headmen to school. Most wound up at the College of William and Mary, where they learned English and English ways. As Spotswood saw it, educating Indian children was an aspect of detribalization because the children would drop their Indian ways and then educate, convert, and temper their own people. Some Meherrin children and possibly even some Tuscaroras wound up at William and Mary. At Ft. Christiana, Spotswood set up a school for the Saponis and Occaneechis. These children became proficient in English and learned English ways, but they did not seem to give up their Indian culture. Saponi parents still taught their children their people's dances, music, stories, and ways of life.[50]

Rev. Giles Rainsford approached King Hoyter about sending his son to school to learn to read and write. Rainsford, who spent months with the Chowans and became adept at their language, said Hoyter was open to the idea. Rainsford volunteered to teach the lad, but Hoyter declined because at the moment the Tuscarora War was raging.[51] Nevertheless, North Carolina ordered all its tributaries to send two children from each nation's principal men to school. Chowan children attended Mr. Mashburn's school at Saram, near the Virginia border. Even the bishop of London noted Mashburn's success, declaring that the Chowan children "are so well disciplined in the Principles of our Religion, and gave before him such an account of the Ground of it, as strangely surprised him."[52] Rainsford reported that King Hoyter himself had some knowledge of Noah and the Flood, but only as an oral tradition passed down to him from father to son.[53] That seemed about the same way Christian settlers knew the story, too.

Among the Machapungas, education went haltingly. In 1764, schoolmaster James Francis at "Attamaskeet" reported that he had a school for Indians and Black people, and although few Black folk attended, six Indian children did. He noted that the Indian boys and girls were very poor. They were seventeen-year-old

Solomon Russell, sixteen-year-old John Squires, thirteen-year-old Betty Squires, thirteen-year-old Polly Mackey, nine-year-old Joshua Squires, and seven-year-old Bob Mackey. Francis worried that Indian parents could not provide for their children, "for if I had not fed them, three fourths of the time they did come, they must have gone with many a hungry belly." Francis asked Rev. Stewart to send 45 shillings to cover the cost of feeding these six Machapunga children for the quarter.[54] Francis was soon transferred to Core Sound, and the school at the Machapungas foundered. Nevertheless, three years later, in 1767, Rev. Stewart was still preaching near Lake Mattamuskeet and there baptized 154 White people, 7 Indians, and a "Mustee" child, meaning a child of Indian and African parentage.[55]

William Byrd believed that educating the Indians was a waste of time. As soon as the Indian child returned to their parents, "instead of civilizing and converting the rest," Byrd lamented, "they have immediately relapt [sic] into infidelity and barbarism themselves." Educated Indians, Byrd believed, "are apt to be more vicious and disorderly than the rest of their countrymen."[56] Byrd voiced fears held by Europeans across North America that Europeanized Indians just became more proficient enemies. So how much Spotswood's education plan affected North Carolina Indians is debatable. In reality, little formal education could be found even among White North Carolinians at this time, and so one would expect virtually none for Indians. There was even less after Spotswood left the Virginia government. Nevertheless, by the end of the eighteenth century, most remaining Indians in eastern North Carolina spoke their Native language and a tolerable English, but interpreters still played a large role when Indians and government officials met. Although the Indians might speak and understand English, only a few could read or write it. Throughout the eighteenth century, most Indians signed legal documents with their mark, usually an X, with their name written out beside it by the court clerk.

If Kings Tom Blount, John Hoyter, and John Durant had wanted to protect their people from the North Carolina government while maintaining as many of the old ways as possible, then they would have to be considered a success. The colonial government was quick to provide redress as best it could. However, the neighbors around the reserves often posed the most vexing problems for the Indians and the government as well. Just as King Blount could approach the North Carolina Governor's Council with problems and petition for redress, so could the settlers. White settlers paid taxes, voted in the Assembly, could hold political office, and so could not be ignored. Nearby settlers complained that Indians set the forest on fire when they hunted, which then spread to the settlers' own valuable timber. They charged that the Indians killed settlers' hogs and cattle. Of course, settlers refused to fence their lands, and these hogs and cows were probably rooting through the Indians' gardens and fields when Indians shot them. They criticized that Indians could be impudent and thieving. Bishop Spangenberg wrote in 1752 that the Tuscaroras "conduct themselves in such a way that the whites are afraid of them. If they enter a house & the man is not home they become insolent & the poor woman must do as they command."[57] One wonders if that was still true in the 1750s or had ever been true, or was just a story that the bishop heard as he made his way through the colony.

The basic truth was that Indians interacted with their neighbors, knew their names, became friends with some, and quarreled with others. Familiarity bred not only friendships, romances, and children but also contempt, complaints, and lawsuits. Whatever the feelings between Indian and settler, whether favorable or not, it did not deter settlers from getting their hands on the Indian land reserves.

5

Fade of the Smaller Tributaries

Like the larger Tuscaroras, the smaller tributaries, such as the Chowans, Meherrins, Machapungas, Yeopims, and Hatteras, also received land reserves, and those lands soon caught the eye of land-hungry settlers. As the eighteenth century progressed and these smaller tributaries fell into poverty, the only wealth they had was their land reserves.

The North Carolina colony's tributaries gave several levels of importance to their reserves. On one hand, the reserves became national lands on which they could be Indians and live somewhat as they wanted. For most, their reserves sat on lands they had once lived on or at least considered their territorial lands. It was home. The lands themselves were also valuable pieces of real estate and in demand by settlers. So they became a sort of bank that the nation's leaders could sell off pieces at a time to raise money to buy food and goods, pay debts, and make improvements. This practice set up a clash within the reserves, with male leaders willing to sell off pieces of the national reserve, while women protested these sales, but with little success.

Settlers in the areas went to great trouble to get their hands on parts of the Indian reserve. Europeans had been acquiring Indians' lands from the very first days of the colony, as when in 1661 George Durant bought a tract of land on the Perquimans River from Kilcacenen, king of the Yeopims. These were Indian lands or their hunting quarters, and these Englishmen had come onto them to build houses and farms. At least in the case of Durant, a transaction had taken place, though we wonder if the Indians understood they were selling away their possession of the land or just the right for these men to use it.

In the long run, it mattered little as behind Durant came thousands more who did not think the Indians had any moral or legal right to the land. The Fundamental Constitutions of Carolina of 1669 supported this notion. Although the Constitutions ordered English settlers to "not expel" the Indians "or use them ill," point 112 declared that no person "shall hold or claim any land in Carolina, by purchase or gift, or otherwise, from the natives or any other whatsoever; but merely from and under the Lords Proprietors."[1] Things worked differently in Carolina. Some settlers purchased lands directly from the Indians, the Lords Proprietors be damned, and usually from Native leaders willing to sell. Sometimes the colonial government advanced private deals, as it had with Capt. Nicholas Crisp in 1714, when it encouraged him to make a settlement with the Tuscaroras to give up their hunting quarters along the Roanoke River. Other times there was not even a purchase as settlers just squatted on or expanded their own claims onto Indian lands. Before the Tuscarora War, the colonial government turned a blind eye to Indians' complaints. This increasing encroachment on lands claimed by the Indians of the coast and Coastal Plain had been one of the causes of the Tuscarora War.[2]

As Indian populations declined, the colonial government might order a resurvey and cut the size of the reserve. Once settlers filled the lands, the deer hide trade diminished as settlers and Indians overhunted deer in the area. As the hunting economy declined and cash was needed in an ever-strengthening British economy, the only thing of value possessed by the Indians was their land reserves. So even while these reserves gave Indians a strong sense of place and history, they also provided them something of tangible economic value, such as political and economic negotiating power, as well as access to cash or goods.

However, possession of reserve lands came at a cost to the Indians. As White settlers came to see it, Indian national identity and Indian lands went hand in hand. Indian allies and those who had been defeated in war had become tributaries and assigned to live on an Indian land reserve. If Indians lived on a reserve, then they were citizens of a recognized Indian nation, possessing a working Indian government with a diplomatic and tributary relationship with the colony. However, when those lands were sold off and the reserve gone, then in White people's eyes that Indian government no longer existed, and its people ceased to be Indians. Indians saw their situation differently—that Indian identity did not necessarily hinge on having or living on a colony-recognized land reserve. Nevertheless, place was an important part of being an Indian in North Carolina, and for many their reserve was a homeland. But as Indians would later find out, the idea of whether they were Indian or not was not always in their own hands.

Over the course of the eighteenth century, the smaller tributaries—the Yeopims, Chowans, Meherrins, Machapungas, and Hatteras—found their reserves under pressure from nearby settlers, and so they began to sell off pieces. When that took place, their identity as Indians also came into question by the colony.

Yeopims

During the Tuscarora war, the Yeopims had sided with the English and along with their Chowan neighbors had made attacks on the Catechna Alliance. Yeopim leader John Durant even captured an Alliance woman and earned £10 when he sold her into slavery. In appreciation of his efforts, the colony named him king of the Yeopims.[3] For a while, King Tom Blount of the Tuscaroras, King John Hoyter of the Chowans, and King John Durant of the Yeopims were the most influential Indian kings in eastern North Carolina, their reserves all in the northern part of the colony and near the colonial capital at Edenton.

However, the Yeopims' location along the north side of Albemarle Sound put them directly in the way of colonial expansion, and their 10,000-acre land reserve caught the eye of nearby settlers. Sometime before 1715, they leased some of their lands to Daniel Civile for two years. But Civile quit paying, and in March 1715 the

Yeopims sued him for £3 sterling to be paid in barrels of corn at 10 shillings per barrel. The court found in favor of the Yeopims and ordered Civile to pay their demand.[4] At the same time, the Yeopims complained that settlers were preventing them from hunting on Currituck Banks and threatening to break the Yeopims' guns if the Indians were found there. The Governor's Council took the Yeopims' side, declaring that they had the liberty to hunt on the banks and that no Englishman had the right to disturb them.[5] Yeopims continued to find favor in the North Carolina courts. The Yeopim John Hawkins sued settler Thomas James for killing a three-year-old heifer and demanded, as the law stipulated, 10 shillings above the price of the animal. Hawkins estimated the cow was worth 5 shillings and so demanded 15. The court agreed, ordered James to pay 15 shillings, and put a lien on James's property until he did.[6]

Then in early 1715, the Yeopims made the fatal decision to go from leasing their lands to selling them. King Durant and his "great men"—John Barber, John Hawkins, Harry Gibbs, and George Durant—all agreed to sell 640 acres of reserve land to William Reed, the president of the Governor's Council. A short time later, the Yeopim leadership sold parcels of land to John Jones, Isaac Jones, and Capt. Richard Sanderson. They also sold the right to the "lightwood" on the land, meaning the resinous pine wood good for making tar and pitch. Now the Governor's Council stepped in, and while it agreed to the sales, as long as none of those sales intruded on the lands of Council president Reed, it ordered the Yeopims to sell no more land without the council's express approval. The Joneses and Sanderson were also ordered to allow the Yeopims to continue hunting on those lands.[7]

Over the next few decades, King John Durant often appeared before the Governor's Council requesting permission to sell off parcels of the Yeopim reserve. The council always agreed. Seemingly the last 50 acres of Yeopim lands were sold for £22, 10 shillings, in 1740 and 1741 by King Durant to Edward Taylor, who had already been leasing Yeopim lands. As the historian Dennis Isenbarger comments, "The Yeopim Indians concluded that they would rather have cash in hand instead of land they could not enjoy and chose to be free from white settlers who did not respect them." After this, the Yeopims disappeared from the colonial records, though Yeopim families still lived in the area. The only record of them left is the community named "Indiantown" in Camden County.[8]

Chowans

In 1677, the Chowans became the first Indian people defeated in war by North Carolina and made into official colonial tributaries. Eight years later the colonial government assigned the Chowans a land reserve of 12-by-12 miles, 144 square miles, on the east side of the Chowan River. Unfortunately, the Chowans lived north of Albemarle Sound and found themselves squeezed by English settlers and enslaved Africans in that most populous part of the colony. The usual Indian killers—sickness, war, rum, and abuse—took their toll, and by the early 1700s colonial counts, the Chowans had been reduced to about sixty people. With this in mind and reasoning that so few people did not need so much land, in 1704 North Carolina unilaterally reduced the Chowan reserve to 6-by-6 miles, or 36 square miles. King Hoyter immediately appealed to the Governor's Council when he saw the surveyors assigning the worst lands to the Chowans. Claiming those lands were "too poor and sandy to raise corn upon," Hoyter demanded better lands be included in the redrawn Chowan tract.[9] Despite the land reduction, the Chowans remained friendly to the colony during the Tuscarora War, with some Chowan warriors under King John Hoyter raiding the Catechna Alliance. John Hoyter had been king of the Chowans before the war, and the colony kept him as the Chowan tributary king afterward.[10]

Like his Tuscarora contemporary, King Hoyter understood his rights as a tributary and the influence he had with the Governor's Council. He always reminded the council of his people's service to the colony during the war—that his warriors had made eight expeditions against the Catechna Alliance and suffered their own farms, houses, and fences burned; their horses, hogs, and cattle stolen or destroyed; their fruit trees cut down. He wanted compensation from the government.[11] And since their reserve lands were bad for growing corn, they would have to rely upon the government all the more. The council sympathized with Hoyter's petition. The Chowans' English neighbors not so much. They accused the Chowans of being hostile and aggressive, destroying the settlers' hogs and cattle, and generally being unreasonable neighbors. In reality, what the settlers disliked most about the Chowans was that Hoyter and his people were active in keeping settlers from expanding onto Chowan lands.[12]

King Hoyter found himself increasingly before the Governor's Council in Edenton defending the integrity of Chowan lands. He complained that the brothers Ephraim and Aaron Blanchard illegally settled on Chowan lands, and he insisted the council evict them. The council ordered the Blanchards to stop any work they were doing on the lands and appear at the next council meeting to discuss Chowan concerns. Not much seemed to have happened because Hoyter was soon back before the council complaining of additional squatters. The settlers must have made some reply, probably pointing to the Chowans as being unreasonable in not wanting to sell their lands. Rather than eject the settlers, the council ordered another survey of Chowan lands. This was done in 1720, and the Chowans lost additional lands as their reserve was cut down from 36 square miles to a little less than 18 square miles.[13] Still, fighting illegal encroachment on their ever-shrinking reserve made perfect sense as King Hoyter and the Chowans realized that money could be made by selling their land. Selling of lands, though possibly short-sighted, was certainly an aspect of Indian independence and sovereignty. It was their land, and they could do with it what they wanted.

By the 1730s, King John Hoyter had died, and his son Thomas Hoyter had become chief. Colonial records did not call him "king," as officials had with his father, but merely "chief," a deterioration in the status of Indian tributaries with the colonial government. That the position went from father to son and not to a sister's son, as in the normal matrilineal succession, indicated that some traditions were already changing. In that year, needing cash and insisting they had too much land and too few people to cultivate it, Thomas Hoyter and the other "chief men of the said Chowan Indians"—James Bennett, Charles Beasley, Jeremiah Pushing, John Robbins, and Neuse Will— began selling off hundreds of acres of the reserve. The men assured the Governor's Council that all the Chowan people supported the sale.[14] One wonders if that was true as women often opposed land sales. Nevertheless, throughout the rest of 1733 the Chowan leadership sold off more tracts: 300 acres on Catherine Creek to Michael Ward for £60; 200 acres, which included part of Chowan Town, to John Freeman for £120 "current money"; and 50 acres on Bennett's Creek to Henry Hill for £50. Henry Hill and his children would become most energetic in acquiring Chowan lands. Also in 1733, the Chowans leased 100 acres to Thomas Tailor for thirteen years for 200 pounds of tobacco per year. In 1733 alone, the Chowans sold off or leased more than 1,100 acres.[15]

The next year the Chowan leadership made another flurry of land sales, some of them to the same buyers. Many of these sales were between 100- and 600-acre increments and going anywhere from £50 for a 100 acres to £140 for 600 acres. Again, the Governor's Council quizzed the Indians on each sale, and the Chowans said they had agreed to each. The council confirmed the sales on January 30, 1735. In 1734 alone, the Chowans sold more than 2,000 acres of land and received just shy of £1,000 proclamation money and sixty barrels of tar. Though the council approved all these sales, it worried about them and now prohibited settlers from purchasing Chowan lands without permission from the governor and the council.[16]

For almost ten years, the Chowans resisted selling any more land. Then on March 22, 1743, they made another rash of land sales of more than 1,000 acres. The Governor's Council approved them all.[17] But things were never simple when it came to land sales. Just one day later, the Chowans complained to the council that back in 1734 they had sold some of their land to James Brown, Richard Minchew, and others, but over the years these settlers had illegally expanded their holdings and wrongly appropriated additional Chowan lands. The Indians asked the council to order these settlers back to their original boundaries.[18] Two days after that, the settlers made their own petition to the council. James Hinton, Henry Hill, Gabriel Lassiter, and Thomas Moore countered that they all had bought land from the Chowans and had paid "a valuable consideration for it," and they wanted "the same Indians might be admitted to acknowledge the said conveyance."[19] These kind of land complaints simmered for years.

Settler Henry Hill and his family developed a rather strange and close relationship with the Chowans. Over the years, the Chowans sold several tracts of land to Hill. In December 1744, the "Great Men of the Chowan Indians" appeared before the council and acknowledged Hill had paid them in full for 640 acres. The council approved the sale and ordered it recorded.[20] However, in March 1745 Chowan James Bennett petitioned the council, saying that Henry Hill had a deed to some Chowan lands that were sold to him by the Indians Thomas Hoyter and John Robbins, who had no authority to sell that land. The council ordered Hoyter, Robbins, and Hill to attend the next council session to explain.[21] Bennett's complaint did not engender much sympathy with the council, but it did muddy the waters. Though the council approved the sale, it did not allow Hill to take possession. Six years would pass, until 1751, before Hill could gain legal possession of the 640 acres of Chowan land and only when Gov. Gabriel Johnston finally stepped in to approve the purchase.[22]

Bennett's petition angered Hill, and bad blood erupted between the two. In July 1747, Bennett appeared before the county court, not the Governor's Council, and accused Hill of unlawfully breaking into his fenced cornfield and "there cut, dug, houghed up and spoiled the corn of the same James." Bennett valued the corn at 50 shillings.[23] However, by 1753 old animosities seemed to have cooled. In early September 1753, Thomas Walton's store was broken into. Jean Brown testified that at about 11:00 p.m. on the night of the burglary she had gone outside to "do her occasions" and heard Henry Hill's son say not to worry as they have time. She went back to bed and a little later heard a noise. Getting out of bed, she saw Hill's son and a slave belonging to James Wilson leaving the store, which had been broken open. Hill's son was going north, and the slave was heading south.[24]

Henry Hill the father, his son, and the slave were arrested. Chowan James Bennett then got dragged into the case. Timothy Walton, son of the store owner, reported that he had met with Henry Hill in jail, who told him a story of alibis gone wrong. Walton said Hill told him that on that Saturday night "one James Bennet, an Indian & the said Henry Hill, was together drinking at the house of the said Henry." Bennett told Hill that Walton's store had been broken into, and he feared that he would be blamed for it. Hill told him to "not be afraid for they can't hurt you." Bennett suggested that they tell the story that "you and me [were] both here drunk together, you can answer for me and me for you."[25] A closeness was developing between Indians and their White and Black neighbors.

Things were swiftly going downhill for the Chowans, though. Losing lands, losing population, what few Chowans remained lived in poverty that was bad even by colonial standards. In September 1752, Moravian bishop Augustus Spangenberg toured the area and said the condition of eastern North Carolina Indians was "deplorable." He noted there were just a few Chowan families left and that most of their land had been taken from them.[26]

Similar reports said the Chowans had been "ill-used by their neighbors."[27] Gov. Arthur Dobb's Indian census of 1755 gave dismal numbers, listing the Chowans as having a total of two men and three women and children.[28] The two remaining men were probably James Bennett and John Robbins as their names appear on future land sales. The women and children were probably Bennett's wife and his two children, James Bennett Jr. and Amos Bennett.[29] However, the governor seemed to have undercounted as over the next few decades many other Chowans, especially women and children, appeared in the records. At the same time, there seems to have been an exodus of adult males from what remained of the Chowan reserve. It is unclear what was happening to the men. Were they dying, moving away, or just lying low out of sight of the authorities? Indian women were becoming heads of households and in some cases heads of nations.

The few adult men left could still cause problems. Chowan women opposed these land sales, but they apparently had no legal standing with the colony and were ignored by the Chowan men and colonial officials. James Bennett and John Robbins, considered the "Chief men of the Chowan Indians," continued selling the people's lands but at lower and lower prices. In 1753, they sold 300 acres to Edward Briscoe for £5.[30] In 1754, with the help of Henry Hill, Bennett and Robbins sold 150 acres along Bennett's Creek to Jacob Hinton for £20 and 200 acres to Richard Freeman, also for £20. The next year, 1755, they sold Freeman an additional 100 acres for £12. Although the governor did not officially approve these sales, they were never contested. Five years later, in 1760, the Chowans sold 600 acres to Aaron Blanchard for £35. This sale in 1760 was the last on which James Bennett's name appeared. He either died soon after this or left the area. Bennett's sons, James Jr. and Amos, continued selling off Chowan lands. In 1763, they sold 700 acres of marshy land to Elisha Hunter for £4, then in 1770 sold 640 acres to Thomas Garrett for £15. The latter sale was the last in which James and Amos Bennett's names appear. After this, only women and children lived on what might generously be called the Chowan reserve.[31] They would work hard to keep what little land they had left, but their gender and skin color would work against them.

Meherrins

The Meherrins, most of whom lived at Meherrin Neck near the confluence of the Meherrin and Chowan Rivers, had a rocky relationship with North Carolina. In 1705, Virginia assigned the Meherrins a circular tract of land with a 3-mile radius around their town of Meherrin Neck on the north bank of the Meherrin River, where it flows into the Chowan River, which actually was within the bounds of North Carolina.[32] The next year, North Carolina accepted the reality of Meherrin lands and ordered them to remain north of the Meherrin River. The Meherrins essentially were Virginia tributaries living in North Carolina, and so they often ignored edicts from North

Carolina. They sat out the Tuscarora War on their land reserve, officially neutral but rather sympathetic to the Catechna Alliance. The Meherrins seemed to be a source of weapons and ammunition for the Alliance during the war. Both Tom Blount and the North Carolina government distrusted them.[33]

King Nick Majors led the Meherrins before the Tuscarora War, but he had sat in on the trial of John Lawson and Baron de Graffenried at Catechna in September 1711 and so became a target of colonial authorities. He had since then disappeared. Captain Roger seemed to be the Meherrins' new leader; his is the only Meherrin name that shows up in the records for the 1720s. No matter, their North Carolina neighbors had little regard for them. Settlers leveled the usual accusations at them of destroying stock and being insolent toward White people. Then in the early 1720s, settlers began squatting on the Meherrin reserve. In October 1723, the Meherrins complained to Virginia about this encroachment. The Virginia Council instructed North Carolina to repeal any land grants that intruded on the Meherrin lands and warned that if the grants were not annulled and the settlers did not stop bothering the Meherrins, then Virginia might have to send its militia into North Carolina and remove them by force. North Carolina ignored the Virginia threat.[34]

Getting no immediate help from Virginia, in April 1724 the Meherrin leadership approached the North Carolina Governor's Council to officially complain that their White neighbors had taken some of their long-held lands. The Meherrins explained that these settlers would not allow them to clear their own lands or plant corn. The council sympathized and informed Surveyor General William Maule to attend the next meeting so they could discuss these encroachments. In the meantime, the council confirmed that the Meherrins should "have the liberty to plant their lands as formerly without molestation from any person whatsoever."[35]

Surveyor General Maule and his deputy, William Gray, finally got around to surveying the Meherrin reserve in 1726, and immediately the Meherrins became alarmed. The two surveyors ignored long-standing Meherrin land claims and began placing settlers on lands the Indians said was theirs. In August, the panicked Meherrins appeared before the Governor's Council to complain about Maule's survey and specifically about the settlers Beal Brown and Edward Powers "molesting them in their settlements and taking up their lands." Brown and Powers made their own protest and said it was the Meherrins who were molesting them. The council ordered all parties to appear at the council meeting in October.[36] When the Indian George Seneca murdered Catherine Groom and her two infant daughters that summer and fled to the Meherrins, the Meherrins, realizing that they needed the goodwill of the colonial government, quickly handed him over to the colonial authorities, who tried and executed him.[37]

At the October council meeting, Maule and Gray made their case that the Meherrins had no legal lands in the colony, certainly no claim that North Carolina had to respect. They used the Meherrins' Virginia tributary status against them, saying that if they were indeed tributaries of Virginia, then they had no right to the lands around their town of Meherrin Neck, which were solidly within North Carolina. It looked as if the Meherrins might lose all their land. Maule and Gray had made a slick legalistic maneuver, and Virginia was powerless to help as any support from the Old Dominion would only strengthen their argument. Shocked and frightened that they might lose everything and with Virginia's promise of support seemingly an empty one, the Meherrins made a momentous diplomatic shift from being a Virginia tributary to being a tributary of North Carolina. Claiming that they had always lived on those lands on the Meherrin River, they now prayed "this Board to take them into their protection as their faithful and loyal tributaries and to secure them a right & property in the said towne with such a convenient quantity of land adjoining to it."[38]

The North Carolina government finally had the Meherrins where it wanted and accepted their offer of tributary status. It ordered Maule and Gray to make a new survey of Meherrin lands between the Meherrin and Blackwater Rivers. A special and separate tract of 150 acres was to be surveyed for Captain Roger "most convenient to his dwelling." There the Meherrins shall "quietly hold the sd. lands without any molestation or disturbance of any persons."[39] The Meherrin reserve would be a tract of land 3 miles up the Blackwater River, then straight across to the Meherrin River down 2 miles to the mouth of the Meherrin at the Chowan/Blackwater River. Three years later, in 1729, North Carolina expanded the reserve, extending its boundaries up to the fork of the Blackwater and Nottoway Rivers, over to Indian Creek, and down to the Meherrin River. All settlers living within these bounds were to move off, and the Meherrins were to have full enjoyment of their lands, settling and farming wherever they wanted within them.[40]

Although the council ordered that the Meherrins not be molested by settlers, it could do nothing about them being molested by their old Indian enemies. Not long after the Meherrins had settled onto their newly surveyed reserve in 1729, some foreign Indians attacked them. It was a terrible blow, with about fourteen Meherrins killed and several taken captive. The Meherrins immediately suspected it was the Saponis and Occaneechis taking revenge for the big attack made eight years earlier at Ft. Christiana. The Meherrins almost got it right. Investigation proved it was the Catawbas who had attacked the Meherrins in revenge for that attack on them at Ft. Christiana. Asked why they had attacked the Meherrins when all knew the attackers at Ft. Christiana had been the Tuscaroras, the Catawbas explained that two White men had told them the Meherrins and Tuscaroras were one in the same. Both were certainly Iroquoian speakers. The Catawba attack terrified the Meherrins. Fearing more might be on the way, they abandoned their town at Meherrin Neck and moved east of the Chowan River. For a while, they found themselves squatting on settler lands, fearing to return to their own reserve. During this time, a few Meherrins worked for the Virginia commission surveying the Virginia–North Carolina boundary. They told their story to William Byrd, one of the commission's Virginia members. Byrd had little sympathy for the Meherrins as "they have ever been reputed the most false and treacherous to the English of all Indians in the neighborhood."[41] The Meherrins would disagree with that view.

Despite the proclamations of the North Carolina Governor's Council, settlers still made claims on Meherrin lands, forcing the council to take another look. The 1729 Laws of North Carolina addressed the Meherrin complaints. This time they expanded the Meherrin reserve, extending their lands farther up the Meherrin and Blackwater Rivers, giving them about 4,480 acres total in Hertford County. Under the new law, the Meherrins were to keep the lands "so long as they should continue a nation and inhabit the same." It seemed the colonial government was already contemplating the day when Indians no longer existed in North Carolina. In addition, all English settlers living within the expanded boundaries were to move off the lands, and only Indians were allowed to live on them. The colonial government appointed John Boude as commissioner to the Meherrins, whom they should contact if any Englishmen intruded onto their lands. Boude would then contact the local constable and have the settlers forcibly evicted. If the settlers refused to leave, they would be fined £5 for a first refusal, £10 for a second, and £20 plus two months imprisonment for a third. The government insisted that the Meherrins should have peaceful possession of their lands, but they could not sell or rent out any of their lands as they were to be communal lands for them. Seeing these legal provisions, Virginia officially gave up its claim that the Meherrins were tributaries of the Old Dominion.[42]

For the next decade or so, the Meherrins lived at peace with their English neighbors. Captain Roger, the Meherrin chief, was no longer mentioned in government documents, so he may have died, but there is no record of who led the Meherrins into the 1730s and after. However, the Meherrins' lands could not protect them from all the sickness, violence, abuse, and alcohol that affected all the Indians of eastern North Carolina. Fearing Catawba raids, some Meherrins set up communities outside the reserve boundaries on Potecasi Creek and even on the east side of the Chowan River. It was just this kind of spreading that angered the North Carolina government.[43]

The troubles began again in 1742. Back in 1729, when the council had expanded the Meherrin reserve, there had been some settler land claims on Indian Creek that should have been nullified by the expansion but had not. Since then, these titles had been sold and resold to other settlers, which worried the Meherrins. In 1742, they began a resurvey to prove these settlers sat on Meherrin lands and hoped to remove them. The settlers, led by Thomas Jernigan, who claimed 575 acres on Indian Creek inside the Meherrin reserve, complained to the council, saying the settlers had long lived here and paid quitrents. The recent Meherrins' survey placed their lands within the reserve boundaries in question, however, and so they were in danger of being driven out. The council tried to find a middle ground. It admitted that the land belonged to the Meherrins per the allocation in 1729, and they should be allowed to enjoy their land in peace—or at least the land that did not have settlers on it. The council ordered the Meherrins to accept the settlers as renters who would pay them £5 Virginia money for every 100 acres the settlers possessed inside the reserve. The council then instructed the Meherrins not to sell any of the lands claimed by the settlers. The controversy showed how powerless tributaries could be when it came to land. Though these lands were Meherrin lands, the Indians were forced to accept the settlers as tenants, could not evict them, and could not sell the land.[44]

Things did not work out. The Meherrins were soon back before the government to prove hardship, claiming that once again "white people" were intruding onto their lands. The term *white people* now began showing up in the records with regularity, revealing a growing mentality in the colony where there were "white people" and everybody else and the Indians were not seen as White people. The North Carolina Legislature turned to John Boude, the commissioner to the Meherrins appointed back in 1729, "to settle the Indians in the quiet possession of their possession, and praying relief thereof."[45] The Meherrins did not think Boude did much to protect their interests, and so their complaints continued. The legislature did pass a bill to prevent further encroachment on the Meherrin reserve, though.[46]

When the French and Indian War broke out in 1754, some Meherrin men served in the Northampton militia. When the war got hot in 1757, the North Carolina government turned to its Indian tributaries, and a party of seven Meherrin warriors joined contingents of Tuscaroras, Saponis, and others to serve with Col. George Washington in Pennsylvania.[47] Unfortunately, this enlistment stripped the reserve of many of its men, and now Meherrin women and children suffered. They appealed to the government, and the North Carolina Legislature ordered provisions be purchased for the Meherrin families.[48] The Meherrin men apparently served well and were soon back home.

Their service notwithstanding, in 1758 the Meherrins were again complaining to the Governor's Council that they were "disturbed in their possession by several persons contrary to an act of Assembly of this Province passed in the year 1729." The council ordered the attorney general to prosecute all those who bothered the Meherrins. This response worked, and the Meherrins kept their lands for a while longer.[49] But times got no better. Meherrin women farmed, and men hunted, but the deer were disappearing. Even the Virginia traders passed the Meherrins by as settlement moved farther west to the Piedmont and mountains. For whatever reason, during the 1760s the remaining Meherrins abandoned their reserve and moved their community south to Potecasi Creek, not far from Ahoskie, North Carolina, where they lived more as individuals but bound through kinship and culture. "Meherrin" does not show up in the records anymore after 1770, and their reserve seemed to be extinguished at that time in the mind of the colonial officials. After the American Revolution, the North Carolina state government refused to recognize the colonial treaties. Historian Shannon Dawdy points out that "as far as white Americans were concerned, the Meherrins and similar peoples no longer possessed a political identity. That did not necessarily reflect the internal perceptions of the Meherrins, which in all likelihood continued some form of traditional council government."[50]

While the colony may not have recognized that a Meherrin nation existed, many Meherrins continued living in Hertford County, which was created in 1759. They were without land, so their White neighbors referred to them as "free People of Color." Despite this designation, a strong Meherrin Indian identity remained, often out of sight of the Meherrins' White neighbors. It was an old North Carolina Indian story.

Machapungas

The Machapungas understood that story. Twelve years after they signed a treaty ending the Tuscarora War, in 1727, they finally got a land reserve, a good-size one at 10,240 acres, or 16 square miles, on the southeastern end of Lake Mattamuskeet, just north of Pamlico Sound in present-day Hyde County. A few Cores who had held out with the Machapungas joined them on the reserve. Immediately after the war, Squire Hooks led the Machapungas, and John Pagett led the Cores. The Cores were Iroquoian speakers related to the Tuscaroras, whereas the Machapungas were Algonquians, and so they seemed often at odds, just as they had been before the war.[51]

One would imagine that the more easterly and isolated Machapungas in the swamps along the shores of Lake Mattamuskeet and the Pamlico Sound would have had a better chance of avoiding the land-hungry. Even in the twenty-first century, that area consists of miles and miles of marsh grass, with few people to be seen. However, no Indian land in North Carolina was free from the settlers' gaze. The Machapungas had been members of the Catechna Alliance and so had waged war against the colony of North Carolina, and they, along with the Cores, were the last to make peace. They were the only members of the Catechna Alliance to survive the Tuscarora War, become tributaries, and have a land reserve recognized by the colonial government. That is a rather amazing testament because all other nations of the Catechna Alliance—the Contentnea Creek Tuscaroras, Bay River Indians, White Oak River Indians, Neuse, and Pamlicos—disappeared both as organized nations and from the colonial records. They were erased as Native peoples.

Upon signing the treaty in 1715, the colony instructed the Machapungas and Cores to settle together on lands along Lake Mattamuskeet. The union was not a natural one. These lands were longtime

Machapunga lands, not Core lands, and the two groups were old enemies. While some Cores may have intermarried with Machapungas, it was not long before most Cores migrated to Indian Woods to live with their Tuscarora kinfolk. By the 1720s, the Cores had disappeared from the records, leaving the Machapungas in possession of their lands near the lake, though place-names such as "Core Banks" and "Core Sound" remain to this day.

After the Tuscarora War, King John Squires led the Machapungas, with John Mackey and Long Tom as his principal men. We are not sure if Squire Hooks and John Squires are one and the same person or different leaders. The Squires, Mackey, and Long Tom families made up the heart of the Machapunga people. We have no records on the size of the Machapunga population after the war, but it was most likely rather small, maybe a few score or so, and this number would decline over the decades. They lived in family homesteads along the many creeks that crisscrossed Machapunga lands rather than around a central village. King Squires's home on New Mattamuskeet Creek served as the nation's capital.[52]

Unfortunately, their English neighbors were always willing to believe the worst about the Machapungas, accusing them of stealing hogs and then beating any Englishman who tried to stop them. Colonists claimed that Machapunga insolence was intolerable, and they demanded the colonial government defend them from these "barbarous heathens." In October 1718, the leaders of Bath town wrote a panicky letter to the colonial government claiming that the Machapungas had taken captives and threatened nearby settlers with destruction. The Machapungas had done no such thing. It was all a hoax concocted by the daughter, son, and two servants of Thomas Worsely to prevent an enslaved Indian named Pompey from being punished for some mischief. It was always easy to blame Indians for any wrongdoing, and settlers were quick to believe such accusations. In reality, the Machapungas were destitute hunters, fishers, and farmers, and the colonial government had to give them ten pounds weight of gunpowder in 1719 for hunting. They posed no threat to their neighbors.[53]

Though the treaty of 1715 had established Machapunga lands between Lake Mattamuskeet and the Pamlico Sound, the reserve had yet to be surveyed. Sometime about 1718, a Machapunga man sold off a parcel of the nation's reserve to settler Richard Jasper. King Squires and Captain Mackey complained to the Governor's Council and requested their lands be surveyed and boundaries made public. The council agreed and declared all surveys and patents of the Machapungas made before November 11, 1718, null and void.[54]

However, no survey seemed to have been made, and six years later King Squires and Captain Mackey went back before the council, again asking for their lands to be surveyed. The council instructed the surveyor general to plot out Machapunga lands and be sure to include in it the settlements in which the Indians currently lived. He should try to use natural boundaries, such as creeks, whenever possible, and provide the Machapungas with 10,240 acres of land, about 16 square miles. It is unclear if a survey was actually made, but in April 1727 the council recognized the reserve as running from where the modern-day town of Engelhard sits on the north to below Wyesocking Bay in the south, with Pamlico Sound on the east and Lake Mattamuskeet on the west. In reality, the Machapungas may have received more land than the 10,240 acres prescribed as they claimed a 45-square-mile tract.[55] In return for this reserve and all the rights that went with it, the Machapungas officially became tributaries of the colony, required to pay to the colonial governor two buckskins every year on September 29, the Feast of St. Michael. Also, every year after this the Machapungas would pay a rental fee of one shilling for every 100 acres. Since the government officially recognized the Machapungas as having 10,240 acres, this annual tribute would come to 102 shillings and change, or a little more than £5, a rather hefty sum for a poverty-stricken people.[56]

The Machapungas reserve soon attracted the interest of nearby settlers. In September 1731, King John Squires, who had complained when a fellow Indian had sold Machapunga land back in 1718, now sold off the first parcel of the reserve. King Squires, along with John Mackey and Long Tom, sold 640 acres to Henry Gibbs of Currituck

Precinct for a down payment of £10 "good lawfull money of the province of North Carolina" and then another £170 to come later.[57] Squires sold his own 150-acre homestead in 1742 to settler Francis Credle for £100.[58] Land sales picked up after this.

The increased number of sales seemed to go along with a declining population. In 1731, Gov. George Burrington listed the Machapungas as one of six Indian nations still living in eastern North Carolina but with only about twenty families on their reserve.[59] Most of these families were Squires, Mackeys, and Long Toms, sometimes shortened to "Tom." Between April and August 1746, King John Squires died. He had led the Machapungas since the end of the Tuscarora War. It appeared that his trusted adviser Long Tom also died in 1746 or left the reserve because his name cannot be seen in the records after this, and his "rice patch" was sold to the settler Casson Brinson for £6 Virginia proclamation money.[60] Leadership now went to the king's son, Charles Squires, who served as leader until 1752, when he was supplanted by his brother, George Squires, who shared leadership of the Machapungas with James Tom.[61]

The Squires brothers seemed to be controversial leaders among their people, especially when it came to their penchant for selling Machapunga lands. Neither Charles nor George seemed to be as traditional as their father, and both had a firmer grasp of the English world the Machapungas now lived in. As early as 1740, Charles Squires purchased 200 acres on Hatteras Island from Joseph Farrow for £100 "lawful money." This purchase does not seem to be for the Machapungas but personally for Squires.[62] In 1752, George Squires, now noted as the "King of the Arrowmusket Indians," offered to lease the entire 10,240-acre reserve to a trio of settlers for ninety-nine years for £88, 10 shillings, 8 pence. Besides the cash payment, if the Indians demanded, the settlers would also pay a rent of one peppercorn every year on the Feast of St. Michael. Along with this rent, the Machapungas would keep their hunting rights on the land. This deal was too much for most Machapunga families, and they protested. The Governor's Council refused to approve the lease, and it never went into effect.[63]

George Squires may have overreached and apparently lost the trust of his people and the colonial government. After 1755, he is not referred to as "king" anymore. George may have fallen even further in esteem because he was sometimes referred to only as the "Proprietor of Arrowmusket." More often he was just listed among other men, such as Charles Squires, Joshua Squires, and Timothy Squires, as "Indians of Arismuskeet" or as the "chief men" of the Machapungas.[64] In 1755, Gov. Arthur Dobbs recorded a total of eight or ten Machapungas living on their reserve.[65] However, six years later, in 1761, he reported the Machapungas could field seven or eight warriors, meaning there was a possible population of twenty-four to thirty-two, more or less.[66] This shows the uncertainness of these colonial counts and how reserve numbers might fluctuate up and down, though the overall trend for all eastern North Carolina Native peoples was downward.

It may have been this dwindling population and the Machapungas' poverty that now made them open to selling the rest of their lands. In March 1756, George Squires, Charles Squires, and John Mackey sold 300 acres to John Jennett and then another 100 acres on Little Creek to John Linton.[67] On June 8, 1761, the Machapungas sold their entire 10,240-acre reservation to the settlers Thomas Jones, William Cummings, and Bartholomew Coin for £100 sterling. Six Machapungas signed the deed: Charles Squires, George Squires, Timothy Squires, James Tom, John Squires, and Joseph Russell. The Machapunga women had little choice in the matter or may not have even known what was afoot as their names do not show up on the document. One wonders if the settlers really knew exactly how much land they were buying because many reserve tracts from 1727 had already been sold. Nevertheless, the North Carolina government approved this sale. Essentially, the Machapunga reserve was no more, at least on paper.[68]

With their lands legally gone, some Machapunga families left the area. The Squires family began to break up. Former king George Squires moved to Tyrell County.[69] While the Machapungas may not have had a reserve, Indians still lived in the area and on those lands.

In 1761, Rev. Alexander Stewart of the Anglican Church visited the Machapungas and reported that a few Roanokes and Hatteras had moved in with them. While there, Stewart baptized two Indian men, three women, and two children.[70] We will return later to the Machapungas as they still have a role in our story.

Hatteras

From their island home, the Hatteras had been some of the first eastern North Carolina Indians to have regular contact with the English when sailors, whalers, and fishermen often stopped on Hatteras Island. Some Indians made close, working, even intimate relations with these mariners, producing bicultural children. The first settlers began making land claims on Hatteras Island in the early 1700s, and movement to the island picked up steam after the Tuscarora War. During this time, the Hatteras were led by King Thom Elks and his family. Over the next few decades, owing to incompetent and sometime fraudulent surveys, these settler land grants began to intrude onto lands claimed by the Hatteras.[71]

In 1756, the Hatteras contested a land claim by Thomas Robb and his family that took part of the King's Point town where the Elks family lived. Conversely, Robb said that it was the Indian town itself that encroached on his lands. An investigation by the colony showed that the Hatteras had no land reserve and that no lands had ever been officially assigned to them. It seemed as if they could lose everything. Fortunately, in 1759 Gov. Arthur Dobbs issued a land patent of about 200 acres to "William Elks and the rest of the Hatteras Indians," which included the Indian town at King's Point.[72] This might well be considered the last Indian reserve created by the colonial North Carolina government. But it also might be considered a land grant to the Elks family specifically, just the same as any other settler might receive. For the next few years, the Hatteras kept their lands, but they began selling off tracts in 1770, 1771, and 1783, and the last part of the Hatteras reserve went to Nathaniel Pinkham in 1802. By then, the Hatteras as a nation had dropped out of the colonial and state records. Most Hatteras had either left the island or had blended in with the local White population. While some stories tell of the Hatteras moving to the mainland and some down to Drowning Creek, the island, because of its isolation, also became a refuge for Indians. The Machapunga George Squires bought land there. So it is just as likely that many of the Hatteras's descendants remain on Hatteras Island today.[73]

Saponis and Occaneechis

Two other Indian peoples associated with North Carolina, the Saponis and Occaneechis, also received some guaranteed lands, but in Virginia. The Saponis and Occaneechis were Piedmont peoples and during the 1600s had moved back and forth between Virginia and North Carolina. They eventually wound up as Virginia tributaries. During the Tuscarora War, the North Carolina government appealed to the Saponis for assistance. The Governor's Council promised that if they moved into North Carolina to help fight "against the heathen," they would be protected and provided for.[74] But the Saponis remained in Virginia. In fact, Gov. Spotswood of Virginia trusted them over all his other tributary Indians and requested they provide twenty warriors to defend the colony if the war spilled over Virginia's borders. The Saponis and Occaneechis moved to Ft. Christiana in southern Virginia, the trading post created by Spotswood and run by the Virginia Indian Company.[75]

At Christiana, the Saponis and Occaneechis prospered, getting favorable trade deals from the Virginia Indian Company. Soon Ft. Christiana boasted more than 300 "Saponies," as the colony referred to all the Indians who lived around the fort. William Byrd later explained, "The most considerable are the Sapponys, the Occaneches, and Steukenhocks, who not finding themselves separately numerous enough for their defence, have agreed to unite into one body, and all of them now go under the name Saponys."[76] However, the Indians themselves still saw individual nations, not necessarily one nation. Protected by the fort's guns, they lived in their traditional longhouses surrounded by a wooden palisade. Spotswood also guaranteed the Saponis a 36-square-mile tract of land and a school for their children. Ft. Christiana soon became a busy marketplace as Tuscaroras, Nottoways, Enos, and Catawbas visited to trade deerskins for guns and goods.[77]

The attack on the visiting Catawbas at Ft. Christiana by the Senecas and Tuscaroras in 1717 proved disastrous for the Saponis and Occaneechis who lived at the fort. The next year, when Virginia abandoned the fort, they not only lost their preferential access to trade goods but, even worse, they lost the defensive capabilities Ft. Christiana had provided. Without that protection, the Saponis and Occaneechis became targets of the Tuscaroras, Meherrins, Nottoways, and Senecas. Blount's warriors launched so many attacks that in 1723 the Saponis made a peace treaty with his Tuscaroras. Even this gesture did not stop the violence. In 1727, Tuscarora warriors attacked a hunting band of Saponis, killing or capturing seven. Blount blamed the attacks on "Northern Indians" as well as on some of his own Tuscaroras who "had revolted from him and now lived as Pirates and Robbers."[78] By 1729, the Saponis began to splinter. Some moved south to join the Catawbas. Some eventually moved to New York to join the Five Nations of the Iroquois. But a third group moved into North Carolina, taking up residence in present-day Granville County, near the headwaters of the Tar River. In 1761, Gov. Arthur Dobbs reported that the Saponis could field twenty warriors, meaning their population was probably between sixty and eighty people. There they laid low for years, almost out of sight of the English and later the Americans. It does not seem that the Saponis ever officially became tributaries of North Carolina and never had a reserve laid out for them. In that same count in 1761, Gov. Dobbs listed the Tuscaroras, Meherrins, and Saponis together and said they all live in the "middle of the colony" near the Roanoke River "and have by law 10,000 acres of land allotted to them in Lord Granvilles District[;] they live chiefly by hunting and are in perfect friendship with the inhabitants." The 10,000 acres mentioned here seemingly belonged to the Tuscaroras, not the Saponis or Meherrins.

The reference, though, does seem to indicate a close relationship between these three peoples.[79]

The Occaneechis followed the Saponis south into North Carolina. An Occaneechi community eventually named "Little Texas" arose in what would become Alamance County, where they would remain for the rest of the eighteenth century. To this day, there is a close connection between North Carolina Saponis and Occaneechis.[80]

Declining Population

During the eighteenth century, while the tributary Indians of eastern North Carolina lost their land reserves, they also lost their population. Illness took out men, women, and children. Rum ravaged individuals, their families, and communities. Attacks by Catawbas and other enemies took a toll. Senecas and New York Tuscaroras visited, as always, and did their usual meddling. Abuse by settlers, such as limiting where Indians could hunt or forage or appropriating their farmlands, also affected the Indians' health. The colonial government still asked for Indians' support in times of war. Because of these challenges, Indian population numbers plummeted. Much of this decline was through death. However, it might also have been due to Indians, in particular adult men, leaving the reserve and living as individuals elsewhere.

As early as 1722, Rev. Thomas Newnam, who preached across northeastern North Carolina, believed the Meherrins and other Indians totaled no more than 300 people.[81] Dr. John Brickell, in his 1730 dinner with Kings Blount, Hoyter, and Durant, believed there were only 1,500 to 1,600 Indians in all of eastern North Carolina.[82] In 1731, Gov. George Burrington noted that there were only six Indian nations left in eastern North Carolina: the Hatteras, Machapungas, Poteskites (Yeopims), Chowans, Meherrins, and Blount's Tuscaroras. All "live within English settlements, have land assigned them . . . and delight in slaughtering one another." According to Burrington, except for the more numerous Tuscaroras, each of the five small nations had no more than twenty families.[83]

Even the Tuscaroras faced their own population decline. In 1731, Gov. Burrington listed the Tuscaroras as still the largest Indian nation in eastern North Carolina, with 200 warriors, which would mean somewhere between 600 and 800 people total. This number was a sharp drop from the thousands who had lived in the area during the 1600s. According to Burrington, the Tuscaroras were once very powerful, but "most of these were destroyed and drove away in the late war." Only King Blount had made peace with the English and had lived in friendship with them ever since.[84] Tuscarora numbers benefited somewhat from a few Chowan, Core, and Saponi families who joined Blount's people. Tuscaroras also left Indian Woods, heading for their kinspeople in New York, south to the Drowning Creek area, as well into what would become Halifax, Warren, and Sampson Counties to join Indian refugee communities or into the settlements as detribalized Indians who lived as individuals, some as holders of small plots of land, some living hand to mouth on the margins of colonial society.[85]

The smaller tributaries seemed most affected. The 1748 militia returns for Northampton County reported that the Meherrins were the only Indians in the county and that they were few in number.[86] In the militia returns for Chowan County for 1754, James Craven reported that the only Indians in the county were the Chowans, "but their strength is nothing, and their condition very deplorable by the artifice & cunning of some of their neighbors. I am informed they consist of two men and five women & children which two white men would at any time overcome."[87]

In 1755, Gov. Dobbs conducted another census of North Carolina Indians, and the drop in their numbers was shocking. The Tuscaroras boasted 100 men and 201 women and children, for a total of 301. Other Indians were almost at extinction numbers. Dobbs said the Chowans of Chowan County numbered five: two men, three women and children. The Meherrins in Northampton County numbered seven or eight warriors, but Dobbs did not record the number of women and children, so the total ranged from eight to possibly twenty or thirty. Then in 1761, Dobbs said there were twenty

Meherrin fighting men. There were only eight or ten Machapunga men, women, and children, and another ten Hatteras on the Outer Banks, though six years later Dobbs recorded seven or eight Machapunga warriors. The Saponis in Granville County numbered fourteen men and fourteen women, though in 1761 Dobbs said they had twenty warriors. If these counts are in any way close to accurate, then the total Indian population of eastern North Carolina north of the Neuse River was around 400 or fewer.[88] In reality, there were more Indians than the governor realized, and many Indian people in eastern North Carolina were not counted. The next few decades showed many more Chowans cropping up than just five, more Meherrins and Machapungas as well.

Nevertheless, there was no doubt that the Indian population of the colony was dropping precipitously. Once numerous Native peoples were slowly fading and being edged out of their lands. The Tuscaroras found themselves facing the same challenges as the smaller tributaries.

6

The Tuscarora Scattering

The Tuscaroras faced many of the same challenges encountered by the smaller tributaries, especially after the death of King Tom Blount. Encroachment on and the sale of Tuscarora lands remained an issue, as did migration away from the Indian Woods reserve.

Just as with the Chowan, Meherrin, and Machapunga, English settlers cast a covetous eye on the Tuscarora Indian Woods reserve as some of the only remaining affordable lands in an area of increasing prices. Others saw the reserves in terms of speculation. Get the lands cheap, watch their value increase as settlers moved into the area, then sell them at a profit to latecomers. In 1721, King Blount complained to the North Carolina Governor's Council that Deputy Surveyor John Grey was laying out settler lands too close to the Tuscarora town of Ooneroy on the Roanoke River. This will cause "feuds and disturbances," Blount warned. Taking his complaint seriously, the council asked that Blount as well as Surveyor General William Maule and Deputy Surveyor Gray meet at Gov. Charles Eden's home in April. There the surveyors were to show their warrants and land entries made within 5 miles of Ooneroy. The governor assured Blount that the surveyors would be given strict instructions to make no surveys or entries within 5 miles of the town and that only the colony's secretary could authorize them. Eden ordered Col. Frederick Jones to lay out the town of Ooneroy per the governor's agreement with Blount.[1] This may have been Blount's first official complaint about encroachment on Indian Woods lands. It certainly would not be the last for the Tuscaroras.

If the April 1721 meeting took place, nothing seemed resolved. The next year Blount returned to the council with a petition from his people complaining that they had difficulty living with the constant encroachments by settlers. He again asked the council to have Indian Woods' boundaries surveyed. Once again, the council ordered Maule and Col. Robert West to lay out the boundaries. They were to take interpreter William Charleton with them to make sure things ran smoothly. The council expected the matter would be settled by the next council meeting. But Maule dragged his feet, and it was not until late 1722 or early 1723 that he and four helpers spent twenty-one days surveying the boundaries of both the Tuscarora and Chowan reserves. Maule said the reserves together totaled 53,000 acres. In 1720, the Chowan lands had been reduced to 11,360 acres. That left 41,640 for the Tuscaroras, about what they had been assigned in 1717.[2] In 1722, North Carolina created Bertie County, which covered the settlements on the west side of the Chowan River as well as Indian Woods.[3] It did not mean much to the Tuscaroras then, but it would later.

Then in 1723 Blount made a decision that would bedevil his people for the rest of the century. In that year, Blount approached the Governor's Council and asked that 600 acres inside Indian Woods known as Quitsney's Meadow be given to their interpreter William Charleton for all the favors he had done the Tuscaroras. Charleton had long been a favorite of Blount from as far back as the Tuscarora War. We know little about him other than that he charged the colony for every day he served in his official capacity as interpreter. Blount nevertheless trusted him, turned to him for advice, and insisted on having Charleton present whenever he met with colonial officials. With hospitality an important Tuscarora characteristic, Blount may have wanted to reward a close friend, maybe even considered a fictive kinsman, and keep him tied to the Tuscaroras. Maybe Charleton hinted that he would like to have Quitsney's Meadow. Whatever the reason, on November 7, 1723, the council approved, and 600 acres inside the Indian Woods reserve were signed over to Charleton. He could settle or dispose of the land as he saw fit. No one back then saw any problem, and Charleton kept the land and passed it on to his son, George Charleton.[4] This land transfer would cause, as Blount prophesied for other settler incursions, feuds and disturbances.

As we have seen, for the next few decades King Tom Blount provided wise and able leadership for the Tuscaroras of the Indian Woods reserve. Under him, the Tuscaroras remained the largest and most powerful Indian nation in eastern North Carolina, with the largest reserve and a good measure of leverage with the colonial government, which always feared Blount might just join with the Senecas and start another Tuscarora War. Then sometime during the first days of March 1739, King Tom Blount of the Tuscaroras died, apparently at his house in the town of Resootka on the Indian Woods reserve. He would have been sixty-four years old or thereabouts. We know nothing else of his death, but old age may have caught up with him. We do not know what became of his body or where it was buried. On March 5, the headmen of the Tuscarora nation appeared before the governor and the Governor's Council to inform them of Blount's death. As tributaries, they asked to be allowed to "choose a king." Gov. Gabriel Johnston agreed and ordered the Tuscaroras to hold an election on the third Tuesday in June 1739 at Resootka and choose a king from among themselves. Once they had made their selection, they should submit the new king's name to the governor "for his approbation."[5]

Elections, at least how the governor imagined them, were unheard of in Tuscarora society. In the old days, certain families or clans may have been expected to provide leaders. Certain individuals, bolstered by their family history, gained the trust of the town by displaying the cardinal virtues of bravery, fortitude, wisdom, and generosity. Personal success as well as the ability to translate one's own beliefs and policies into benefits for one's people brought one more authority. But in this new day, as tributaries Tuscarora leaders needed to possess additional characteristics. They had to know how to navigate through the English colonial world as well as be acceptable to Carolina authorities. Gov. Johnston and the council wanted a compliant Tuscarora leader who not only understood he was an ally, client, and tributary but was also powerful and respected enough to keep his people loyal, peaceful, and under control. They would never approve of anyone who showed even the slightest anti-English attitude.

Unfortunately, we do not know whom the Tuscaroras chose and Johnston approved. The next mention by name of a Tuscarora leader appeared nine years later, in 1748, in the colonial records, with James Blount being noted as "Chief of the Tuskerora Nation."[6] Was James the son of King Tom Blount, as the English counted succession? Or Tom's sister's son, as the old matrilineal tradition demanded? Or a brother? Were there other leaders in the nine years between King Tom and Chief James? We just are not sure.

After King Blount

The death of King Tom Blount was a blow to the Tuscarora nation and to all remaining Indians of eastern North Carolina. It marked the passing of a generation. He had been born in 1675, when the Tuscaroras were independent and powerful, the most numerous Indian nation on the Coastal Plain, a people who dominated their neighbors, both Indian and English, and whose language was the Indian lingua franca of the region. By his death in 1739, only a few Tuscaroras could remember those days. He had led what was left of a much-diminished Tuscarora people in North Carolina, tributary vassals to the colonial government. King Tom Blount had proved to be a wise and energetic protector of his people. He had prevented them from going into a disastrous war alongside the Catechna Alliance in 1711 and from being extinguished as a people, like so many of those towns and nations that had joined the Alliance. He had kept them as independent as possible. Though he handed King Hancock over to colonial authorities and eventually allied with the Carolina government, he had tried mightily, and apparently successfully, to avoid attacking other Tuscaroras. After the war and now a tributary, he had negotiated with colonial authorities over lands and rights and had stood before the Governor's Council to defend his people. Needing

Blount as an ally and fearing what might happen if he were to ignite another war, the North Carolina government had gone out of its way to provide justice and keep him happy. More importantly, he had prevented English settlers from encroaching on Tuscarora lands. But as those Indians and Englishmen who could remember the destruction the war brought passed away, as memories faded, then the Tuscaroras, like all Indians of eastern North Carolina, found justice, respect, and compassion harder to find among the English.

The most serious threat to the Tuscaroras was the same that afflicted the other Indians: pressure on their land by settlers. While King Blount was alive, he had managed to protect Indian Woods' boundaries and keep the council's sympathy. In 1732, Thomas Pollock Jr., son of Thomas Pollock, who had been governor during the Tuscarora War, complained to the council that he owned some land in Bertie County on the Roanoke River but that the Tuscaroras claimed it, though he had no idea how they got the claim. Because of their claim, Pollock said he could not settle the land until the Tuscaroras gave it up. Unable to settle it, he faced it being taken from him as a lapsed patent. Even then, he still had to pay quitrents on the undeveloped land. He asked the council to allow him not to pay the quitrent and prevent his claim from being declared lapsed. With King Blount still alive, the council made no move to force the Tuscaroras to negotiate or give up their claim. All they could do for Pollock was declare that his claim would not be declared lapsed, but he would still have to pay the quitrent.[7] Certainly, other settlers made similar claims about where the boundary of Indian Woods ended and their own lands began.

Blount had his own complaints. In 1735, the recently appointed governor, Gabriel Johnston, visited Indian Woods to listen to Blount rail against settlers selling rum to his young men, which prevented them from hunting and taking care of their families. He insisted that White traders overcharged them for goods and that ferrymen on the Roanoke River refused to carry them across. He explained how settlers pressed the boundaries of his reserve, encroaching on lands that belonged to the Tuscaroras. Gov. Johnston listened, but all he could do was appoint a Commission of Indian Affairs to look into the issues.[8]

Governor, council, and commission walked warily as long as Blount lived. But once he died in 1739, all bets were off. Nevertheless, the name "Tuscarora" carried weight late into the eighteenth century. In 1741, the council ordered a survey of Tuscarora lands to prevent encroachments and disputes with the "white people" living around the Tuscaroras. The survey was to be recorded with the Secretary's Office and a copy given to the Tuscaroras with the secretary's seal on it.[9] It does not appear that the survey was made as Tuscarora complaints about settler encroachment continued. Settler Humphrey Bates drew the most ire. Back in 1723, King Blount had transferred 600 acres of Indian Woods land to interpreter William Charleton. Charleton passed it on to his son, George, who several years later, sometime before 1748, sold half the tract, 300 acres, to Humphrey Bates. Suddenly, a stranger, an English settler who had no real connection to the Tuscaroras, claimed a tract of land inside the Tuscarora reserve.[10] Tuscaroras did not like having Bates living among them.

In 1748, the council resolved to settle Tuscarora boundaries. The Laws of North Carolina of 1748 devoted the entire chapter IV to the Tuscaroras and showed that despite Blount's death the colonial government considered the Tuscaroras important and potentially dangerous allies who needed to be mollified. The council ordered another survey, and the Laws of 1748 recognized Indian Woods fronting the north side of the Roanoke River and encompassing parts or all of Quitsnay Swamp, Roquist Swamp, Deep Creek, and a "great spring." From later reports, it appeared that the new survey cut about 10,000 acres or so from Indian Woods, making the Tuscarora reservation about 30,000 acres. These lands were to be confirmed to James Blount, "Chief of the Tuskerora Nation," and its people, heirs, and successors forever. This is the first mention of a successor to King Tom Blount. Unlike his predecessor, James Blount was not labeled a "king."[11]

The council came down firmly on the side of the Tuscaroras, prohibiting any person from purchasing Indian Woods lands and determining that all such sales would be considered null and void. Any person buying Tuscarora land would be fined £10 proclamation money for every 100 acres they purchased. Also, settlers living within these newly surveyed Tuscarora lands were to vacate those lands by March 25, 1749. If they had not done so by that date, then they would be fined 20 shillings proclamation money for every day they remained on Tuscarora land. Addressing another complaint by the Native peoples, the law stipulated that if any person let their cattle, horses, or hogs range onto Tuscarora lands, as many settlers did, they would be liable for the same penalties and forfeitures as if their animals had ranged upon a fellow colonist's land. The unfenced cattle and hogs of settlers had long been a threat to Indian gardens and fields. The council's laws made a strong statement for Tuscarora rights. "The said Indians shall and may enjoy the benefit of the laws . . . in the same manner as the white people do or can, any law, usage, or custom to the contrary, notwithstanding."[12] This was an important declaration of Indians as equal with White people before the law and as subjects of His Majesty. At least in theory. All this equality went out the window if a person was not counted as an Indian anymore.

The next year, 1749, the council showed it meant what it said about respecting the integrity of Indian Woods by declaring that the Tuscaroras were to "occupy and live upon the same, and to prevent any person or persons taking up lands or settling within the said bounds."[13] Humphrey Bates, who held 300 acres of Indian Woods land, may have been the Tuscaroras' target. Once Bates heard of the law, he appealed to the council to make an exception for him and allow him to remain on the land. He muddied the waters enough to be allowed to stay there, and the Tuscaroras fumed over his presence.[14]

Even at midcentury, the Tuscaroras posed a threat in the mind of the colonial government. The shadow of the French and their success in creating Indian allies in Louisiana probably stoked this fear. As the governor and council saw it, even with King Blount gone, it would not be wise to push the Tuscaroras too far. Bishop August Spangenberg visited the Tuscaroras in 1752. His guide was the trader

Thomas Whitmel, a member of the recently created Commission of Indian Affairs, whom Spangenberg said could speak fluent Tuscarora and so was the official interpreter for the nation. As they toured Indian Woods, Spangenberg wrote that the Tuscarora population was small and that they had no king, but rather a captain who was appointed by the colonial government. However, there were "also some individuals who live among them as chiefs." The Tuscaroras, he said, were "very poor and oppressed by the Whites," and little effort had been made to Christianize them.[15]

Spangenberg believed that it was the Tuscaroras' alliance with the Six Nations of the Iroquois in New York that gave them more power than their numbers should. The bishop said the Tuscaroras "suffered from this relationship very much" because although both nations made war on the Catawbas, it was the Tuscaroras who bore the brunt of Catawba counterattacks. Nevertheless, when Spangenberg met with Tuscarora leaders during his tour, they gave him a threat to pass along to the Catawbas. He should tell them that the Tuscaroras had plenty of young men who knew the way to Catawba Town and could go and return there within twenty days. Up to now the Tuscaroras had remained quiet and not bothered the Catawbas except to hunt a little in Catawba territory. They would remain quiet as long as the Catawbas also remained quiet. But if the Catawbas wanted to become troublesome, then Tuscarora warriors would find their way to Catawba Town.[16]

Spangenberg believed it was this aggressive attitude that made the Tuscaroras different from the Indians he encountered up north. In Pennsylvania, he said no White people feared the Indians unless the Indians were drunk. However, the Tuscaroras of North Carolina "conduct themselves in such a way that the Whites are afraid of them. If they enter a house & the man is not at home they become insolent & the poor woman must do as they command." Up north, a White man drove a party of Senecas off his land "like sheep before him & thus rid himself of the nuisance." However, dealing with the North Carolina Tuscaroras could be dangerous. Spangenberg had heard reports of Indians stealing stock and even murdering White men. The

Indians had lost the Tuscarora War and so had lost their land, which, he acknowledged, had "created a bad feeling not only among those tribes immediately concerned but with all the rest. This feeling of animosity will not speedily die out."[17] Despite Tuscarora aggressiveness, Spangenberg reported that the Indians who remained in eastern North Carolina, remnants of those who had made war against the colony in 1711, "are treated with great contempt & will probably soon be entirely exterminated."[18] Seen as dangerous but treated with contempt? One wonders who Spangenberg was listening to.

Spangenberg's prediction about the extinction of the Tuscaroras was premature. Still, in this new day the Tuscaroras' old survival strategy of factional opposition, which had allowed them to survive the war and its peace, also contributed to internal discord and a splintering of the Indian Woods Tuscaroras. By the 1750s, Tuscarora communities could be found in North Carolina, South Carolina, and New York. Some Tuscarora men and families lived along Drowning Creek in southeastern North Carolina and in other swamps, streams, and woods in eastern North Carolina. So there was an inherent tension in Tuscarora society, and it again reared up at Indian Woods.

In March 1753, a faction of Tuscaroras petitioned the Governor's Council "that their king had in a clandestine manner leased [part of Indian Woods] to John McGasky contrary to their inclination." They cited the Laws of 1748, which prohibited this kind of thing. Even rank-and-file Tuscaroras now saw the English government as a mediator in Tuscarora affairs, but old-style Tuscarora factionalism was at work in this case. As James Blount was realizing, being leader of the Tuscaroras could be a miserable and difficult job as one had to appease the English, one's kinfolk, and the Tuscarora people as a whole, all while advancing one's personal ambitions. Sometimes all these could not be reconciled. The willingness of Tuscarora factions to oppose their leadership did not make things easier. The North Carolina government had no desire to get too involved in internal Tuscarora affairs, but it could not allow discontent to fester. On March 29, the council ordered the creation of a commission composed of the interpreter Thomas Whitmel, William Taylor, and John

Hill to determine what was going on at Indian Woods. Two months later the commission made its report and came down hard on Chief James Blount and in full support of the opposing Tuscarora faction. The commission ordered McGasky to "quit his claim and all pretention to the said land by virtue of the said lease." McGasky made an appeal, but the council rejected it and "ordered that the judgement of the said commissioners be confirmed and that the said John Mc-Gasky do remove himself and his effects off and from the said Indian lands accordingly."[19]

When Arthur Dobbs took office as the new colonial governor in October 1754, the Tuscaroras and other eastern North Carolina Indians visited to "make their acknowledgements" but also to inform the governor of the problems facing them. Dobbs, an engineer by training and an amateur scientist by inclination, observed that the Tuscaroras consisted of about 100 men and 200 women and children, showing a sharp drop in population over the previous few decades. His official Indian census next year listed the Tuscaroras at 301 people. In contrast, the Cherokees alone, Dobbs noted, could field 2,590 warriors. At this first meeting, the Tuscarora leaders complained that settlers to the north had now stopped them from hunting in their usual winter grounds. Dobbs assured the Tuscaroras that he would redress "any wrong done to them." He also announced that he had, "by the consent of the Assembly, given them a small present of about £25 value to shew our other Indian allies that we are desirous of their living with us as brethren, and sharing in all our privileges." Understanding the need for Indian allies, Dobbs pondered raising settler quitrents to pay for more gifts for the Indians.[20]

French and Indian War

Behind the colony's newfound concern over its Indian tributaries was the French and Indian War. Throughout the first half of the eighteenth century, France had expanded down the Mississippi River Valley, creating the colony of Louisiana, establishing alliances and trade relations with the Native peoples of that huge area, and all the while trying to box in England's American colonies and lure away its Indian allies. The French menace frightened England's Atlantic colonies as they realized France had done a good job of securing Indian allies. Rivalry over strategic points in western Pennsylvania in 1754 started the shooting war. Soon French troops, Canadian colonial militia, and their Indian auxiliaries were attacking English strongpoints. Colonial troubles worsened when the French and Indians ambushed an expedition led by British Gen. Edward Braddock in July 1755 in southwestern Pennsylvania, killing the general and forcing his troops back into Maryland. By 1756 and 1757, England and France were officially at war, and the colonial French and Indian War exploded into the global Seven Years War. For the colonies, the year 1757 looked bleak as the war seemed to be going France's way. Down in North Carolina, Gov. Dobbs focused most of his attention on the Cherokees, who were split, with some factions supporting the French and others the English.[21]

Officials did not worry too much about French influence among the Indians of eastern North Carolina. They were just too far east. But "foreign" Indians raiding from outside the colony could not be discounted, especially because Senecas, Tuscaroras, and other Iroquois from New York still visited North Carolina. Just as important was the belief that it would take English-allied Indian warriors to defeat French-allied Indian warriors. Hundreds, if not thousands, of Indian allies would be needed. Even then, an expedition to take the French Ft. Duquesne, present-day Pittsburgh, was in the planning stages. So royal governors were instructed to shore up their Indian alliances and begin recruiting for the upcoming campaign.[22]

Dobbs made the rounds of the colony's tributary Indians, condemning the French, extoling the British, and requesting the Indian nations' warriors help toss the French out of western Pennsylvania. Col. George Washington of Virginia sent a letter to the Tuscaroras asking for their active assistance. He urged them to "take up the hatchet" and join the colonies in a war against the French.[23] The Tuscaroras proved willing. In late March 1757, Chief James Blount and Captain Jack led thirty-seven Tuscarora warriors to Williamsburg,

Virginia. On March 29, Chief Blount, Captain Jack, the Tuscarora warriors, seven Meherrin warriors, two Saponis, and thirteen Virginia Nottoways met with the Virginia Council. Blount reminded the officials that the Tuscaroras had long ago made peace with White people and given up violence, even burying their guns and tomahawks, metaphorically speaking. But after hearing of all the offenses the French had committed against the Tuscaroras' English allies, they would take up their weapons again and join the English until their enemy had been beaten. Elated, the officials asked what the Indians needed so that it could be immediately supplied. Weapons, ammunition, clothing, and war paint, Blount replied.[24] The Cherokees added another 150 warriors. Even the Catawbas, long the enemies of the Tuscaroras, sent a contingent. All were soon on their way to rendezvous with colonial forces. With so many Tuscarora and Meherrin men gone from home, the North Carolina Assembly appropriated £40 proclamation money to provision the wives and children of the warriors.[25]

Over the summer, the Tuscaroras and other Indians led raids against the French and their Delaware and Shawnee allies, conducting operations in Virginia, Maryland, and Pennsylvania. The offensive did not go off without a hitch. Lt. Gov. Robert Dinwiddie of Virginia complained that the Cherokees, Catawbas, and Tuscaroras were "not to be govern'd, nor will they tarry any time to do us service. The Catawbas and Tuscaroras have return'd home." The Cherokees remained at Winchester, "but they are a dissatisfied set of people." Virginia sent £500 worth of goods in hopes of making them happy.[26] Despite complaints on both sides, the Tuscaroras, Meherrins, and Saponis served in Washington's Virginia regiment during his attack on Ft. Duquesne and were instrumental in taking that fort.[27] Unfortunately, bad treatment of the Cherokee allies by settlers resulted in the Cherokees taking up arms against the English in what has been called the Anglo-Cherokee War of 1758–61. Tuscarora warriors would play a minor role in that conflict as well.[28]

Tensions back on Indian Woods required Chief James Blount to leave Captain Jack in charge of the warriors in the field and return home in late 1757. He found strained relations with the Tuscaroras' White neighbors. Good service in war did not seem to translate to good feelings by their neighbors. While James Blount was gone, White settlers accused some of the remaining Tuscarora men of becoming aggressive. Settlers wrote of Indian men barging into their homes and behaving "themselves in a very ill manner." Indians and settlers pulled guns on each other. Then in May the Tuscarora James Strawberry had murdered the Englishwoman Elizabeth Knott near the Cashie Creek bridge by striking her three times on the back of the head with a piece of lightwood. Strawberry never explained his motive, and Knott was a stranger just passing through Bertie County on her way to Virginia. Strawberry, sometimes known as James Shrewsbury, was arrested and held in the Chowan County jail. Sheriff William Halsey asked the Committee for Public Claims to compensate him for feeding the accused murderer as well as another 40 shillings for Col. William Eaton, who served as the interpreter during the Strawberry trial. Strawberry went to trial in October and was quickly convicted and executed.[29]

As in the case of the other tributary Indians of eastern North Carolina, hanging onto their reserve remained the most urgent issue the Tuscaroras faced. Chief Blount was no sooner back from the Ft. Duquesne expeditions than he appeared before the governor and council, asking them to "grant a patent or some better title for our land for the white folks tells this is good for nothing and they come and settle without leave, fall our timber and drive stocks of all sorts. We hope care will be taken to protect us in quiet possession of our lands from the White people abusing us."[30]

Adding to Tuscarora troubles was that the council and Assembly no longer met exclusively in Edenton, only about 40 miles from Indian Woods. There the Tuscaroras were regular visitors, and so their concerns were often in front of the colonial government. But as settlers spread across the length and breadth of North Carolina, the governor, council, and Assembly began meeting in various towns across the colony: Edenton, New Bern, Bath, even Brunswick Town and Wilmington far to the south on the Cape Fear River. Over the course of the eighteenth century, each of these towns would temporarily serve as the colonial capital. In 1757 and 1758, the government was sitting at New Bern. Twice in 1758, in May and November, James Blount led delegations of Tuscaroras to New Bern to lay their complaints before the council. The longer distance was an inconvenience for the Tuscaroras as it meant longer travel times and longer stays in town. It was also an inconvenience for the government, which had to provide provisions for them. As the council noted, the Tuscaroras were becoming "burthersome to several private persons with whom the said Indians are acquainted, therefore moved that persons be appointed to provide necessary provisions for the said Indians during their say in town." These providers would then be reimbursed by the colonial government. The council turned to Thomas Whitmel and William Williams to supply the Tuscaroras in New Bern. Whitmel and Williams were essentially acting as Indian agents.[31]

As usual, it was the settler Humphrey Bates who sent James Blount again and again before the council. The Tuscaroras had long protested Bates's presence on 300 acres inside Indian Woods. The council agreed, but Bates made no effort leave and time and again avoided being forced off the land. In 1758, Bates petitioned the council to see his side of things and order the Tuscaroras to leave him alone and let him enjoy his land in peace. He even produced William Charleton's grandson, George Charleton, who swore the land legally belonged to Bates. Nevertheless, the council again supported the Tuscaroras, ordered Bates to leave, and instructed the colony's attorney general to prosecute Bates unless he did.[32] Bates ignored the order, and the Tuscaroras nagged the governor for the next several years.[33]

The Tuscaroras also believed the colony had not fulfilled its promises about the French and Indian War expeditions and their service during the Anglo-Cherokee War in 1761, when about fifty warriors were sent to the Piedmont to prepare for an attack on the Cherokees and help build roads. The war ended before they could see action.[34] Several Tuscarora warriors complained they had not received the pay promised. In 1762, the Assembly appointed a commission to investigate. It took one day for the commission to conclude that the Tuscaroras' complaints were groundless. They had already received £7, 10 shillings, from Capt. Charles Cogdell. The investigation also turned up a bill of £15, 3 shillings, from Timothy Clear for providing the Indians with provisions and liquor during their time in the capital. The Assembly approved paying Clear from the Contingency Fund.[35]

By the mid-1760s, several things were bearing down on the Tuscaroras that would reshape their society and Indian Woods. First came a shift in Indian status and relations with the colony, county, and empire as a whole. Second came a push by the New York Tuscaroras to lure their North Carolina kinfolk to move north and join the Sixth Nation of the Iroquois. Along with these came a decline in the North Carolina Tuscarora population, which meant not only more loss of reserve lands but also a colonial reassessment of Tuscarora Indian identity.

With the end of the French and Indian War, England acquired a vast empire, and so the relations changed between it and its American colonies. They changed for the Indians as well. On one hand, England now tried to limit the individual colonies from dealing with Indians, especially powerful Indian peoples who could pose military threats, such as the Six Nations of the Iroquois, Cherokees, Shawnees, Creeks, Choctaws, and others. Early in the war, to rally their Indian allies and to bring about a more unified imperial Indian policy, England created two American departments to handle and regulate Indian affairs. William Johnson, a former trader with the Iroquois who had married into a Mohawk family, was appointed superintendent of the Northern Department, north of the Potomac River. John Stuart eventually headed the Southern Department, south of the Potomac. The French and Indian War, the Anglo-Cherokee War, and the subsequent Pontiac's War west of the Appalachian Mountains in 1763 had taught the English the peril and expense of ignoring Indian complaints and allowing Native peoples to be abused. The imperial superintendencies were an attempt not only to regulate Indian affairs but also to take them out of the hands of the colonies, something the colonies did not necessarily appreciate. As King George III informed Gov. William Tryon of North Carolina in 1765, illegal and fraudulent settlements on Indian lands needed to be removed and prosecuted by law. From now on, only people properly licensed to purchase Indian lands could do so. And before the governor provided such a license, he needed to clear it with the Commission of Trade and Plantations. This process, the British government hoped, would keep peace with Indians, who constantly complained about land loss.[36]

It also meant that the Crown's relations with Indians would become more regimented, more authoritarian. With the French expelled from North America after the end of the French and Indian War, the English no longer saw the Indians as valuable allies; after all, the Catholic threat in New France had been removed, and Canada was now English, as were all the lands west to the Mississippi River. There seemed less need to appease these Indians. Seen less as valuable allies and more as threats to White settlers, English authorities increasingly refused to accept Indians as subjects of the king, protected by common law, and entitled to the same rights as any Englishman, as North Carolina had proclaimed back in 1748. Although they might fear Indians' warlike capabilities, they increasingly saw them as lesser individuals with fewer rights. Indians were not White or Protestant, nor did White people think Indians possessed English views of constitutional liberty and so could never really be true subjects of the Crown. The concept of "race" as a determinant of intelligence and morality was coming to the fore.[37]

Second Tuscarora Migration

The Tuscaroras had their own role to play in England's postwar plans. In 1763, Johnson of the Northern Department and Stuart of the Southern Department decided it would be best for imperial interests if the North Carolina Tuscaroras moved north to join their kinfolk in New York. However, Stuart worried that the North Carolina Tuscaroras' excessive debt to settlers might prevent them from leaving. Now came talk of the Tuscaroras selling their Indian Woods lands to finance the move, and in 1764 an agreement was made with Thomas Whitmel, Thomas Pugh, William Williams, and John Watson to purchase Indian Woods. For whatever reason, though, the North Carolina Assembly rejected the proposal.[38]

In May 1766, a delegation of nine New York Tuscaroras appeared in North Carolina, led by a *diagawekee*, or sachem, named Isaac. They had been sent by William Johnson to convince the North Carolina Tuscaroras to move to New York. This was an attempt to bolster Iroquois population and warrior numbers, which had suffered during the French and Indian War. In the earlier migrations of 1715, North Carolina Tuscaroras had contributed about 600 warriors, 400 older men and boys, and 500 women and girls to the League of the Longhouse. Now the Iroquois came calling again, but there were only about 230 Tuscarora men, women, and children living on Indian Woods by government counts. Isaac, the delegation leader, arrived before Gov. William Tryon at Brunswick Town on the Cape Fear River, suffering from the mumps. Gov. Tryon took in the sachem and slowly nursed him back to health. "I found him not only humanized but also civilized," Tryon remarked. During his stay, the *diagawekee* explained his mission. He proposed selling or leasing part of Indian Woods to pay for the removal. Then he presented the governor with several strings of wampum. Impressed, Tryon asked that he be given a Tuscarora name. Isaac gave him his own title— *diagawekee*—which was to honor Tryon's care for him during his illness. This term was probably a derivative of "Deganawida," the name of the Great Peacemaker of the Iroquois. According to Tryon, all North Carolina governors were to wear the title of *diagawekee* from then on. While the sachem recovered, his diplomatic entourage went to live at Indian Woods, where they made the case for the Tuscaroras' removal to New York.[39]

The Iroquois diplomats must have been persuasive because in July 1766 Chief Thomas Basket—Chief James Blount was apparently dead—and a delegation of Tuscarora leaders approached the

North Carolina Governor's Council and Assembly and asked them to approve the sale of their lands so most of them could move to New York. They reminded the officials that fifty years earlier a good number of their people had moved to that colony, where the Tuscaroras became the Sixth Nation of the Iroquois Haudenosaunee. Up in New York, their kinfolk had heard of their poverty, how the deer had been hunted out, and so hoped to convince them to move north, where the deer were plentiful and life was good. Now, 156 Tuscaroras from Indian Woods agreed to relocate to New York, but they needed money for moving expenses. With this in mind, they hired some trustees—Robert Jones, who was the colony's attorney general, William Williams of Halifax County, and Thomas Pugh of Bertie County—to lay out some tracts of land totaling not more than 640 acres and sell them at public auction. Money from this sale would pay off any current Tuscarora debts, fund the cost of the move, and, if any were left over, be distributed to those Tuscaroras who wanted to remain in North Carolina. Separate tracts of land would be given to the trustees for their good service.[40]

Gov. Tryon seemed amenable, but because the colonial government had created the Tuscarora reserve, the Governor's Council and Assembly would have to agree to the plan. The two governmental bodies raised no objections and said they would follow Tryon's lead. However, the Tuscaroras wanted to move that summer, but surveying and selling the tracts at auction could take years. So the auction idea never got off the ground. The three trustees would instead lease 8,000 acres of Indian Woods for 150 years in return for £1,500 cash and an annual payment of a single peppercorn to be given to the Tuscaroras every September 29 on the Feast of St. Michael.[41]

Gov. Tryon saw the deal in starker terms. He said the three Englishmen advanced the Tuscaroras the money to buy wagons and provisions for the trip, and the Tuscaroras put up 8,000 acres of their lands as collateral. Tryon feared that the Tuscaroras would have to sell off more of their land to repay this loan.[42] Thirty-six Tuscarora leaders and principal men recorded their names or marks on the agreement. The document is one of the few on which we get to see so many Tuscarora names and how they referred to themselves in these diplomatic procedures: James Allen, John Wiggins, Billy George, Snip Nose George, Billy Cain, Charles Cornelius, Thomas Blount, John Rogers, George Blount, Wineoak Charley, Billy Basket, Billy Owen, Lewis Tuffdick, Isaac Miller, Harry, Samuel Bridgers, Thomas Seneca, Thomas Hewit, Billy Sockey, Billy Cornelius, John Seneca, Thomas Basket, John Cain, Billy Dennis, William Taylor, Owens, John Walker, Billy Mitchell, Billy Netoss, Billy Blount, Tom Jack, John Lightwood, Billy Roberts, James Mitchell, Captain Joe, and William Pugh. The three Englishmen would split the 8,000 acres among themselves. But Robert Jones died that summer and willed his share of the lands to his sons, Allen and Willie Jones. Nevertheless, the lease, or debt, went through. The governor approved it in November 1766, and the Board of Trade in London did so in 1769.[43]

Those 156 or so Tuscaroras were long gone by then, most of them moving to New York by September 1766, led by Isaac the sachem and his diplomats. They had been advanced almost £2,000 proclamation money to make the move. The Tuscaroras had essentially financed their own removal from North Carolina, seventy years or so before the great Southeastern Indian Removal of the 1830s, which culminated in the tragic Cherokee Trail of Tears. More than 150 Tuscaroras meandering north would have presented quite a caravan. Rev. William Smith, traveling along the "frontiers" of North Carolina, remembered it. "I saw above 200 Indians, being the body of the Tuscarora Nation, moving from Carolina to be incorporated with the 6 Nations, and to live near Sr. Wm. Johnson. I talked a good deal with some who understood English, and I believe a school among them would be of great use."[44]

The long trek took months, and the Tuscarora migrants did not always have an easy trip. Despite having a safe-conduct pass from Superintendent William Johnson, the Tuscaroras were attacked by settlers at Paxton, Pennsylvania, who stole six horses and plundered many of the goods they had leased their lands to purchase. Though the Six Nations complained to Johnson about this attack, the Tuscarora migrants, finding themselves with few provisions, little clothing, and depleted ammunition were forced to spend the winter at Shamokin, an Indian town on the Susquehanna River in central Pennsylvania. Johnson had to send food and ammunition so the men could hunt for their families. They would not make it to New York until early the next year, and Pennsylvania did not reimburse the Tuscaroras £50 for their stolen goods until a year after that.[45]

An advance party of twenty Tuscaroras arrived at Oughquago, an Oneida Iroquois town near present-day Windsor in southern New York, in February 1767. There Johnson welcomed them and met with a Tuscarora chief named Aucus al Kanigut. It is unclear who this migrating chief was, but here in his new home among his New York kinfolk, he was going by his traditional Tuscarora name and not the Anglicized names so common in North Carolina. Kanigut handed Johnson several belts of wampum, thanked him for allowing them to move north, and hoped to remain here. In Carolina, the chief told Johnson, "they lived but wretchedly being surrounded by white people, and up to their lips in rum, that they could not turn their heads any way but it ran into their mouths. This made them stupid, so that they neglected hunting, planting, etc." They feared that if they were forced to return to North Carolina, they might "fall into the same error again, as we understand they have liquor in plenty among them. . . . We request you would give us some medicine to cure us of our fondness for that destructive liquor." Kanigut called Johnson "Brother" and reminded him that they had listened to him from afar by not attacking the Catawbas when he told them not to. Also, during the recent French and Indian War, several of their young warriors were killed serving the British. That should prove their loyalty. Now that there was peace, all they wanted to do was hunt and plant, but they needed Johnson to provide them with utensils and provisions until they could recover from their trip. "We must all suffer, having nothing left us after our long journey."[46] They would be allowed to remain in New York, joining their Tuscarora kinspeople and the Six Nations of the Iroquois. But they would not forget the Tuscaroras they left behind in North Carolina.

Dissolution of Indian Woods

Their departure that summer left 104 Tuscarora men, women, and children on Indian Woods, as counted by Gov. Tryon. With more than half their people moving away, splitting families, clans, and the nation itself, the remaining North Carolina Tuscaroras experienced an upheaval. Leadership was lost. Of the thirty-six Tuscarora principal men who signed the removal petition, twenty-six apparently left for New York. Of the men who signed, only Capt. Thomas Basket, William Taylor, Billy Roberts, Lewis Tuffdick, Capt. Thomas Blount, Billy Dennis, John Caine, Billy Blount, and James Mitchell remained. Future chief Whitmel Tuffdick, who had not signed the original removal petition, also remained at Indian Woods. Capt. Thomas Basket now served as the chief of the Indian Woods Tuscaroras. In early November 1766, Capt. Basket and the remaining ten Tuscarora leaders appeared before Gov. Tryon, asking for assistance. Basket, addressing his "Brother" Tryon, assured him and the English king of their loyalty. They presented a few deerskins as a sign of their tributary status and begged Tryon to forgive the "smallness of the present," blaming it on poverty as "we are mostly old men, unable to hunt, our young men having gone to the norward with the Northern chief, Tragaweha," probably a different pronunciation of *diagawekee*.[47]

Basket asked Tryon to confirm the recent lease of 8,000 acres of Indian Woods to Jones, Pugh, and Williams, but he was more concerned about settlers' attitudes toward the Tuscaroras. "We are by education and custom unable to acquire a livelihood otherwise than by hunting; and as ill-natured persons frequently take away and break our guns, and even whip us for pursuing game on their land, we beg of your Excellency to appoint Commissioners (as heretofore) to hear our complaints, and redress our grievances." A particular grievance was toward Sarah Bates, wife of the now deceased Humphrey Bates, who still sat on 300 acres of Tuscarora lands. The government had ordered the Bates family off the land several times, yet in 1766 they remained. Capt. Basket brought up the issue again: "As our bounds are now become more circumscribed, we choose, and if [she] should refuse so to do, on a friendly application, we must request you to direct the Attorney General to eject her." Basket urged Gov. Tryon to act with all deliberate speed as "those Indians whom we have left at home are old men and children, incapable of providing for themselves, if cold weather should come on." Moved by the captain's speech and the condition of the Tuscaroras, Tryon ordered food and clothing be given to Basket and his principal men. Within a month, Tryon and the Assembly confirmed the 8,000-acre lease.[48]

The migration of more than half their people to New York proved to be another downturn for the North Carolina Tuscaroras. With only about a hundred remaining in the colony, or at least counted by the colony, the Tuscaroras were not the valuable allies or fearsome enemies they once were. If anything, the colony saw them as deadweight and an unnecessary expense. The Tuscaroras now found themselves on the same path to national disappearance and disputed Indian identity that the Machapungas, Meherrins, and Chowans had walked. As the colonial government lost interest, Indian issues shifted away from the Governor's Council and into the county courts. Although in July 1767 King George III instructed North Carolina officials not to grant anyone any land within or next to lands occupied by Indians, this command seemed more directed at dealings with the Cherokees.[49] The Tuscaroras became afterthoughts as North Carolina officials in the late 1760s and the 1770s joined the other colonies in their march toward revolution and independence.

As planters expanded into Bertie County, the Tuscaroras found their lands under siege. Even when Indians' complaints made it to the courts, juries of planters and settlers were usually in no mood to rule in the Indians' favor. Adding to this toxic swill was White supremacy, which was increasingly turned on the Tuscaroras as some married or produced children with African Carolinians. For many Whites, the Tuscaroras and other Indians of eastern North Carolina now looked a lot like Africans and not as they thought Indians should. But the Tuscaroras still had Indian Woods, had a recognized government, and were one of the colony's official tributaries, which meant they were Indians, at least as most North Carolinians defined them.[50]

And the Tuscaroras still had some pull with the colonial government. In 1769, their long battle with the now dead Humphrey Bates over his land in Indian Woods apparently came to an end. The land was occupied by his wife, Sarah, who had taken up with the Pamlico planter John Allen. Now the colony's attorney general prosecuted Sarah Bates and John Allen for trespass on Tuscarora lands and ordered them out of Indian Woods.[51] This time it worked.

This may well have been one of the last victories for the Tuscaroras. Stuck in poverty, the remaining Tuscaroras began to sell lands for needed cash. On December 18, 1773, just two days after the Boston Tea Party in Massachusetts, the "chief of the Tuscaroras" appeared before the Governor's Council to complain that William King had "entered upon and laid waste upon the lands lying on the north side of the Moratuck [Roanoke River]." However, the council investigated and determined that the Tuscaroras had already sold those lands to Col. Needham Bryan by the "failure of that nation of Indians." So King was actually laying waste to Bryan's lands, not the Tuscaroras'. The council determined the Tuscaroras had no standing for this complaint but did order King to get off Bryan's lands.[52] What exactly "failure of that nation of Indians" meant is unclear, but probably a land forfeiture due to an unpaid debt.

This loss seemed to start a run by Tuscarora men to lease their remaining lands long term. On December 2, 1775, as revolutionary fever heated up in the colony, the Tuscarora leadership—Whitmel Tuffdick, Wineoak Charles Sr., Wineoak Charles Jr., Billie Roberts, Lewis Tuffdick, West Tuffdick, Billie Blunt Sr., Billie Blunt Jr., John Rodgers, John Smith, Billie Pugh, Billie Baskett, John Hicks, Samuel Bridgers, John Owen, James Mitchell, Isaac Cornelius, Thom Thomas, and Walter Gibson—leased 2,000 acres of Indian Woods to Thomas Pugh, William Jones, and William Williams for ninety-nine years for an annual rent of eighty Duffield blankets, eighty Oznaburg shirts, eighty pairs of boots "to be made of half thicks which said shirts & boots are to be suitable for the Indians according to their different sizes," 50 pounds of gunpowder, and 150 pounds of shot. These items would be delivered each year to Whitmel Tuffdick, the new chief of the Tuscaroras.[53] That the Tuscaroras were asking for trade goods but not cash at this late date indicated their needs as well as the uncertainty over the value of North Carolina proclamation money and British pounds in light of the American Revolution. Asking for eighty sets of these goods seems to indicate that only eighty Tuscaroras lived at Indian Woods.

Just a week and a half after leasing the 2,000 acres to Pugh, Jones, and Williams, that same Tuscarora leadership now leased an undetermined amount of acreage to William King—the same William King whom the Tuscaroras had two years earlier accused of laying waste to their lands. But land deals made for strange allies, and the agreement stated that the lease would run for ninety-nine years and that King and his heirs would pay an annual rent of £15 proclamation money.[54]

Though North Carolina declared its independence from Britain on April 12, 1776, the change in government did not stop the pressure on Indian lands or Indians' complaints about it. On February 10, 1777, these "Chieftans & heade men of a nation of Tuscarora Indians inhabiting on Roanoke River in Bertie County" made an official ninety-nine-year lease with settler Zedekiah Stone of an undetermined amount of Indian Woods lands along Acorn Branch. However, Stone had to agree "to give no disturbance [or] molestation" to the Indians Joseph Lloyd, Thomas Smith, and Sarah Hiatt. The lease seemed to arise from work that Stone had done for the Tuscaroras but that they could not pay for, so he took a cheap lease of land in lieu of a cash payment. Stone and his heirs were to enjoy the land, but at the end of the ninety-nine years it was to revert to the Tuscaroras "for their village & cultivation." Stone also had to agree that he and his heirs were "never to molest" the Tuscaroras or disturb them in "any of their lands now enjoyed by them without their consent."[55]

More leases were on the way in 1777. On March 28, The Tusca-roras leased about 100 acres between Black Creek and the Roanoke River for ninety-nine years to Thomas Pugh. Pugh and his descen-dants were to pay £8 proclamation money at the end of every year to the Tuscaroras and their descendants.[56] On September 7, Tuscarora leadership leased 60 acres to Titus Edwards for £1,000 North Caro-lina "current money" as well as £5 a year for ninety-nine years.[57]

In reality, the Tuscaroras lost more lands than the leases and sales recorded. Settlers might lease or purchase 100 or 200 acres, but they often spilled over the bounds and appropriated far more acreage than what was recorded, sometimes as much as double the amount. Rarely were these tracts surveyed in a timely manner, if at all. It was often this overflow of settlers' tracts that sent Tuscarora leaders to the council and courts to complain about encroachment. All Indians of eastern North Carolina faced this illegal expansion by settlers and lost far more lands than lease or sales agreements stipu-lated. As we have seen with settlers such as Humphrey Bates, when the Indians protested the loss of their lands this way, settlers delayed, filed their own lawsuits, or just ignored government orders to leave and remained on these lands for years.[58]

Even as North Carolina declared its independence from Britain and created the state of North Carolina, problems with some of these leases cropped up as Tuscaroras complained that they were not re-ceiving the rents due them and had trouble collecting. Chief Tuffdick, who pledged his Tuscaroras' loyalty to the new American govern-ment, petitioned Gov. Richard Caswell about these problems. Cas-well passed the complaint to North Carolina's new state Senate. On December 22 and 23, 1777, the state House and Senate took up the Tuscarora complaints and again came down strongly on the side of the Indians. The House issued a resolution "that all persons be and they are hereby prohibited from making entries in the Tuscarora lands in Bertie County." It then appointed a commission composed of Wil-liam Williams, Thomas Pugh, Zedekiah Stone, and Simon Turner—both Pugh and Stone were lessees of Tuscarora lands—"with power to superintend and take of their affairs, and they, or a majority of them, shall and may demand and receive any rents now due or which may become due to said Tuscaroras." The commissioners could issue warrants against those settlers in debt to the Indians and who had defaulted. The commissioners were also to "prevent ill-disposed persons from bringing spirituous liquors for sale on the lands now in the possession of the said Tuscaroras." The Senate concurred.[59] On the surface, this seems a win for the Tuscaroras, but in reality a commission was now appointed to act as a guardian of the Tuscarora lands, collecting rents and acting as an enforcer, something the state felt the Tuscaroras could not do for themselves.

That the Old North State saw the Tuscaroras as incapable of handling their own affairs was evident in the North Carolina Laws of 1778. Chapter XVI, "An Act for quieting and securing the Tuscarora Indians, and others claiming under the Tuscaroras, in the Possession of their Lands," was one of the largest sections of these laws. First, it confirmed the Tuscarora lands to Whitmel Tuffdick, chief or headman of the Tuscaroras, and the Tuscarora Indians living on the lands guaranteed by the Laws of 1748. These lands were exempted from quitrents and any type of poll taxes. Also, as the Tuscaroras are "by nature ignorant, and strongly addicted to drinking, may be easily imposed on by designing persons, and unwarily deprived of their said lands," the law ordered that from this point on there could be no more individual purchase or lease of any Tuscarora lands, no person could settle, cultivate, or oversee any part of the lands, and any purchases or leases should be declared null and void. Anyone caught buying or renting Tuscarora land would be fined £300 pounds proclamation money for every 100 acres of purchase or lease. One-half of this fine would go to the Tuscaroras, the other half to the person who sued. However, the law stipulated that the Tuscaroras could sell or lease their lands as long as they had the consent of the North Carolina Assembly.[60]

Then the law took up the matter of Tuscarora lands already leased. It recognized and declared legal the lease of Robert Jones Jr., William Williams, and Thomas Pugh in 1766 for 8,000 acres of

Tuscarora land for £1,500 for 150 years and stated that their heirs were confirmed in it and should pay the usual taxes on it. It also noted that the Tuscaroras had made a few leases to other White people since 1766, which were also confirmed to them and their heirs and should be taxed accordingly. However, once these leases ended, the lands were to revert to the state of North Carolina "if the Nation is extinct."[61]

In a major change, the state now ordered the Bertie County court to handle Tuscarora complaints of land fraud. Relegating the Indians to the county courts was bad enough, but the colonial government also made it harder for Indians to get justice. Back in 1762, North Carolina had passed a law declaring "that all Negroes, Indians, mulattoes and all of mixed Blood descended from Negro or Indian Ancestors, to the Third Generation, exclusive, Bond or Free, shall be deemed and taken to be incapable in Law to be witnesses in any cause whatsoever, excepting against each other."[62] Indians and Black people now could not testify in court against White people. The possibilities for abuse seemed endless. It would certainly be harder for Indians to protect the integrity of their lands from White settlers if they could not testify against them in court.

Now, if the Tuscaroras accused a White man of encroachment or fraud, they were to tell the commissioners, who would then go to the Bertie County court and testify in their stead.[63] The court would then call up a twelve-man jury to hear the case and determine the outcome. The Bertie court would oversee the commissioners, appoint new members for those who died or resigned, and ensure their good behavior by threat of removal for malfeasance.[64]

In a final statement, the Laws of 1778 determined that all "the lands now belonging to, and possessed by the said Tuscaroras, shall revert to, and become the property of the state, whenever the said Nation shall become extinct, or shall entirely abandon or remove themselves of the said lands, and every part thereof."[65] Already the state was preparing for the day when there would be no more Tuscaroras. Worse, Bertie County, not the state government of North Carolina, was to become the caretaker of the Tuscaroras. These laws signified a tremendous loss in status for the Indians. Rather than a sovereign, albeit a tributary, nation and people, they were now wards of the county.

A deficiency in the Laws of 1778 was that though they established that Bertie County courts would handle Tuscarora complaints, empanel jurors, and call witnesses, they did not impose fines or penalties on jurors or witnesses who refused to show up. The laws did not provide any support for the county court when dealing with Tuscarora issues. Chief Tuffdick complained that this lack of support caused Tuscarora concerns not to be heard in a timely manner as juries and witnesses refused to attend hearings. The state remedied this oversight with another set of laws in 1780 that penalized witnesses and jurors up to £100 if they failed to appear for Tuscarora trials unless they could show sufficient excuse. Witnesses and jurors who did attend would receive a stipend of £10 a day during their attendance, though this was to be paid by the party bringing the suit, meaning the Tuscaroras. The trial could be held on Tuscarora lands in Bertie County at a place selected by the commissioners.[66]

The first Bertie County case for the Court of Indian Commissioners took place on February 24, 1781, apparently at Indian Woods. The case dealt with the executors and lands of William King. The Tuscaroras complained that the now deceased King had illegally held some lands that they wanted returned, but his executors were committed to keeping their hold on the contested tracts. This time the twelve jurors, all White freeholders, showed up. After hearing testimony, they sided with the Tuscaroras. The Indian Commissioners' Court ruled that William King, "in his life time had no right to the premises in dispute nor his Executors since his death." The lease was, the court determined, not only fraudulent but fraudulently obtained. The Tuscaroras were to take possession of their lands.[67]

That the Tuscaroras were successful in court may well have been due to the close relationship they had with the commissioners, in particular Zedekiah Stone, who had long served in that post. He had also made a ninety-nine-year lease of some Tuscarora lands back in 1777, so he had his own eyes on Indian property and may well have seen King's claim as competition. It would not be improbable that the commissioners, led by Stone, would and could push the jury in the Tuscaroras' favor. In February 1782, Stone bound himself and his successors to an indenture in which he agreed to pay the headmen of the Tuscaroras, including Whitmel Tuffdick, Sam Robarts, Louis Tuffdick, Isaac Cornelius, West Tuffdick, John Randal, William Pugh, Watt Gibson, and "the rest of the Tuscarora Nation of Indians and their successors," £20,000 specie and £12 a year "so long as the said Zedekiah Stone and his heirs and assigns do tend a certain tract of land in the county aforesaid [Bertie] known by the name of the Corner Tract." Stone would give much of this tract to his son, David Stone, who later became governor of North Carolina.[68] The £20,000 specie seems an incredibly large amount of money, and one wonders what was behind it. Was this large number just a way to show Stone's permanent leasing of these lands? There does not seem to be any evidence that the Tuscaroras in fact received the money.

It may have been that the Tuscaroras realized they had a friend in Zedekiah Stone and his family. They certainly needed one. The Tuscaroras had worked ceaselessly to get Humphrey Bates and William King off their lands but now welcomed Zedekiah Stone and his family to lease their own tracts of Indian Woods. In July 1787, Whitmel Tuffdick, Louis Tuffdick, Wyatt Tuffdick, William Basket, Walter Gibson, Samuel Tuffdick, George Blount, and Lyle Blount, all "Chieftains and head men of the Nation of Tuscarora Indians" in Bertie County, sold to Thomas Stone, either a brother or son of Zedekiah, "all the trees that is standing and laying down" along Turner Mill Creek for £10 North Carolina current money, to be paid to them in hand. These trees were more than likely to be used for tar and pitch production. When state authorities questioned the Tuscarora leaders, they said they were satisfied with the agreement.[69] Two years later, records indicated the Tuscaroras received £15 from Zedekiah Stone for the previous year's rent and another £10 for his ninety-nine-year lease of timber on the Roanoke River low grounds.[70]

Then, for the next decade or so the Tuscaroras seem to drop out of the new state's records. We know little of what was happening at

Indian Woods during this time, but probably the same things that had happened to the Chowans, Meherrins, and Machapungas: population decline from alcoholism, poverty, emigration from the area, land loss, marriages to and intimate relations with non-Tuscaroras, all while being seeing less as Indians and more as People of Color. Now maps showed only one Tuscarora settlement in Bertie County, and its name was merely recorded as "Tuscarora town." No other Indian towns by name were shown in eastern North Carolina.[71] In December 1801, David Stone, son of Zedekiah Stone and a US senator from North Carolina, reported that "the collection of rents is very badly managed in the hands of those people," meaning the Tuscaroras. Stone recommended that all lands remaining in Tuscarora hands, including those currently leased out that would revert to them, be sold, the money used "to give decent support to those few Indians who live here," and any balance used to create a public school in the county.[72]

Frightening events the next year would speed up Stone's proposal. During the spring of 1802, rumors of slave rebellions in the making spread across northeastern North Carolina and terrified the White population. By March, planned slave insurrections had been "discovered" in the counties along the north bank of Albemarle Sound. Though evidence was sketchy, and no violence by the enslaved had taken place, seven slaves were executed. The panic soon spread to Bertie County when a scribbled note was found in a cotton bale near Colerain in northeastern Bertie County. The "Colerain Letter" contained the names of fifteen enslaved Africans who planned to ignite an insurrection on June 10, 1802. According to the letter, the plan, more of a fantasy or maybe what White people imagined enslaved men would want, was to burn buildings, kill all the White men and old Black women, take the White women for wives, and make the young Black girls serve them. They would then be free and could live like White planters.[73]

At about the same time, another plot was "discovered" at Windsor, near the Indian Woods reserve. An enslaved man named Sam, who belonged to the planter Samuel Johnson, testified that an enslaved man named Gain, who belonged to David Turner, and another named Jumbo from the Outlaw Plantation near Windsor had acquired some guns and powder and planned on launching attacks across Bertie County. Rumors alleged that the nearby Tuscaroras were to rise up with the enslaved and join them in killing their White neighbors. Despite some severe interrogations in which torture was used, no evidence could be found for an actual slave conspiracy around Windsor. Nevertheless, White people in Bertie County, in no mood for logical thinking, connected this plot to the Colerain plot and went into a frenzy of vigilante violence. Eleven Bertie County slaves were tried and sentenced to death by the courts, scores more were killed by mob violence, and hundreds abused and harassed. Though we have no firm evidence, possibly some of those killed were Tuscaroras.[74]

Now their White neighbors turned a baleful eye on the Tuscaroras. Though the Indians were never proven to have been part of any plot, just the idea that they could have joined with the enslaved was enough to make most of their White neighbors feel that now was the time to deal with what remained of eastern North Carolina's last tributary nation. This belief spurred the idea that the Tuscaroras should sell off what remained of Indian Woods and leave the area. In fact, the North Carolina Assembly confirmed earlier leases and encouraged the Tuscaroras to lease more land if they wanted.[75]

Final Migration North

Then out of the blue, rescue appeared for the Tuscaroras. In early 1803, Chiefs Sacarusa and Longboard of the New York Tuscaroras visited Indian Woods and offered to take the remaining North Carolina Tuscaroras back to New York. Even after the migration of Tuscaroras to New York in 1766, kinship kept the lines of communication open between the two groups. Visitors from New York were not uncommon at Indian Woods and probably vice versa. It would seem reasonable that the New York Tuscaroras had been monitoring the deteriorating situation of the North Carolina Indians

and became especially worried about their kinspeople being impli-
cated in a slave rebellion. Ten to twenty families on Indian Woods
seemed amenable to relocating north. Even they realized that their
situation in North Carolina was becoming untenable. No longer did
their White neighbors see them as Indians but as People of Color and
closely associated with African Carolinians, if not actually as African Carolinians. Angry neighbors threatened the Tuscaroras with
enslavement, which seemed a reality in light of the recent conspiracy
beliefs. It seemed the right time for the Indian Woods Tuscaroras to
join their kinfolk in New York.[76]

The Tuscaroras gave the two New York chiefs the authority to
negotiate with the state government for them. What had happened
to Whitmel Tuffdick and the other leaders in Indian Woods? Were
they dead? Had they left the area? The state records concerning Tuscaroras get scarce during the 1790s and 1800s. A few Indian families
who seemed more like free People of Color did not garner much interest from the state government. However, the 4,000 acres or so of
Indian Wood lands still got the attention of state officials, and now it
seemed a resolution about those lands was imminent.

The Assembly welcomed Sacarusa and Longboard's arrival, and
negotiations began on the fate of Indian Woods. The Tuscaroras
wanted to sell the 4,000 acres that they currently owned and controlled. However, over the years they had leased much to White settlers. The Assembly stipulated that all leases would officially end in
just over a hundred years, in July 1916, and the land would be taken
over by the state. The state government appointed a committee to act
for it, while Sacarusa and Longboard negotiated for the Tuscaroras.
A sale was eventually hammered out in which the Tuscaroras sold
their remaining 4,000 acres to the state for $21,146. The Tuscaroras
had now sold off the last of their North Carolina lands. Because this
deal concerned Indian lands, it had to be approved by the US secretary of war, who happily did.[77]

Sometime during that summer of 1803, Sacarusa and Longboard
led the remaining Tuscaroras, or at least all those who wanted or
could go, up to their reserve in New York, not far from Niagara

Falls. Like those who had migrated earlier, they left behind houses, fences, burial grounds, ceremonial grounds, and the old spirits they associated with the land. Some Tuscaroras remained in Bertie County—we are not sure how many—but as individuals and so were seen by the state not as Indians but as People of Color. Other Tuscaroras also lived as individuals in nearby counties and down on Drowning Creek. Nevertheless, now, as the state saw it, Tuscarora lands and government had been extinguished and were no more. The Tuscarora nation in North Carolina, according to the state, was officially extinct.

We know nothing of the migration of these last Tuscaroras that summer of 1803. In anticipation of their arrival, the New York Tuscaroras negotiated an expansion of their 3-square-mile reservation and in 1804 purchased an additional 7 square miles. The money for this purchase came from the funds the North Carolina Tuscaroras received for their final lease. However, these last North Carolina Tuscaroras were seemingly not welcomed as enthusiastically by their northern kinsmen as were those of the migration in 1766 and so may have had a rougher time fitting in. Many New York Tuscaroras had converted to Christianity and had acculturated to more American ways. They saw these North Carolina Tuscaroras as rustic and somewhat uncivilized. There may also have been a racial aspect to their reception as many North Carolina Tuscaroras may have appeared more African American than their New York kinspeople were used to. Some of these North Carolina Tuscaroras, unhappy in New York, joined other Tuscaroras in Canada on the Grand River.[78]

All vestige of a once independent Tuscarora nation in North Carolina was gone. But that does not mean that all Tuscaroras were gone. Some did not leave but remained behind, landless and living as free People of Color around Bertie and other counties. As the historian Arwin Smallwood points out, "Their departure did not end Indian culture and life in Indian Woods" because enslaved people who had both Tuscarora and African or European ancestry kept Native culture alive.[79] Many remembered they were Tuscaroras or of Tuscarora descent, and through them a Tuscarora identity and presence continue in the area and down on the Lumber River to this day. But because they were without lands or leadership, their White neighbors did not think "Indian" when they saw them.

Even the issue of Tuscarora lands in North Carolina did not end so easily because earlier leases by the Indians to White settlers kept the Tuscaroras tied to the state. In 1814, Sacarusa and Longboard sued the heirs of William King for unpaid rent. Back in 1775, King had leased a tract of Indian Woods for ninety-nine years, paying the Indians £15 proclamation money each year. King died, and his heirs took over the lease. But after the Tuscaroras left Indian Woods in 1803, the King heirs did not pay their rent anymore as they said there was no one left to pay it to. Sacarusa and Longboard sued the heirs for back rent from 1803 to 1814. The heirs claimed they should not have to pay because the Tuscaroras did not live on the land anymore. However, the North Carolina Supreme Court ruled in favor of the Tuscaroras, saying the lands had been guaranteed to the Tuscaroras in 1717, in 1726, and again in 1748. These lands were Tuscarora lands whether they lived on them or not, and the King heirs were required to pay the back rent.[80]

Fourteen years later, in November 1828, Sacarusa and Longboard informed Secretary of War Peter Porter that they were returning to North Carolina to come to a final settlement on Indian Woods lands. In 1829, the remaining Tuscarora lands, including all those that had been leased out, were put under the supervision of Alfred Slade. A special committee headed by George E. Spruill examined the Tuscarora claims and recommended the final liquidation of all Tuscarora land. In November 1831, North Carolina paid $3,250 for the remaining Indian Woods acreage, about 8,000 acres. This transaction ceased all claims to all remaining Tuscarora lands as the government "legalized claims by White residents of Indian Woods to Indian lands." This money went to the Tuscaroras in New York.[81] The days of the tributary Indians in eastern North Carolina and their reserves had ended. And that was that. After 1,000 years or more of living in North Carolina, 120 years after the start of the

Tuscarora War, 92 years after the death of King Tom Blount, the Tuscarora nation in North Carolina had come to an end.

However, not all Tuscaroras were gone. Nor were all Meherrins, Chowans, Machapungas, or others as enclaves of people who considered themselves Indians were scattered across eastern North Carolina. But for the North Carolina government and their White neighbors, these Native peoples, without their reserve lands or governments, were no longer Indians. Making the situation worse for these Native peoples was that as their neighbors also saw them, they did not look much like Indians anymore but more like Africans or African Carolinians, who at worst were enslaved property, at best free People of Color with few rights that must be respected.

7

From Native People to People of Color and Back

From the very first meetings between North Carolina Natives and Europeans, skin color had been a subject of interest. Giovanni da Verrazzano in 1524 noted the dark color of Indian skin and believed the Indians marveled at his whiteness. Arthur Barlowe, during the first 1584 Roanoke reconnaissance, wrote of the Indians' yellowish color. One unfortunate consequence of this focus on skin color was that once the tributary Indians sold off their last bits of reserve land, they ceased being Indian in the eyes of North Carolina and now became People of Color.

Changing Ideas of "Race"

As Barlowe and other Europeans of the 1580s would have seen it, skin color was determined by where one was born. Africans were dark because Africa was hot and tropical and so burned their skin. Hot weather made Africans lazy and shiftless, as Europeans saw it. People from Europe were white-skinned because they came from northern climes, and, they liked to claim, it was that bracing weather that made them industrious and productive. As for American Indians, the English of that early day believed they were born white but became darker because they lived their lives outdoors slathered in bear oil. William Strachey, a Jamestown official in 1610, said the coastal Algonquians "are generally of color brown, or rather tawny" but that they are not "naturally born so discolored." Rather, "they

186

are from the womb indifferent white, but as the men so do the women dye and disguise themselves into this tawny color."[1] A white European could become darker if they lived the life of an Indian or African, while Africans and Indians could become lighter and more industrious if they moved to northern areas. So in this era, "race" was cultural, not biological, and Indians and Africans could become "white" and "civilized" to English ways.[2] Sir Walter Raleigh's appointment of the Croatoan Manteo to serve as his lord of Roanoke and Dasemkepeuc was a good example of this view.

By the mid-eighteenth century, the increasing number of European settlers and enslaved Africans entering North Carolina coincided with a shift in the idea of "race" and skin color. Now arose the idea that "race" was a product of biology. As historian Kirsten Fischer explains, "Philosophers in England and northwestern Europe divided the world's people into groups and debated the possibility that distinct human species, each with their own physical, moral, and mental abilities, had evolved from separate origins." White, Black, and Red were now seen as immutable, and one's race and skin color could never change. Skin color now determined one's intelligence, physical abilities, morality, industriousness, goodness, and badness; and in the case of North Carolina and most of England's southern colonies, it determined one's place in society, even whether one was free or enslaved.[3]

Modern scholars now reject the concept of "race" because all humans, no matter their skin color or ethnicity, are genetically the same. But race was real for the English colonists in the 1700s, and now real racism and White supremacy came to North Carolina. White settlers saw Africans and Indians as inferior to White Europeans and therefore open to enslavement and loss of rights. Although Indians and English settlers might be subjects of the same king, the settlers did not really imagine they were equal in this respect. Indians had to be respected only as long as they were powerful. Some might display noble traits, but that was just a disguise for imagined Indian treachery. Even worse from the settler point of view was that by the late 1700s eastern North Carolina Indians were losing any noble characteristics owing to alcohol, sickness, violence, abuse, and inter-marriage with Africans and African Carolinians. At the same time, Indian trade dependency on the English made Indians detestable in the English mind. Then again, the English never associated nobility with Africans. So by the mid-1700s, although North Carolina was a triracial society of Indians, Africans, and English, by no means were these groups seen as equal or similar.[4]

Thomas Jefferson, one of colonial America's premier scientific writers and third president of the United States, played up this new concept of race. Writing in his 1786 *Notes on the State of Virginia*, Jefferson advocated marriage between Indians and White people but made a distinction between pure Indians or Indians who had mar-ried with White people and were worthy of assimilation into White society and those Indians who had married with Black people and so became contaminated, as he saw it, and were not necessarily Indians anymore and so could never assimilate. For Jefferson, Indians in gen-eral were equal to White people in intelligence and imagination and more so in bravery, endurance, and love of family. Because of these similar qualities, Jefferson believed Indians and White people should mix, blend, and become a single people.

However, for Jefferson the only Indians worthy of intermarriage with White people were those powerful peoples west of the Appala-chian Mountains, such as the Shawnees and Cherokees, who had, he believed, remained racially pure or had intermarried only with White people. In his list of quality Indians of eastern America, he made no mention of any Indians of Virginia or the Carolinas other than the Cherokees and the Catawbas. Not making his list were the Tuscaroras, Meherrins, Chowans, Hatteras, Mattamuskeets, Occa-neechis, Saponis, or any Indians of the Virginia and North Carolina Coastal Plain. The reason for this omission, historian Arica Cole-man explains, was that for Jefferson these Coastal Plain nations had become too mixed with Africans to be considered Indians anymore. Black people in America, Jefferson said, were less than White people and Indians in intellect, imagination, and beauty. He could not sup-port the intermarriage of White people with Black people because their children would remain inferior. Coleman succinctly explains Jefferson's and other White people's views this way: "Red blood" ennobled; "Black blood" contaminated. Jefferson himself said as much, explaining that the Romans could free their slaves and then intermarry with no stain, "but with us a second is necessary, unknown to history. When freed, he [the enslaved Black] is to be removed beyond the reach of mixture."[5] Mixture took place anyway.

Indians, Africans, and English

Part and parcel of this new concept of race based on skin color was that in the American colonies Africans and Indians could be legally enslaved, whereas people adjudged White could not. Indians in North Carolina and across the American South developed a complex relationship with the chattel slavery expanding across the region. Long before Europeans arrived on the continent, Native peoples had taken war captives. Some of these captives would be tortured to death as vengeance to restore harmony to the family and town. Others would be adopted into their captors' families and do the work that all Indians did: clearing, planting, hauling, hunting, skinning.[6] In earlier times, there was little profit in having too many captives in one's household, so the enslavement of others was not widespread in early North Carolina Native society. The coming of Europeans and their desire for captives to be made into enslaved workers added a new dimension to Native warfare. With a South Carolina market for captives to send to Barbados and other colonies, Indians now made war for the purpose of taking captives, then exchanging them with English slave merchants for guns, powder, and manufactured necessities. In turn, these slave merchants sold these captured Indians to England's Sugar Islands and to buyers in other colonies, including North Carolina.[7]

Enslaved Indians remained a common sight in North Carolina for much of the late seventeenth and eighteenth centuries. John and Anna Lear up on the Chowan River owned three enslaved Black individuals, Charles, Manuell, and Manuell's wife, as well as two enslaved Indians, Dinah and Harry.[8] James Cole of Pasquotank precinct owned one enslaved Indian and two enslaved Black people, all three of whom he accused of breaking into his house and plundering a trunkful of clothes.[9] When Capt. Nicholas Jones settled in the colony, along with the many enslaved Africans he listed for headright purposes were also Betty, an Indian woman, and Peter, an Indian man.[10]

It was not long before enslaved Indians, often women, and enslaved Africans, usually men, worked alongside each other in the colony's homes and fields. Intimate relations between them took place, and bicultural children resulted, who learned something of their parent's Native and African cultures. Colonial officials were vastly interested in the color of people's skin and had categories in which they could place a person because of these characteristics. However, these categories were not necessarily rigid. At one end—or, rather, at the top of the social pyramid, as the English believed—sat White people. Anyone could be White if they were not enslaved and had skin light enough to be deemed white to other White settlers. Of course, this was a racial construct because at some point a person's skin color would be too dark to be considered White or too white to be Black. Where that line lay, no one was sure as it was based on appearance. Toward the other end of the spectrum—or at the bottom—sat Indians, or "pure Indians," as Jefferson believed, and Africans, people considered to be Black or "Negro," the term used in colonial days.[11]

Skin color, facial features, and hair texture marked these two peoples, and eastern North Carolina Indians' residence on Indian reserves helped identify them as Indians. Then came people "in between" Black, White, and Red. Some might sit somewhere between White and Indian and African. For others, as Jefferson noted, they were less than pure Indians or pure Africans. If a White person and a Black person produced a child, colonial authorities usually assigned that child the title "mulatto." Another category was "mustee," which was usually assigned to the child of an Indian and a Black person but sometimes to a child born of an Indian and a White person. These "mixed" categories were often nebulous, used interchangeably, and changed on an individual basis. Most White people of the colonial South were interested in "mixed" people but did not necessarily care if they had Indian or African parentage. Both were equally negative, as they saw it. North Carolina took its cue from South Carolina, which said that when it came to a non-White person, if they were not fully Indian, then they should be considered Black.[12] In contrast, skin color was not important among matrilineal Indians because any child born to a Tuscarora or Machapunga or Chowan mother was a member of her clan and a citizen of her nation and so was an Indian.[13]

The Tuscaroras and other Indians of the area had probably met their first Africans as enslaved helpers to Virginia Indian traders leading horse caravans to their villages. Harry, the runaway slave engineer, had been taken in by the Contentnea Creek Tuscaroras and helped design and build the European-style fort at King Hancock's town of Catechna. Unfortunately, the Catechna Alliance also handed Harry over to Col. John Barnwell after the peace treaty in mid-1712, who immediately executed him. One wonders how the Tuscaroras thought of their relationship with Harry, a relationship in which they could hand him over on English demand. They also agreed to hand over King Hancock. Yet the Tuscaroras had freed the two enslaved Africans taken upriver by Christoph de Graffenried when they had captured him and John Lawson in 1711. We have no knowledge of what became of them. Indians certainly saw Africans when they visited the towns and settlements that sprang up on the Coastal Plain. Southern colony officials always worried about Indians and Africans allying and then making war on the European settlers. To keep an animosity between Indians and Black people, some colonies used Indians as runaway slave catchers and used Black people to help attack Indians.[14]

For enslaved Africans, Indian Woods and the other tributary reserves must have looked like havens of freedom. It is possible some Africans sought freedom there, but this was a risky undertaking. Some settlers accused the Tuscaroras of harboring runaway slaves, then again some Indians might catch a slave and return them to the plantation for a reward. Freedom could not be guaranteed to an

African runaway heading to the reserves.[15] Historian Arwin Smallwood, a descendent of Indian Woods Tuscaroras, writes that though White people wanted their slaves returned, they feared going into Indian Woods to search for them lest they be confronted by a mob of angry Indians.[16] It is unclear whether reserve Tuscaroras ever held enslaved Africans of their own or how many Africans, enslaved or free, spent time on the reserves. As we will see, some certainly did spend time there because intimate relations between Tuscaroras and African Carolinians took place. By the mid-1700s, if one visited the Tuscarora towns of Ooneroy and Resootka, one would find mainly Indians but also probably a few White, Black, and some "mixed" or bicultural peoples who lived among them.

Neighboring White settlers certainly imagined that their escaped slaves found homes on the reserves. They accused King Tom Blount of harboring runaways on Indian Woods, smuggling them out of Bertie County, and providing escape directions for slaves on the run. However, the slaves Blount was accused of harboring seemed to be enslaved Indians rather than enslaved Africans. As we have seen, when Blount and his Tuscaroras raided into South Carolina, they often captured enslaved Indians and brought them back to Indian Woods. Several settlers accused Blount of harboring runaway enslaved Indians at Resootka. Several times the North Carolina Governor's Council ordered Blount to return these enslaved Indians, but Blount delayed, blamed the Senecas, and nothing happened. The enslaved Indians in question never seem to have been returned to their owners.[17] There were probably many others who did not make the colonial records.

Despite the treaty demands that the Indians return all slaves looted from the English during the Tuscarora War, one might understand Blount's desire to free enslaved Indians. They may have been family, clan kin, or other Tuscaroras. After all, Blount's own wife and children had been captured during the war and would have been sent to the slave pens had the colony not intervened. Maybe Blount realized the injustice of Indian slavery, particularly in light of how many Tuscaroras had been marched off to the Charles Town slave markets after the Battle of the Neoheroka Fort in 1713. Taking and harboring enslaved Indians may have been his people's strike against slavery. Then again, during the Tuscarora War Blount did deliver some Indian slaves to Gov. Thomas Pollock. Maybe his attitude changed after the war.

Whatever their beliefs, the Tuscaroras and other tributaries could not help coming into regular contact with Africans and the English. As settler farms and plantations butted up against the Indian reserves, it was almost impossible to keep the three peoples apart. They met, gossiped, joked, brawled, traded, schemed, and had intimate relations. Dwindling Indian population numbers made it harder for Indians to find eligible marriage partners within their individual nations because soon all were connected as kinfolk. It was possible that some intimate relations took place between kinfolk, willingly or unwillingly. Marrying other eastern North Carolina Indians alleviated the taboo of marrying kinfolk. This became a reality in North Carolina, and it made no difference if they were Iroquoian, Algonquian, or Siouan speakers. Cultural intermixing became a survival strategy. In the mid-1700s, several families of Hatteras moved onto the Machapunga reserve and intermarried, bringing in the surname "Collins." Similarly, a few Machapunga men moved to Hatteras Island and married Hatteras women.[18] Some Chowans, Saponis, and Cores relocated to live with the Tuscaroras at Indian Woods.[19] Celia Kearsey, a Tuscarora woman born on the Indian Woods reserve said her mother was Tuscarora and her father, Thomas, a Weyanoke from Virginia. In the 1750s, Celia married James Lowry, part Indian and part White, and they moved to Drowning Creek in southeastern North Carolina. Other Tuscarora individuals and families also moved to Drowning Creek and married Indians there and so gave rise to Tuscarora families living along the Lumber River in Robeson County, North Carolina.[20] Families of Saponis and Occaneechis from Granville County and even Nansemonds from Virginia also migrated to the Drowning Creek Indian communities.[21]

A growing population of White settlers on the borders of the Indian reserves could provide mates for Indian men and women, and some did. But the number of Indian and White marriages in eastern North Carolina was not overwhelming. Intimate relations took place, as in John Lawson's story about meeting auburn-haired, gray-eyed Hatteras, whom he says stemmed from their intermarriage with European survivors of the Lost Colony. But Hatteras also married and mixed with English mariners and settlers on Hatteras Island. Before the Tuscarora War, bicultural children resulted from the liaisons between the Indian "Trading Girls," who made temporary marriages with lusty Englishmen when they arrived in Indian towns with libidos raging.[22]

Unlike in the case of the Cherokees, where British traders spent many long months in their distant mountain villages and so married Cherokee women, few long-term marriages developed between British traders and eastern Indian women. Part of this may have been location. The Indian towns of eastern North Carolina were not that far from the Virginia trade centers, and so there was no need for a trader to live in the towns for any length of time. In the colony of North Carolina, trade with the Indians was almost nonexistent before the Tuscarora War, and so there was little interaction between settlers and Indians. After the war, when the planter and farmer population grew around reserve borders, some intermarriage between Whites and Indians took place. As we saw, James Lowry, who married the Tuscarora woman Celia Kearsey, said his mother was Indian and his father White.[23] When Rev. Alexander Stewart visited the Machapungas in 1763, he reported that the Indians were "intermixed" with White people.[24] But it is unclear whether "intermixed" meant "intermarried" or just "living among each other." Down on Drowning Creek, by the 1790s about 16 percent of the households had spouses who were of different ethnicities.[25]

It just does not appear that many English men and women took wives and husbands from the nearby Indian populations and vice versa, or if they did, then the practice was not widespread. This may have stemmed from an English racial and class bias. Indians were not White, nor were they Christian, and most were certainly poor. As the eighteenth century muddled along, White people increasingly saw them as a servant underclass good enough for sex but not worthy enough for marriage. According to William Byrd of Virginia, settlers disdained to marry Indians, but he felt this view was shortsighted. Intermarriage, he believed, would have made the Indians less angry at their land being taken from them and would have whitened the colonies. "For if a Moor may be washt white in 3 generations, surely an Indian might have been blancht in two."[26] Byrd's comment implies another reason why White people in eastern North Carolina did not marry Indians. Jefferson and his White neighbors came to believe that Indians, instead of being "washt white," were being "washed Black." Since Indians were increasingly mixing with local Black people, they were becoming less noble and more inferior, maybe even criminal, as White people characterized them. Nevertheless, some White people did have intimate relations and even marriages with Indians and Africans, more often than officials hoped or liked.[27]

There seemed to be enough interracial relationships on the lower end of society between White women, often poor indentured servants, and Indian or African men that it worried North Carolina authorities. Wanting to nip these relationships in the bud, in 1715, just after the end of the Tuscarora War, the North Carolina government ruled that any indentured servant woman who bore a "bastard child" with a Black, mulatto, or Indian person would have two years added to her indenture, or she could pay a £6 fine to the local Anglican church. It is revealing that there was no corresponding rule regarding a White man having intimate relations with an African or an Indian woman.[28] If an Indian, African, or a mixed-race man or woman married a White person and produced children, then the colonial government tried to make life as difficult as possible for that family. In 1723, the North Carolina Legislature passed "an Additional Tax on all free Negroes, Mulattoes, Mustees and such Persons Male & Female, as now are or hereafter shall be intermarried with any such Persons resident in this government." Any of these people twelve years of age or older were required to pay this additional tax, which was not levied on White settlers.[29] About this same time, the government also stipulated that "no Negroes, Mulattoes, Mustees or Indians shall be capable of voting for Members of the Assembly."[30]

Skin color, facial features, class, and concepts of inferiority and superiority were becoming markers of who deserved civil rights and who did not. In 1741, the colony stiffened the bicultural child rule and stipulated that not only would any White servant woman who delivered a child born with an African, mulatto, or Indian have two years added to her indenture, but also her child would be held as a servant until they were thirty-one years old. That same law also prohibited any colonial official from knowingly marrying "a white man with an Indian, Negro, Mustee, or any person of Mixed Blood" and made every offense subject to a fine of £50 proclamation money.[31] These restrictions indicate that sexual relations between White women and African and Indian men were common enough and of enough concern to the authorities that they passed laws to officially prohibit such relations. Poor Black people, poor Indians, poor mulattos, poor mustees, and poor White people often found love and comfort with each other at the bottom of colonial society.

Yet there was no law preventing Indians and Africans from marrying or cohabiting with each other, so Indians might have intimate relations with other Native peoples, Africans, African Carolinians, mustees or mulattos, enslaved or free. The Indian slave trade and African slavery initially brought these two peoples together. As we have seen, planters and farmers in eastern North Carolina kept both enslaved Indians and enslaved Africans. However, as Indian numbers decreased, the African and African Carolinian population far outpaced that of the Indians in eastern North Carolina. In 1730, when eastern North Carolina Indians numbered fewer than 2,000 souls, there were about 6,000 Africans. There were 19,000 Black people by 1755, about 40,000 in 1767, and 66,000 in 1775. In the first US census conducted in 1790, North Carolina listed 100,572 enslaved people and 288,204 White people.[32]

As Indians became increasingly connected through kinship, some looked to other Indian peoples and White people, but others needing spouses and comfort looked to the ever-increasing population of Africans and African Carolinians, both enslaved and free. As the historian Theda Perdue explains, "Kinship, not physical features, distinguished one [Native] individual from another, and the Africans whom Indians incorporated had matrilineal ties to [Indian] clans through birth or adoption."[33] Similarly, in Southern slave society bondage was also matrilineal. A child born to an enslaved mother was automatically enslaved as well; a child born to a free woman would be free. With the matrilineal eastern North Carolina Indians, a child born of an Indian mother was automatically a member of her family, clan, town, and people. It made sense for an enslaved African man to produce children with a free Indian women because their children would be not only free but also members of an Indian nation. Gender imbalances among enslaved Africans and Indians in these early years dictated intimate interracial relations as enslaved Africans in general tended to be male and most enslaved Indians were females, the very people who had done the farming and production in their Native homes. Among enslaved Africans, there were always more men than women, so there were always going to be some men who could not find mates unless they looked outside their ethnic group.[34]

Adding to the attraction between Indians and Africans was the similarity in their cultures. Religious ideas, oral traditions, methods of basket weaving, boatbuilding, cooking, as well as the use of herbal medicines were similar enough to make it easier for Indians and Africans to form friendships, intimate relations, and even marriages.[35] How widespread these relationships and marriages between Indians and Black people were in colonial North Carolina is not known. Were they common or uncommon? That they took place is beyond doubt as White neighbors commented on how Indians had mixed with Black folk, but numbers are impossible to come by because officials, although very interested in Black or Indian people's intimate relations with White people, took little note of those between Indians and Africans.

Still, every now and again the mask slips, and we see evidence of these Indian–Black relationships, usually through their bicultural, "mixed-race" children. In 1719, Rev. Taylor reported his baptizing successes up near the Chowan River to his superiors. Among the thirty-six he baptized, most were White children, but he also baptized a young, enslaved mustee woman and three mustee children. This was Chowan territory.[36] In its June 1764 edition, the *North-Carolina Magazine* of New Bern ran an ad in which a slave owner wanted the return of his runaway mustee slave, who possessed "greatly the Looks and Colour of an Indian."[37] In 1776, Richard Blackledge of Craven County bequeathed, among the many distributions of land and slaves in his will, to his son-in-law, Spires Singleton, some land near Lake Mattamuskeet as well as five slaves, including a mustee girl named Amelia.[38] We know from indenture records, which sometimes noted a child's parents, that some Machapunga women married or had intimate relations with White and Black men.[39] As will be seen, evidence of Indian and Black intimate relations and the children they produced will become more apparent as Americans hoped to lay claim to the last of the eastern North Carolina Indian reserves.

Decline in Status

The tributary Indians' liaisons with Africans and African Carolinians coincided with a distinct slide in how colonial officials and settlers viewed them. As the generation of strong leaders such as King Blount, King Hoyter, and King Durant passed, as Indian population numbers spiraled downward, as Indian poverty increased, as Indians and African Carolinians produced children, and as fewer White people remembered that Indians were once formidable enemies and not just servants, local White people lost both their fear and their respect for their tributary Indian neighbors. By 1790, there had been generations of White settlers and many newly arrived immigrants who never encountered an Indian, at least as they imagined Indians. They had, however, much contact with Africans and African Americans. It was not that far of a jump to lump all dark-skinned people—Indians, Africans, and people in between—together as "People of Color."

Evidence of this slide in the colony's thinking toward Indians can be seen in the government's shifting of the legal jurisdictions that dealt with Indians. In the past, when King Blount or King Hoyter had a problem, he appealed directly to the governor or the powerful Governor's Council. The council was essentially the colony's upper legislative house, composed of wealthy and powerful settlers appointed originally by the Lords Proprietors and then later by the governor or king. They advised the governor, and the governor might sit in when the Indian kings came before the council. In the years following the Tuscarora War, the council had been particularly good about giving justice to the colony's tributaries. It might also appoint commissioners to mediate with specific Indian nations over certain issues. But by the mid-eighteenth century, Indians issues were shifted to the county courts.

Instead of belonging to a sovereign tributary nation deserving of diplomatic recognition, Indians were increasingly seen as residents of the county. Indian leaders speaking for their peoples and individual Indians speaking for themselves now appeared before the judges and juries of the county court, where many were not friends of the Indians and did not see them as deserving of equal justice with White settlers. Increasingly, Tuscaroras and other tributaries found their claims, particularly against White debtors, dismissed and then might have court costs charged to them. The county courts might also be called upon to mediate disputes among Indians of the same nation and of different nations as well.[40]

Indians came to fear the county courts, anticipating they would not receive justice. Making it more difficult was a law of 1762 that forbade Indians, Black people, and in-between peoples from testifying against White people in court. To get around this law, these tributaries turned to trusted White friends to intercede for them. When an Indian complained that settler Richard Edge had taken his gun, he asked settler Thomas Jarvis for help. It was Jarvis who filed suit in Albemarle County for the Indian. The tactic worked, and the gun was returned. Settler Jonathan Jennings did a similar service for another Indian when he filed suit against Matthew Winn for the return of the Indian's sow. Another White man, Thomas Barcock, testified in the Indian's behalf and identified the sow as belonging to the Indian. Some Indians even hired White lawyers to plead their case. Indian John Hawkins hired attorney Thomas Swann to sue Thomas James in General Court for the cost of a heifer that James had killed. Swann got Hawkins's restitution for him.[41]

One of the more mysterious things taking place on the North Carolina reserves in the second half of the eighteenth century was the disappearance of adult Indian men. We do not know what was happening to them. Were they dying? Being enslaved? Leaving the reserve to live down at Drowning Creek? Maybe living nearby but off the reserve? Were these absences just periodic, and the men missing only when White people took reserve counts? Were they abandoning their families and community, or was their absence a strategy to help their family? We just do not know. Of course, not all adult Indian men left their reserves—after all, male children grew into adults—but in the documents of the latter part of eighteenth century we see more and more Indian women going before the courts and interacting with colonial and state officials. Some women, in the absence of men, became the unofficial leaders of their Indian nation. Without Indian men, these women married or cohabited with local Black or White people. Surnames were now often passed from mother to child rather than from father to child.[42]

The counties took a dim view of this absence of Indian men and the rise of Indian women, who increasingly made decisions for their family and people. Their disapproval was not necessarily an anti-Indian attitude but a push for patriarchal rights. In 1762, North Carolina passed the Act for the Better Care of Orphans. The act prioritized father's rights over those of a mother. Only fathers could be primary guardians, not mothers, and any child without a father could be considered an orphan, even a White child with a White mother. These fatherless children could be forcibly apprenticed to guardians until they were eighteen years old if they were female and twenty-one if they were male. Free-born mulatto and mustee females could be forcibly apprenticed until they were twenty-one. In 1796, the legislature added to the law, stating that any child whose father had been missing from the family for more than a year and had left the child in a destitute situation could be forcibly apprenticed.[43] Together, these two laws severely affected the Chowan and Machapunga women, probably Tuscarora women as well, whose adult men had disappeared.

Among the Chowans, county courts began taking children from their mothers and forcibly apprenticing them to local White people. As the county rationalized it, since Chowan men had abandoned the reserve and left women as the head of families, taking these children, mainly young boys, helped the family by providing fewer mouths to feed. It also gave the boys a trade or at least some work that would keep them out of trouble and off the county dole. For the last few decades of the eighteenth century, we see Indian boys being indentured out as apprentices.[44] In 1779, fourteen-year-old Benjamin Robbins was apprenticed to James Garrett until he was twenty-one. Per the indenture contract, Benjamin was to faithfully serve his master, "his secrets keep[,] . . . not absent himself from his master's service without leave, frequent public houses, contract matrimony, nor commit fornication during the said time." As an apprentice, Benjamin was to be taught to read and write and learn the plantation business.[45] Eleven-year-old James Robbins was to learn the "art and mystery of a tanner."[46] Ten-year-old Samuel and Jethro Robbins were to become house carpenters.[47] Other Chowan boys such as Lewis Robbins, Josiah Bennett, Joseph Bennett, and George Bennett found themselves apprenticed to shoemakers and coopers. These forced apprenticeships showed just how powerless the Chowans had become, especially Chowan women. As the historian Warren Milteer points out, county officials might remove these children in a fit of pique or to punish the Chowans for past sins. "Apprenticeships crippled the Chowans' abilities to maintain independent households[,] . . . challenged Chowan women's parental rights and claims to their children's labor[,] . . . [and] helped destroy the last symbol of Chowan autonomy, the reservation."[48] They also separated Indian children

4. Indenture of the Native child Joshua Longtom. Native children, such as the ten-year-old Machapunga boy Joshua Longtom, were often forcibly taken from their families by the colonial and state government and apprenticed to learn a trade, in Joshua's case as a mariner. This violent act was a method of Indian erasure. *Source*: Indentures of Joshua & Jordan Longtom, May 19 and Sept. 18, 1804, Apprentice Bonds and Records, Hyde County Records, North Carolina State Archives, Raleigh. Photograph by the author.

from their Indian culture, essentially detribalizing them and hastening them on to the classification "People of Color."

Machapunga families also became targets of forced apprenticeships. In 1804, Ship Master Stephen Fletcher asked the local court to let him take as an apprentice ten-year-old Joshua Longtom, "a base born Indian son" of the Machapunga woman Jenny Longtom and an unknown White father. The court agreed, and Joshua was apprenticed to Fletcher until he was twenty-one years old to become a "seaman & mariner." At the same time, Ship Master Little John Pugh offered to indenture thirteen-year-old Price Longtom and his nine-year-old brother, Jordan Longtom, both "base born sons of Polly Longtom," an Indian woman, and a Black father. Both Price and Jordan were apprenticed to Pugh until they were twenty-one years old to learn how to become watermen.[49] Other Machapunga boys apprenticed in 1804 included Shadrach Mackey and Simpson Mackey, each referred to as a "base born person of Cullor."[50] Children with Machapunga surnames—"Longtom" and "Mackey"—continued to be forcibly apprenticed up into the 1830s: twelve children with the surname "Longtom" and another twelve with the surname "Mackey." Ten children with the Hatteras surname "Collins" were apprenticed in Hyde County. Descendants of the Machapungas, Hatteras, and Roanokes all made up a considerable part of the People of Color population in Hyde County.[51]

Of Land, Gender, and Skin Color

Not only were the county courts taking their children from Indians, but the Indians also still needed to appeal to the courts over the land issues that bedeviled them. As the number of Indians declined and they posed no military threat to the colony, the only thing they had of value was their lands.[52] With the deer hide trade in eastern North Carolina declining, and as cash became the coin of the realm, as we have seen, Indians began leasing or selling off parcels of their reserves for money. Some money was used to purchase provisions and supplies; some to pay legal costs, fines, and taxes; some to leave the area; and some for personal enrichment. Sometimes the nation supported these sales; at other times, factions formed to oppose them. In other instances, legal chicanery separated Indians from their lands. It seems almost trite to say that loss of their lands over the course of the eighteenth century and the rise of White supremacy caused severe hardship to the Indians of eastern North Carolina by leaving them poverty-stricken and erasing them as Indians in the eyes of the state and White society.

Among the Machapungas, with the absence of adult men it was the women who presided over the last days of their reserve and existence as a tributary Indian people recognized by the colony. The last official act between the North Carolina government and what could be considered the Machapunga nation came on November 21, 1792, when four Machapunga women—Patience Mackey, Mary Longtom, Jean Longtom, and Marthy Longtom, along with three children, Tabithy Mackey, Timothy Mackey, and John Longtom—offered to sell the entire 10,240-acre reserve to the settler Hutchens Selby for £50. There is much to raise eyebrows here. This seems to be the third time that the Machapungas had either sold or tried to sell or lease their entire reserve: in 1752, in 1761, and now again in 1792. This does not count the many individual tracts sold during the previous decades. It is unclear if the sale in 1792 was a sly Indian trick to make money by selling land the Machapungas did not own or whether the Indian women just did not know what their male leaders had sold or kept over the years. Also, this was now after the revolution, and only the US government was constitutionally able to purchase Indian land. Nevertheless, the sale was recorded in the Hyde County records. It is unclear if Selby knew the land he "bought" had already been sold or whether the Machapunga women ever got their £50.[53] After this "sale" in 1792, the Machapungas as a nation or people disappeared from the North Carolina government records. Despite this "erasure," many Machapunga women and children remained in the area, as we see from the indenture records.[54]

The Chowans faced the same challenge. By the 1780s, the destruction of the Chowan reserve was almost complete. These last land sales are a muddle, and not all Chowans agreed with them. It was possible that those selling the land may not have had the actual authority to do so, but postrevolution White Americans purchasing lands did not care as long as they had a bill of sale. The county courts would not oppose the sales, and the Chowan women were powerless to stop them. Members of the Robbins family seemed to realize that rather than retain a reserve, they needed to do what settlers did and make a private purchase. In 1782, James, Benjamin, Patience, Sarah, Nanney, Elizabeth, Dorcas, and Christian Robbins purchased 30 acres of land from Henry Hill. This tract came to be called "Indian Town," which sat in the south-central part of the recently formed Gates County.[55]

It was fortunate the Chowans bought the separate "Indian Town" because in 1790 settlers William Lewis and Samuel Harrell proposed to buy the final remnants of the Chowan reserve for 100 Spanish-milled dollars. James Robbins, Benjamin Robbins, George Bennett, and Joseph Bennett, the "Chief men and representatives of the Chowan Indian nation," sold them the last 400 acres of the reserve.[56] But this transaction was dicey as under the new US Constitution only the national government could purchase Indian lands. Lewis and Harrell appealed to the North Carolina Legislature with a theory that was novel but took an axe to Chowan identity. Yes, the two men said, they had purchased "Indian" lands, but the Chowans were not really Indians anymore. They argued that the "whole of the said Chowan Indian men is dead, leaving a parcel of Indian women, which has mixed with negroes, and now there is several freemen and women of mixed blood as aforesaid which have descended from the said Indians, and the said freemen as aforesaid considering themselves heirs to the aforesaid Indians and entitled to small remnants of the aforesaid tract."[57] As Lewis and Harrell saw it, the Chowan representatives listed in the sale were not pure Indians anymore, but Black or at best mustees or mulattos who had married into the Chowan nation. Historian Warren Milteer Jr. cuts through this eighteenth-century legal jargon, explaining that by claiming that the Chowans had mixed with Black people, the two buyers were saying the Chowans really were not Indians anymore in the eyes of White people, and so the constitutional prohibition on private purchases of Indian lands did not apply here. Lewis and Harrell were purchasing land from free Black people, People of Color, not Indians, they claimed. The North Carolina government accepted the two settlers' reasoning and allowed the purchase to go through. All that remained to the Chowans were the 30 acres of Indian Town.[58]

For the next twenty-five years, the last of the government-recognized Chowans lived at Indian Town, led by the matriarch Nan Robbins. We know little of their life in these few years, but it seemed poverty-stricken and hand-to-mouth. With so few Indian marriage partners nearby, Chowan women married local African Carolinians. Some Chowans continued to live at Indian Town, but others, such as Christian Robbins, left and settled elsewhere as individuals. In 1795, Benjamin Robbins, a Chowan who lived as an individual in Gates County, was allowed to vote in an election for the US House of Representatives. He was the only Chowan voter in the county.[59]

But trouble was on the way for Indian Town. In 1815, when Dorcas Robbins and John Robbins could not pay a $20 promissory note, Gates County auctioned off a 6-acre parcel of Indian Town, and neighbor John Walton was the highest bidder. One wonders if this Walton was a descendant of Thomas Walton, whose store had been burgled back in 1753. John Walton now owned a big part of Indian Town and convinced some Chowans, such as Christian Robbins, who did not actually live there, to sell their interest in the town. Through this approach, Walton acquired another 5 acres. Walton now convinced the Gates County Court to divide what was left of Indian Town into individual Chowan allotments. Nan Robbins and the other Chowan women protested, saying Walton had no valid claim, and, besides, they were not shareholders; rather, Indian Town was communal Chowan national lands and so could not be divided. Indian Town, they said, belonged to all the Chowan people. Walton appealed. The court agreed with him and ordered Indian Town divided between Walton and the Chowans Nan, Sarah, Elizabeth, and heirs of Patience, Lewis, Judith, Thaney, and Feasey Robbins. Walton then

sued these remaining landholders for court costs. The court agreed
with him and ordered the Chowan women to pay $18.07. They were
unable to come up with the money, so in 1821 the court seized the
Chowan lands in Indian Town, put them up for auction, and John
Walton bought them. It was a great piece of legal chicanery. Now the
very last piece of the Chowan homeland was gone.[60] The Chowan
women, seen as People of Color, were landless and homeless.

In North Carolina's view, the Chowan nation, like all the other
tributary nations and their reserves, had become extinct, and so the
Chowans disappeared from state records. Only the names "Chowan
River" and "Chowan County" recalled their existence. But this
was not exactly true. Though the last of their land had been sold or
taken, many Chowans still lived in the Chowan–Albemarle region.
Their sense of place as well as their kinship bonds remained strong,
especially among numerous Robbins family descendants. But from
the view of the North Carolina state government and the Chowans'
White neighbors, the Chowans, now without Indian lands and an Indian government and "mixing" with local African Americans, were
not Indians anymore but People of Color. Of course, the Chowans
did not see themselves as such, and memories of their people, nation,
place, and history persist to this day.[61]

People of Color

As Milteer points out, according to the settlers, "native peoples who
no longer possessed these lands could no longer be Indians under the
colonizer's definition. . . . Without a land base, they lost the feature
that distinguished them from other nonwhite people." Government
records only rarely noted whether a person was an Indian Person
of Color or an African Person of Color, though individuals in the
community might know, and memory was an important way of iden-
tifying who was who and who had free or enslaved parents, grandpar-
ents, and great-grandparents. By the late eighteenth century, White
North Carolinians in the eastern part of the state did not see Indians;
rather, they saw Black people: at best free People of Color, at worst

slaves bound for life.[62] There seemed an almost nefarious process to it: relieve Indians of their lands, erase their identity as Indians, then limit their rights by assigning them as "People of Color."[63]

For North Carolina and the American South, by the end of the eighteenth century the label "Person of Color" applied to all non-enslaved, non-White people, and now that group included many people who considered themselves Native Indian peoples. By this time, most People of Color in eastern North Carolina were of mixed descent, meaning they were of Indian–Black, Indian–White, or Black–White ancestry and were just as likely to have mixed parents.[64] It was also economically profitable to declare Indians to be People of Color as it helped settlers evade the US Constitution's prohibition on private citizens buying lands from Indians.

Every now and then the North Carolina records give a peek at this reclassifying process. In 1794, brothers George and Joseph Bennett, two Chowans from Gates County, applied for "freedom papers" that verified their status as free men and would allow them to move to Virginia. The documents declared each of the men as a free-born son of an Indian man and a "free woman." Their Indian ancestry had been recognized. Then, a few years later, George returned to Gates County to live among his Chowan kinfolk. The 1810 US census declared George Bennett and his Chowan kinfolk to be "free colored" persons. The only thing that had changed was that an earlier White person saw him as Indian and a later White Person believed him a Person of Color. It was that simple.[65] In 1795, a Bertie County court clerk declared a Chowan named "John" to be either a "mulatto" or an "Indian." However, John's attorney described him as a "free man of color."[66] For some, it could go the other way. The 1790 census described the Hatteras families of Duncan and Basnett as "mulatto." Ten years later, the 1800 census listed the same families as "white."[67]

What did it mean to be a free Person of Color in the late eighteenth and early nineteenth centuries? For North Carolina, free People of Color could be, as Milteer explains, "those assumed to be free people of African descent, free people of Native ancestry whom the state did not recognize as politically autonomous, free persons with heritage in the East Indies, and a variety of individuals with mixed ancestry." Milteer points out that free People of Color were legally closer to White people than to slaves. They could own property, seek redress in the courts, earn and keep their wages, have their connection to their children recognized, and leave the state without permission—all things unavailable to the enslaved. Because of this distinction, free People of Color did not make any great coalitions or associations with enslaved people.[68] Yet they had also lost all the rights Indian tributaries once had to petition the government, have their complaints heard by the governor and Governor's Council, have their lands protected, be seen as subjects of the British monarch, and, later, have diplomatic standing with the US government.

Once Indians lost their reserve lands and were reclassified as People of Color, their history in North Carolina ceased being that of Indians and instead became part of the history of People of Color in the Old North State. According to North Carolina, by the early 1800s the only Indians left in the state were the Cherokees out in the mountains because they were seen as Jefferson's "pure Indians," with a functioning government and powerful enough to make the government think twice before starting an expensive war with them. Other than the Cherokees, only White people, the enslaved, and free People of Color remained in North Carolina. But many of those labeled as People of Color did not forget their Indianness. Not all Tuscaroras left for New York with Chiefs Sacarusa and Longboard in 1803. Some Bertie County slaves and free People of Color counted themselves as Tuscaroras or descendants of Tuscaroras. The same could be said of the other Indians of eastern North Carolina. Once they sold off the last bit of Meherrin or Machapunga or Chowan lands, they disappeared as Indians in the state's eyes and records but physically did not disappear from eastern North Carolina. Saponis and Occaneechis, who never had an official reserve but settled in the Carolina Piedmont, always considered themselves Indians.

Enclaves of Indian people living as People of Color could be found in counties across eastern North Carolina, such as Tuscaroras in Bertie County and down in Robeson County. There were Machapunga descendants in Hyde County. In Hertford County remained Meherrins, while Chowan peoples lived in and around Gates County. In Halifax and Warren Counties lived descendants of Saponis, Tutelos, Nansemonds, and Tuscaroras—all later taking the name "Haliwa-Saponi." People who thought of themselves as Saponis could be found in Person County, and those who defined themselves as Occaneechis were in Alamance and Orange Counties. The Coharies of Sampson County claimed both Tuscarora descent and descent from the Neuse, who had relocated to the Little Coharie River in that county. No matter what their White neighbors said, they saw themselves as Indians or of Indian descent. Still, it was a long and difficult process to break out of the biracial White–Black system established in the South. Each eastern North Carolina "tribe" often had difficult internal discussions about expressing an Indian identity, especially among members of families who felt more of an affinity for the African American community.[69]

How much of Native Indian culture remained in these peoples was debatable. As we have seen, skin color played little role in being Indian. Identity rested more on one's family, town, people, lands, culture, and history. Unfortunately, this notion of identity was running against the tide as the South became a two-"race" White and Black society. If one was not White, then one must be Black. Yet we have to wonder whether during the summer, late on Saturday nights, did slaves or People of Color gather around a fire deep in the woods to step to a Tuscarora dance that remembered their victories? Did a grandmother cure her sick grandchild with a tincture recalled from her own Chowan grandmother? Did a waterman paddling on the Pamlico chant a Machapunga fishing song? Did an enslaved Indian African mother teach her daughter a Meherrin lullaby? According to Smallwood, in what was once Indian Woods in Bertie County these biracial Tuscaroras who possessed part-African and part-European ancestry passed on their religious beliefs, farming techniques, even methods of cooking. They would combine their Indian, African, and European cultures to create a unique culture of their own. "The residents of Indian Woods would remember their Indian ancestry but forget their nation."[70]

Indians could also be found in those refugee communities down on Drowning Creek, later named the Lumber River, and among the swamps and creeks of Robeson, Scotland, Hoke, Cumberland, Sampson, Bladen, and Columbus Counties. This area had long been a no-man's land between the Tuscaroras to the north and the Catawbas, Cheraws, Waccamaws, and other Siouan speakers to the south and west. After the Tuscarora and Yamasee Wars, Indian survivors, including Cheraws, Tuscaroras, and other Indian peoples, sought refuge in these rather swampy lands, meeting up with the remnants of people who already used the area, such as the Cape Fear Indians and Waccamaws. It seemed a natural place for an Indian refuge. Swampy waters interspersed with patches of high ground did not make it ideal for cash-crop farming, so it did not attract many White settlers. Also, for many years the area was part of a border dispute between North Carolina and South Carolina, which also made English settlers hesitant to take land there. So Indian individuals and families from many different peoples gravitated to Drowning Creek, the Green Swamp, and various creeks in southeastern North Carolina. Here they made new connections with the land, and it became a new homeland sacred to them.[71]

That Tuscarora families eventually wound up on Drowning Creek is beyond a doubt. Genealogical research traces such Drowning Creek families named Lowry, Locklear, Chavis, and Cumbo back to the Tuscaroras. Even the White neighbors of these Indians of Robeson County often identified them as Tuscaroras.[72] Oral tradition has Tuscaroras from Bertie County moving south to Drowning Creek as early as the mid-1700s, if not earlier. This migration would not be unusual as Indians sought to live among other Indian peoples in an increasingly Black and White North Carolina. The Great Slave Conspiracy of 1802 in Bertie County may well have sent other Tuscaroras to southeastern North Carolina, where growing communities of Indian peoples lived. Chief Leon Locklear of Robeson County said his ancestors were from Indian Woods and in 1803 were out on a long hunt. When they returned, they found that Sacarusa and Longboard had led all the other Tuscaroras away to New York. Finding all their people gone, Locklear's Tuscarora ancestors migrated to Robeson County and joined the Indian people there. Locklear still called Indian Woods home.[73] These refugee communities would have been an attractive destination for eastern North Carolina Indians. They were by far the largest Indian presence in eastern North Carolina and by the mid-1800s were becoming increasingly active in reestablishing their Indian identity and rights.

Soon a host of connected Indian communities composed of different Indian peoples had arisen along the Lumber River and the swamps it created. They also drew in a few White people and African Americans. Their existence was an excellent example of Indian ethnogenesis at work, where new Indian peoples and communities were created out of different peoples and communities. There have long been tales of Roanokes, Hatteras, Saponis, Waterees, Neuse, Cape Fears, Virginia Pamunkeys, and even the English survivors of the Lost Colony joining these Robeson County Indian communities. The Coharies of nearby Sampson County also have a tale of being connected to the Lost Colony.[74] These Indian—or People of Color—communities gained an unsavory reputation among their White neighbors. The militia returns of 1754 noted that on "Drowning Creek on the head of Little Pedee, 50 families[,] a mixt crew, a lawless People, possess the Lands without patent or paying quit rents; shot a Surveyor for coming to view vacant lands being inclosed in great swamps."[75]

Nearby in Bladen and Columbus Counties were remnants of Cape Fear Indians, Waccamaws, Woccons, and other Yamasee War refugees who eventually took the name "Waccamaw Siouan." They were descendants of Siouan-speaking peoples who had tended to be tributaries of South Carolina during the colonial period.[76] Some also claimed Tuscarora ancestry. Indian ancestry continually showed up among North Carolina People of Color. The famed abolitionist, Union spy, and African American politician Abraham Galloway, who was born enslaved in Smithville (Southport), North Carolina, in

1837, had Indian ancestry from his enslaved Black mother. His father was a White boat pilot from a well-off Smithville family.[77]

Since Indian history was now subsumed under the history of People of Color, it is difficult to get a good handle on Indians' numbers in the early 1800s. The North Carolina government made no effort to differentiate between People of Color who were Indians or of Indian ancestry and People of Color who were of African ancestry. So eastern North Carolina Indians suffered the same segregation, discrimination, and violence as Black Carolinians at the hands of White people before, during, and after the Civil War. Because they were considered Black, some Indian individuals and families gravitated toward African American communities and their experience. The family of Hiram Rhodes Revels, a US senator for Mississippi during Reconstruction, was connected to the Indians of southeastern North Carolina, but he is considered an African American, and his work was among African Africans.[78]

Then in 1835 North Carolina rewrote its state constitution and enshrined White supremacy by taking away voting rights from free People of Color. Article 1, section 3, paragraph 3, read: "No free negro, free mulatto, or free person of mixed blood, descended from negro ancestors to the fourth generation inclusive, (though one ancestor of each generation may have been a white person,) shall vote for members of the Senate or House of Commons."[79] The new constitution said nothing about Indians because the state did not believe any existed other than the Cherokees, and Cherokees were not really a part of North Carolina, as the state saw them. All eastern North Carolina Indians had been defined as free persons of mixed blood or as mulattos. Though the constitution said nothing of Indians, it would affect all those who claimed they were Indians because many remaining Indians in eastern North Carolina might have an African ancestor in their family tree over the past four generations—and a White one as well. Not only did the new constitution prohibit People of Color from voting, but it also prevented them from carrying weapons without a court license and from serving in the militia.[80] There was a terrible irony here that at the exact same time the US government was pushing "civilization" on the Cherokees and trying to turn them into Anglo-Americans, the state of North Carolina was turning eastern North Carolina Indians into African Americans. In many ways, the Indian peoples of eastern North Carolina had "achieved" what President Andrew Jackson had envisioned for Indians: that they give up their Indian identity and place themselves as individuals under the laws of the state they lived in.

Not all Indians accepted their new designation quietly. In 1850, the authorities arrested Blake Robbins for illegally carrying a firearm in violation of the 1835 laws. They considered Robbins a free Person of Color, and it was illegal for a Person of Color to carry a firearm unless he had obtained a license from the county court. Robbins had no such license but insisted that he was a Chowan and so did not need one. His case gradually climbed through the courts, until in 1852 the Superior Court finally ruled nolle prosequi, thereby abandoning its prosecution of Robbins. The court accepted that Robbins was indeed an Indian and that the law did not apply to his brand of People of Color.[81]

Nevertheless, it was Robbins's case that proved the rule. As the state of North Carolina saw it, except for in a few individual cases, such as Robbins, there were no more Indians in eastern North Carolina. There were only slaves and free People of Color.

Indian Resurgence

However, the Indian presence was too overwhelming to be ignored, and within thirty years or so after the Robbins ruling, the state was forced to recognize that Indians lived in eastern North Carolina, particularly in Robeson County along the Lumber River. Down in Robeson County, the Indian peoples had a contentious relationship with their White neighbors, who saw them as insolent People of Color. Violence and murders became common. During the Civil War, the Confederacy conscripted many Robeson County Indian men to work on Confederate Ft. Fisher at the mouth of the Cape Fear River, where they faced overwork, abuse, and sickness. After the Civil War, the Indian Henry Berry Lowry and his band waged a guerrilla war against the local authorities who oppressed his people. Despite the violence, most Indians of Robeson County were hardworking small farmers, field hands, or sharecroppers who remembered their Indian ancestry and took pride in their Indianness no matter what their White neighbors said.[82]

Eventually, their Indian identity could not be overlooked. In the 1880s, local state representative Hamilton MacMillan decided that the Indians of Robeson County must have descended from the Croatans of the Outer Banks, whom MacMillan believed had taken in the Lost Colony back in 1587. He convinced the North Carolina State Legislature to officially designate the Indians of Robeson County as the Croatan Indians. Though "Croatan" was an inaccurate name, it was still a recognition of their Indianness, something different than "People of Color." As such, the Croatans of Robeson County founded their own Indian schools and Indian churches, even creating their own college, the Croatan Normal School, to train Indian teachers.[83] Over the next seventy years and through several name changes, the Croatans would become the Lumbee Tribe of North Carolina, recognized as Indians by both the state of North Carolina and the federal government. There is still a strong Tuscarora presence in that area alongside that of the Lumbees.

The naming of the Croatans was the beginning of an Indian resurgence in eastern North Carolina that carried over into much of the twentieth and twenty-first centuries. By the mid-twentieth century, these Indian enclaves re-created their own tribal governments and reasserted an Indian name and identity. The Indians of Sampson County, who claimed descent from the Tuscaroras and Neuse, took the name "Coharie" because their community lived on Little Coharie River. They soon opened the East Carolina Indian School at Clinton. Indians in Halifax and Warren Counties asserted their Saponi and Tuscarora identity and created the Haliwa-Saponi tribe. The Waccamaw Siouans arose in Columbus County. The Person County Indians retook the name "Sappony," while the Occaneechis reorganized from Indian communities in Alamance, Caswell, and

5. Likely Waccamaw Siouan families and children outside the Waccamaw Siouan School in Columbus County, North Carolina, c. 1920s. Native schools like this one existed in Native enclaves after the land reserves had been sold off. Courtesy of the State Archives of North Carolina, Raleigh.

Orange Counties. The Meherrins, from their enclave in Hertford County, reorganized their government. All these groups eventually became recognized as Indians by the state of North Carolina and have seats on the North Carolina Commission of Indian Affairs, created in 1971.[84] Other Indian communities, at least at this time, are still fighting for state recognition, such as Tuscaroras in Bertie and Robeson Counties, Chowans in the Albemarle, and Machapungas out near Lake Mattamuskeet. It is strange that other than the Meherrins, none of the tributary Indian nations of eastern North Carolina that survived the Tuscarora War and once possessed extensive land reserves—the Tuscaroras, Machapungas, Chowans, Hatteras, Yeopims, and Cores—have reappeared or are recognized as Indian peoples by the state of North Carolina in the early twenty-first century. That may change in the future.

Unfortunately, those Indians recognized by the state of North Carolina, other than the Cherokees, are not recognized as Indians or as Indian tribes by the federal government's Bureau of Indian Affairs. Even the Lumbees, who were recognized as Indians by the federal government in 1956, were not recognized as an Indian *tribe* or *nation* and so were expressly prohibited from receiving any of the benefits that federally recognized Indian tribes might receive from the Bureau of Indian Affairs. The reason for this nonrecognition was that these eastern North Carolina Indians became associated with People of Color, and so in the eyes of White Americans and the US government they lost their Indian identity. Of course, we have seen where this falsehood came about, but it is carried on to this day when skin color negates Indianness, kinship, sense of place, and history.[85]

Despite all the work of the colonization process—the abuses, the Indian slave trade, the military conquest, enclosure on ever-shrinking reserves, the wiping out of Indianness by declaring Indians to be People of Color—Indians returned to eastern North Carolina. In reality, they had never left.

Conclusion

The one-two punch of the colonization process and race-based chattel slavery just about erased the Indians of eastern North Carolina. Just about, and it was close, but not quite.

From the English point of view, the colonization process in North Carolina worked as it was supposed to and all too well. Despite early setbacks at Roanoke Island in the 1580s, by the latter decades of the seventeenth century, England had taken possession of the land, chartered a colony, set up a colonial government, attracted settlers, and established a meager but functioning economy. Now it had to begin the process of turning the Native peoples who lived there into tributaries, which would open up more land for more settlers and, it hoped, more profitable opportunities.

Though the Tuscarora War of 1711–15 cost the English many lives and much treasure, it also smashed Indian power in eastern North Carolina and opened settlement south to the Cape Fear River and west to the Piedmont. Hundreds of Native peoples were killed, hundreds more enslaved and marched off to the Charles Town slave markets, and just as many displaced and seeking refuge wherever they could. Those Indian nations that survived the war—the Tuscaroras, Meherrins, Chowans, Hatteras, Cores, Yeopims, and Machapungas—signed treaties with the colony in which they submitted themselves as tributary-paying vassals and were assigned land reserves where they were to live as they wanted but within the confines of English and colonial law.

The Tuscarora War sobered the colonial authorities, while the destruction the war brought speared an icicle of fear into their hearts.

For decades after the war, North Carolina authorities worried that if they pushed their tributaries too far, then the tributaries might join with the Senecas and go on another rampage. So during those first postwar decades, colonial authorities were most attentive to the complaints of their tributary Indians. They tried to give them justice and protect them from settler abuses, even providing food and goods during hard times. Tributaries such as King Tom Blount knew his rights and worked them well. He could go before the powerful Governor's Council, be heard by it, and usually get favorable results. By 1750, one would say that in eastern North Carolina the colonization process was humming along at top performance. The Indians had been conquered, turned into tributaries, and assigned lands, so they became reliable allies who caused little trouble to the colony. This is what Richard Hakluyt and other early proponents of English colonization had envisioned for Indigenous peoples. Though conquered, at least they were still seen as Indians. However, the one thing of value these tributaries had, their land reserves, caught the eye of settlers. Poverty-stricken, these Indians gradually sold off their reserves until all lands were gone, and they were landless. Indians without Indian lands became something else in the eyes of the colonial and state government and in the eyes of their White neighbors as well.

Then came the other punch in the form of race-based slavery. A multitude of sins have been attributed to slavery, and it has deserved each accusation and more. One more evil it spawned was what it did to the Native peoples of eastern North Carolina. Indians were the first peoples enslaved by Europeans in the Americas. The Spanish, French, and English all practiced Indian slavery, and in the English colonies South Carolina made a business of it by arming its Indian allies and then turning them loose on other Indians across the Southeast. In North Carolina, the deadly and incessant slave raids proved one of the causes of the Tuscarora War, which in turn led to the conquest of the Indians of eastern North Carolina, who now became colonial tributaries. For the first half of the eighteenth century, enslaved Indians were a common sight on North Carolina plantations and farms.

However, enslaved Indians could not provide enough of the workforce White planters wanted, so the planters turned to enslaved Africans. It was not long before enslaved Indians and enslaved Africans met on these farms and plantations, had intimate relations, and produced children. Similarly, as the African and African Carolinian population swelled in eastern North Carolina, tributary Indians on their land reserves also met, interacted with, and made their own relations with Africans, producing Indian-African children. Some Indians had relationships with local White people and birthed Indian-White children. African, African Carolinian, and Native men had intimate relations with White women as well, often indentured servants, and created children with them, much to the consternation of the colonial government, which tried to prohibit these "interracial" sexual relationships and the children they produced. Officials became very interested in these children of difference "races," as they thought of them back then. Everyone in North Carolina and the South as a whole found themselves categorized as White or Black or Indian, and their "mixed-race" children were labeled "mustees" and "mulattos."

By the latter decades of the eighteenth century, as Indian numbers dwindled and the Black population and White supremacy increased, eastern North Carolina became a two-skin-color region, White and Black. Anyone not considered White was labeled a Person of Color, which included not only Black people and "mixed-race" mustees and mulattos but also Indians. As Indians and Africans cohabitated, had intimate relations, and produced children, these children increasingly came to be seen as People of Color, not Indian. Compounding this trend was that by the end of the eighteenth century most tributary Indian land reserves had been sold off. As settlers and North Carolina officials saw the situation, Indians without Indian lands were not Indians anymore but People of Color. By 1835, when North Carolina revised its constitution, it considered there were no more Indians in the state, except for a few Cherokees out in the distant mountains, many of whom would be dealt with by the Trail of Tears three years later. Aside from White people and the enslaved, there were only "free negros, free mulattos, or free persons of mixed blood," none of whom could now vote or carry weapons without a permit.[1] So not only did the institution of slavery enslave North Carolina Indians, it also tried to erase them as Indians.

This type of erasure has sometimes been referred to as "paper genocide" or "documentary genocide," where a people's ethnicity gets erased by county clerks or other state officials who decide what "race" someone is. As we saw with the Chowan Bennetts and Robbins and the Machapunga Mackeys and Longtoms, their ethnicity was up to memory, opinion, and the judgment of others. With the only two categories being White and People of Color, officials now deemed Indians extinct in the eastern part of the Old North State as they had no more Indian land reserves and no more Indian governments. For a while, Indians became part of the history of the People of Color of North Carolina and the South, with all the good and the bad that entailed, including the slave South, the Civil War, Reconstruction, and then the coming of the Jim Crow laws, segregation, and severe discrimination.

If North Carolina Indian history had ended in 1835, then one would have to agree that the colonization process that the English had set in motion back in the 1580s was a resounding success and then some. Indians had been conquered, became loyal tributaries and military allies, lost their lands, and were eventually either killed off or their Indian identity erased. Of course, just declaring someone not to be an Indian anymore and only recognizing them as Black or as a Person of Color did not mean they were not actually Indian. By the late 1700s and early 1800s, there were plenty of Native people in eastern North Carolina, but the state saw them as People of Color. That's where North Carolina differs from the colonial experience in more northerly colonies, though the latter had their racial issues as well. The coming of African slavery to the colony and the ability of North Carolina to erase "Indians" and redefine them as "People of Color" with the same lack of civil and political rights as African Americans was one of the most nefarious and far-reaching effects of the colonization process on Native peoples.

Here was a perhaps unarticulated consequence of the colonization process: not just the disappearance of Indians but also an identity genocide in which a person's Indian identity was erased, and in the mind of the state and its White residents it was replaced with a Black or African American identity. The state, not the Indians themselves, declared who was Indian and who was not. Skin color became the marker between "White" and "Black," whether one had political and civil rights or not, and often whether one was slave or free.[2] So while the state might say there were no Indians in eastern North Carolina, as we have seen, that was not true. In truth, North Carolina's nineteenth-century biracial society was just too narrow to hold Indians in.

By the 1880s, North Carolina had to recognize that Indians had not disappeared in eastern North Carolina but had been there all along and were making a resurgence. They fought against the loss of their Indian identity, but it was only when their voices grew loud enough and the evidence overwhelming that the state of North Carolina began to change its policy and again recognize them as Indians. Convincing the federal government and their White neighbors that Indianness does not rest on skin color is still a work in progress. One of the greatest tricks played by North Carolina authorities was convincing people that Indians had ceased to exist. In the end, the colonization process, as lethal as it was, was not wholly successful because Indian peoples remain in eastern North Carolina to this day.

Notes

Bibliography

Index

Notes

Abbreviations

CCR	Colonial Court Records, State Archives of North Carolina, Raleigh
CRNC	*Colonial Records of North Carolina*
CRNC2	*Colonial Records of North Carolina*, Second Series
GASR	General Assembly Session Records, State Archives of North Carolina, Raleigh
NCHGR	*North Carolina Historical and Genealogical Register*
SPG	Society for the Propagation of the Gospel in Foreign Parts

Introduction

1. Michael Leroy Oberg, *Dominion & Civility: English Imperialism & Native America, 1585–1685* (Ithaca, NY: Cornell Univ. Press, 1999), 16–18.

2. Wesley Frank Craven, *The Southern Colonies in the Seventeenth Century, 1607–1689* (Baton Rouge: Louisiana State Univ. Press, 1949), 361. See also W. Stitt Robinson, "Tributary Indians in Colonial Virginia," *Virginia Magazine of History and Biography* 67 (Jan. 1959): 56–57; Verner W. Crane, *The Southern Frontier, 1670–1732* (New York: Norton, 1981), 162–65. More nuanced are Helen C. Rountree, *Pocahontas's People: The Powhatan Indians of Virginia through Four Centuries* (Norman: Univ. of Oklahoma Press, 1990), 91–94, and Frederic W. Gleach, *Powhatan's World and Colonial Virginia: A Conflict of Cultures* (Lincoln: Univ. of Nebraska Press, 1997), 184–85, 196–97, both of which see tributary status as an attempt to protect Indians while at the same time make them toe the English line.

3. Francis Jennings, *The Invasion of America: Indians, Colonialism, and the Cant of Conquest* (New York: Norton, 1975), 123–25; Kristalyn Marie Shefveland, *Anglo–Native Virginia: Trade, Conversion, and Indian Slavery in the Old Dominion, 1646–1722* (Athens: Univ. of Georgia Press, 2016), 4, 6; J. Leitch Wright, *Only Land They Knew: The Tragic Story of the American Indians in the*

Old South (New York: Free Press, 1981), 92–93, 225–26; Aziz Rana, *The Two Faces of American Freedom* (Cambridge, MA: Harvard Univ. Press, 2010), 32–34.

4. Michelle LeMaster, "In the 'Scolding Houses': Indians and the Law in Eastern North Carolina, 1684–1760," *North Carolina Historical Review* 83 (Apr. 2006): 193–232; Bradley J. Dixon, "'His one Netev ples': The Chowans and the Politics of Native Petitions in the Colonial South," *William and Mary Quarterly*, 3rd Series, 76 (Jan. 2019): 41–74; James H. Merrell, *Indians' New World: Catawbas and Their Neighbors from European Contact through the Era of Removal* (New York: Norton, 1989), 157–60; Jenny Hale Pulsipher, *Subjects unto the Same King: Indians, English, and the Contest for Authority in Colonial New England* (Philadelphia: Univ. of Pennsylvania Press, 2005), 19–20, 30–33, 35; Kristofer Ray, "Constructing a Discourse of Indigenous Slavery, Freedom and Sovereignty in Anglo-Virginia, 1600–1750," *Native South* 10 (2017): 28.

5. Martha W. McCartney, "Cockacoeske, Queen of Pamunkey: Diplomat and Suzeraine," in *Powhatan's Mantle: Indians in the Colonial Southeast,* ed. Peter H. Wood, Gregory A. Waselkov, and M. Thomas Hatley (Lincoln: Univ. of Nebraska Press, 1989), 173–95; Merrell, *Indians' New World*, 139–42, 157.

6. Oberg, *Dominion & Civility*, 91 (quote); Chapman J. Milling, *Red Carolinians* (1940; reprint, Columbia: Univ. of South Carolina Press, 1969), 60, 228; Yasu Kawashima, "Legal Origins of the Indian Reservation in Colonial Massachusetts," *American Journal of Legal History* 13 (Jan. 1969): 43–44; Rountree, *Pocahontas's People*, 91–92; Arwin D. Smallwood, "A History of Three Cultures: Indian Woods, North Carolina, 1585 to 1995," PhD diss., Ohio State Univ., 1997; George Stevenson Jr., "Indian Reservations in North Carolina," *Carolina Comments* 57 (Jan. 2009): 26–31.

7. Richard White, *The Middle Ground: Indians, Empires, and Republics in the Great Lakes Region, 1650–1815* (Cambridge: Cambridge Univ. Press, 1991).

8. Kathleen DuVal, *The Native Ground: Indians and Colonists in the Heart of the Continent* (Philadelphia: Univ. of Pennsylvania Press, 2006), 5.

9. Winthrop D. Jordan, *White over Black: American Attitudes toward the Negro, 1550–1812* (Chapel Hill: Univ. of North Carolina Press, 1968), 90.

10. Henry F. Dobyns, *Their Number Become Thinned: Native American Population Dynamics in Eastern North America* (Knoxville: Univ. of Tennessee Press, 1983), 42.

11. Timothy Silver, *A New Face on the Countryside: Indians, Colonists, and Slaves in South Atlantic Forests, 1500–1800* (New York: Cambridge Univ. Press, 1990), 38–29; Robbie Ethridge, *From Chicaza to Chickasaw: The European Invasion and the Transformation of the Mississippian World, 1540–1715* (Chapel Hill: Univ. of North Carolina Press, 2010), 159.

12. Jack D. Forbes, *Black Africans and Native Americans: Color, Race, and Caste in the Evolution of Red–Black Peoples* (New York: Blackwell, 1988), 190–92, 199.

13. *Return of the Whole Number of Persons with the Several Districts of the United States*, US Census, 1800, Dec. 8, 1801, at www2.census.gov/library/publications/decennial/1800/1800-returns.pdf; Forbes, *Black Africans and Native Americans*, 198–99.

14. James H. Merrell, "The Racial Education of the Catawba Indians," *Journal of Southern History* 50 (Aug. 1984): 363–84; William G. McLoughlin, "Red Indians, Black Slavery and White Racism: America's Slaveholding Indians," *American Quarterly* 26 (Oct. 1974): 367–85; Gary B. Nash, *Red, White and Black: The Peoples of Early America* (Englewood Cliffs, NJ: Prentice-Hall, 1974), 290–97; Claudio Saunt, *Black, White, and Indian: Race and the Unmaking of an American Family* (Oxford: Oxford Univ. Press, 2005); Christina Snyder, *Slavery in Indian Country: The Changing Face of Captivity in Early America* (Cambridge, MA: Harvard Univ. Press, 2012), 122–23; Gerald M. Sider, *Lumbee Indian Histories: Race, Ethnicity, and Indian Identity in the Southern United States* (Cambridge: Cambridge Univ. Press, 1993), 177–79; Arica L. Coleman, *That the Blood Stay Pure: African Americans, Native Americans, and the Predicament of Race and Identity in Virginia* (Bloomington: Indiana Univ. Press, 2013).

15. Daniel H. Usner Jr., *Indians, Settlers, & Slaves in a Frontier Exchange Economy: The Lower Mississippi Valley before 1783* (Chapel Hill: Univ. of North Carolina Press, 1992); Arwin D. Smallwood, "A History of Native American and African Relations from 1502 to 1900," *Negro History Bulletin* 62 (Apr.–Sept. 1999): 22; Tiya Miles, "Native Americans and African Americans," in *The New Encyclopedia of Southern Culture*, vol. 24: *Race*, ed. Thomas C. Holt, Laurie C. Green, and Charles Reagan Wilson (Chapel Hill: Univ. of North Carolina Press, 2013), 114–16.

16. Malinda Maynor Lowery, "On the Antebellum Fringe: Lumbee Indians, Slavery, and Removal," *Native South* 10 (2017): 43; Coleman, *That the Blood Stay Pure*, xvi, 53, 66.

17. Warren Eugene Milteer Jr., "From Indians to Colored People: The Problem of Racial Categories and the Persistence of the Chowans in North Carolina," *North Carolina Historical Review* 93 (Jan. 2016): 28–57; Patrick H. Garrow, *The Mattamuskeet Documents: A Study in Social History* (Raleigh: North Carolina Department of Cultural Resources, 1975); Jeremiah James Nowell Jr., "Red, White, and Black: Race Formation and the Politics of American Indian Recognition in North Carolina," PhD diss., Univ. of North Carolina, Chapel Hill, 2000; Forest Hazel, "Looking for Indian Town: The Dispersal of the Chowan Indian Tribe in Eastern North Carolina, 1780–1915," *North Carolina Archaeology* 63 (Oct. 2014):

34–64: Gregory Ablavsky, "Making Indians 'White': The Judicial Abolition of Native Slavery in Revolutionary Virginia and Its Racial Legacy," *University of Pennsylvania Law Review* 159 (Apr. 2011): 1520–22; Daniel R. Mandell, *Behind the Frontier: Indians in Eighteenth-Century Eastern Massachusetts* (Lincoln: Univ. of Nebraska Press, 1996), 182–96; Coleman, *That the Blood Stay Pure*, 1–10.

18. Snyder, *Slavery in Indian Country*, 8 (quote); Malinda Maynor Lowery, *Lumbee Indians in the Jim Crow South: Race, Identity, & the Making of a Nation* (Chapel Hill: Univ. of North Carolina Press, 2010), 12.

19. Malinda Maynor Lowery, *The Lumbee Indians: An American Struggle* (Chapel Hill: Univ. of North Carolina Press, 2018), 6–7, 42–45.

20. Usner, *Indians, Settlers, & Slaves*, 1–2.

21. Though the concept of "race" has long been discredited, for the people of eighteenth- and nineteenth-century North Carolina it was real. As they saw it, "White" people possessed certain immutable characteristics, and "Black" people did as well. Since "White" and "Black" became common designations during the period covered by this book, I have capitalized both, as is standard procedure now. I use "Indian," "Native American," and "Native people" interchangeably but have tried to use Indian national names—Tuscarora, Machapunga, and so on—when I need to be very specific. "African," "African Carolinian," and "African American" are also used, along with "Black," "Person of Color," and "People of Color," which were official designations during the period discussed. Readers will also find that I provide personal names of people whenever possible, such as the names of Indians who sold away land and who bought the land. In a few instances, there might be a long list of names because I believe providing the names of these historical players to be a help to Indians, African Americans, and White people in this local area to find their ancestors. For many Indians of eastern North Carolina, the Indian resurgence over the past century is still a work in progress, and finding ancestors is an integral part of it. I am glad to provide any help I can for these Native peoples of eastern North Carolina to reassert or reclaim their Indian identity.

1. Of Vassal States and the Colonization Process

1. Lawrence C. Wroth, *The Voyages of Giovanni da Verrazzano, 1524–1528* (New Haven, CT: Yale Univ. Press, 1970), 134.

2. Wroth, *Voyages of Giovanni da Verrazzano*, 136.

3. Arthur Barlowe, "Arthur Barlowe's Narrative of the 1584 Voyage," in *The First Colonists: Documents on the Planting of the First English Settlements in North America, 1584–1590*, ed. David B. Quinn and Alison M. Quinn (Raleigh: North Carolina Department of Cultural Resources, 1982), 2.

4. Melissa Darby, *Thunder Go North: The Hunt for Sir Francis Drake's Fair & Good Bay* (Salt Lake City: Univ. of Utah Press, 2019), 29.

5. Thomas Harriot, "A Briefe and True Report of the New Found Land of Virginia (1588)," in *First Colonists*, ed. Quinn and Quinn, 73.

6. Jennings, *Invasion of America*, 105.

7. Cecil Jane and E. G. R. Taylor, "Third Voyage of Columbus Carta," in *Select Documents Illustrating the Four Voyages of Columbus*, 2 vols. (London: Hakluyt Society, 1929–32), 2:66; Stephen Greenblatt, *Marvelous Possessions: The Wonder of the New World* (Chicago: Univ. of Chicago Press, 1991), 52–54, 56–57, 77, 167 n. 6; John H. Elliott, "The Seizure of Overseas Territories by European Powers," in *Theories of Empire, 1450–1800*, ed. David Armitage (Aldershot, UK: Ashgate, 1998), 140; Robinson, "Tributary Indians in Colonial Virginia," 50.

8. "Doctrine of Discovery, 1493," Gilder Lehrman Institute of American History, at https://www.gilderlehrman.org/history-by-era/imperial-rivalries/resources/doctrine-discovery-1493; Anthony Pagden, "Dispossessing the Barbarian: The Language of Spanish Thomism and the Debate over the Property Rights of American Indians," in *Theories of Empire*, ed. Armitage, 159–61, 167; Greenblatt, *Marvelous Possessions*, 61–62.

9. Richard Hakluyt, "Letters Patents of King Henry the Seventh granted unto John Cabot and his three sonnes, Lewis, Sebastian, and Sancius for the discoverie of new and unknown lands. March 1496," in *Hakluyt's Voyages: The Principal Voyages, Traffiques & Discoveries of the English Nation*, ed. Irwin R. Blacker (New York: Viking Press, 1965), 17–18.

10. Richard Hakluyt, "Second Voyage of Master Martin Frobisher, made to the West and Northwest Regions in the yeere 1577, with a description of the country and people. Written by Master Dionise Settle," in *Hakluyt's Voyages*, ed. Blacker, 187–88.

11. Richard Hakluyt, "The Letters Patents granted by her Majestie to Sir Humfrey Gilbert knight, for the inhabiting and planting of our people in America. June 11, 1578," in *Hakluyt's Voyages*, ed. Blacker, 210.

12. R. F. Foster, *The Oxford History of Ireland* (Oxford: Oxford Univ. Press, 1989), 46–48, 52–53 (quote), 75; Steven G. Ellis, *Ireland in the Age of the Tudors 1447–1603: English Expansion and the End of Gaelic Rule* (London: Addison Wesley Longman, 1998), 22–24.

13. Ellis, *Ireland in the Age of Tudors*, 15, 281–82; Karen Ordahl Kupperman, *Roanoke: The Abandoned Colony* (Lanham, MD: Rowman & Littlefield, 1984), 11–12.

14. Richard Hakluyt, *Discourse of Western Planting, 1584*, in *The Original Writings & Correspondence of the Two Richard Hakluyts*, ed. E. G. R. Taylor

(London: Hakluyt Society, 1933), 211–13, 317, 319; Kupperman, *Roanoke*, 28–34; Oberg, *Dominion & Civility*, 18–22.

15. Hakluyt, *Discourse of Western Planting*, 211–13, quote on 213; Kupperman, *Roanoke*, 28–34; Seth Mallios, *The Deadly Politics of Giving: Exchange and Violence at Ajacan, Roanoke, and Jamestown* (Tuscaloosa: Univ. of Alabama Press, 2006), 62.

16. Gary B. Nash, "The Image of the Indian in the Southern Colonial Mind," *William and Mary Quarterly* 29 (Apr. 1972): 198–204; Karen Ordahl Kupperman, "English Perception of Treachery, 1583–1640: The Case of the American Savages," *Historical Journal* 20 (June 1977): 264–68.

17. Barlowe, "Arthur Barlowe's Narrative," 10; Ralph Lane, "Narrative of the Settlement of Roanoke Island, 1585–1586," in *First Colonists*, ed. Quinn and Quinn, 29–36; Lee Miller, *Roanoke: Solving the Mystery of the Lost Colony* (New York: Penguin, 2000), 271–72; "Journal of the 1585 Virginia Voyage," in *First Colonists*, ed. Quinn and Quinn, 18; Thomas C. Parramore, "The 'Lost Colony' Found: A Documentary Perspective," *North Carolina Historical Review* 78 (Jan. 2001): 77; Peter H. Wood, "The Changing Population of the Colonial South: An Overview by Race and Region, 1685–1790," in *Powhatan's Mantle*, ed. Wood, Waselkov, and Hatley, 43–51; Brandon Fullam, *Manteo and the Algonquians of the Roanoke Voyages* (Jefferson, NC: McFarland, 2020), 133–38; Helen G. Rountree, with Wesley D. Taukchiray, *Manteo's World: Native American Life in Carolina's Sound Country before and after the Lost Colony* (Chapel Hill: Univ. of North Carolina Press, 2021), 118–42.

18. Harriot, "A Briefe and True Report," 67.

19. Stephen R. Potter, *Commoners, Tribute, and Chiefs: The Development of Algonquian Culture in the Potomac Valley* (Charlottesville: Univ. Press of Virginia, 1993), 17–18; Mallios, *The Deadly Politics of Giving*, 12, 17–18; Kim Sloan, *A New World: England's First View of America* (Chapel Hill: Univ. of North Carolina Press, 2007), 121, 123, 131, 139; Robinson, "Tributary Indians in Colonial Virginia," 53.

20. Barlowe, "Arthur Barlowe's Narrative," 4.

21. Barlowe, "Arthur Barlowe's Narrative," 4.

22. Barlowe, "Arthur Barlowe's Narrative," 8.

23. Sloan, *A New World*, 85; Lowery, *Lumbee Indians*, 6; Fullam, *Manteo*, 162–63.

24. Barlowe, "Arthur Barlowe's Narrative," 6.

25. Barlowe, "Arthur Barlowe's Narrative," 4.

26. Barlowe, "Arthur Barlowe's Narrative," 4–12.

27. Lane, "Narrative"; Michael Leroy Oberg, "Gods and Men: The Meeting of Indian and White Worlds on the Carolina Outer Banks, 1584–1586," *North*

Carolina Historical Review 77 (Oct. 1999): 367–90; Kupperman, *Roanoke*, 82–84.

28. Fullam, *Manteo*, 131.

29. Lane, "Narrative," 29–31, 35, 36 (quote); Fullam, *Manteo*, 143.

30. Lane, "Narrative," 39; Mallios, *Deadly Politics of Giving*, 66–73; Michael Leroy Oberg, *The Head in Edward Nugent's Hand: Roanoke's Forgotten Indians* (Philadelphia: Univ. of Pennsylvania Press, 2008), 80–100.

31. Lane, "Narrative," 40–45.

32. John White, "John White's Narrative of the 1587 Virginia Voyage," in *First Colonists*, ed. Quinn and Quinn, 102.

33. Fullam, *Manteo*, 50.

34. Oberg, *Head in Edward Nugent's Hand*, 120–21.

35. White, "John White's Narrative of the 1587 Virginia Voyage"; John White, "John White's Narrative of the 1590 Virginia Voyage," in *First Colonists*, ed. Quinn and Quinn, 117–30. For some of the best works on England's Roanoke expeditions and their effect on the Indian peoples of the area, see David Beers Quinn, *Set Fair for Roanoke: Voyages and Colonies, 1584–1606* (Chapel Hill: Univ. of North Carolina Press, 1985); Oberg, *Head in Edward Nugent's Hand*; Kupperman, *Roanoke*; Miller, *Roanoke*; and Fullam, *Manteo*.

36. John Smith, *The Generall History of Virginia, the Somer Iles, and New England, with the Names of the Adventurers and Their Adventures* (1624), vol. 2 of *The Complete Works of John Smith*, 3 vols., ed. Philip L. Barbour (Chapel Hill: Univ. of North Carolina Press, 1986), 193, 215; John Lawson, *A New Voyage to Carolina* (1709), ed. Hugh Talmage Lefler (Chapel Hill: Univ. of North Carolina, 1967), 69.

37. Sloan, *A New World*.

38. Mr. Francis Yardley to John Farrar, Esq., May 8, 1654, in *Colonial Records of North Carolina*, 26 vols., ed. William L. Saunders (1886; reprint, Wilmington, NC: Broadfoot, 1993), 1:18, hereafter cited as *CRNC*.

39. Gov. Yardley report, 1655, Nathaniel Batts Papers, PC 1293.1, State Archives of North Carolina, Raleigh; W. P. Cumming, "The Earliest Permanent Settlement in Carolina: Nathaniel Batts and the Comberford Map," *American Historical Review* 45 (Oct. 1939): 83–87.

40. Deed of sale of land from Kilcacenen to George Durant, Mar. 1, 1661, in *CRNC*, 1:19.

41. Fundamental Constitutions of Carolina, drawn up by John Locke, Mar. 1, 1669, in *CRNC*, 1:187–205.

42. Fundamental Constitutions, in *CRNC*, 1:204 (quote), 202.

43. Fundamental Constitutions, in *CRNC*, 1:202.

44. Fundamental Constitutions, in *CRNC*, 1:204.

45. "Instructions given by us the Lords Proprietors of Carolina unto the Governor and Councill of that Parte of Our Province called Albemarle," Nov. 21, 1676, in *CRNC*, 1:230–31.

46. Nash, "The Image of the Indian," 208–10; LeMaster, "In the 'Scolding Houses,'" 201–2, 212–13; Robinson, "Tributary Indians in Colonial Virginia," 53–54.

47. *William Powell, The Proprietors of Carolina* (1963; reprint, Raleigh: North Carolina Department of Archives and History, 1968), 3, 4, 10; Hugh T. Lefler and William S. Powell, *Colonial North Carolina: A History* (New York: Scribner's, 1973), 32–33.

2. Resistance and Conquest in North Carolina

1. Jonathan Edward Barth, "'The Sinke of America': Society in the Albemarle Borderlands of North Carolina, 1663–1729," *North Carolina Historical Review* 87 (Jan. 2010): 12.

2. Noleen McIlvenna, *A Very Mutinous People: The Struggle for North Carolina, 1660–1713* (Chapel Hill, NC: Univ. of Chapel Hill Press, 2009), 14, 46–70; Barth, "'The Sinke of America'"; Kirsten Fischer, *Suspect Relations: Sex, Race, and Resistance in Colonial North Carolina* (Ithaca, NY: Cornell Univ. Press, 2002), 24–29; Robert Earle Moody, "Massachusetts Trade with Carolina, 1686–1709," *North Carolina Historical Review* 20 (Jan.–Oct. 1943): 44.

3. James D. Rice, *Tales from a Revolution: Bacon's Rebellion and the Transformation of Early America* (Oxford: Oxford Univ. Press, 2012), 3–18.

4. Rice, *Tales from a Revolution*, 42–43, 46–48, 100, 123–24; Shannon Lee Dawdy, "The Meherrin's Secret History of the Dividing Line," *North Carolina Historical Review* 72 (Oct. 1995): 394.

5. "Treaty between Virginia and the Indians, 1677, in the Virginia Colonial Records," *Virginia Magazine of History and Biography* 14 (Jan. 1907): 280–96; Rountree, *Pocahontas's People*, 87, 100–101; Michael J. Puglisi, "'Whether They Be Friends or Foes': The Roles and Reactions of Tributary Native Groups Caught in Colonial Conflicts," *International Social Science Review* 70 (1995): 76–77.

6. Barth, "'Sinke of America'"; McIlvenna, *Very Mutinous People*, 46–70.

7. Representation to the Lords Proprietor, c. 1679, in *CRNC*, 1:260; introduction to *Colonial Records of North Carolina*, Second Series, 10 vols., ed. William S. Price, Jr. (1968; reprint, Raleigh: North Carolina Department of Cultural Resources, Division of Archives, 1974), 5:x, hereafter cited as *CRNC2*; Alan D. Watson, *Society in Colonial North Carolina* (Raleigh: North Carolina Department of Cultural Resources, 1996), 3; Jeffrey J. Crow, Paul D. Escott, and Flora J. Hatley, *A History of African Americans in North Carolina* (Raleigh: North Carolina Department of Cultural Resources, 1992), 3.

8. Lars C. Adams, "'Sundry Murders and Depredations': A Closer Look at the Chowan River War, 1676–1677," *North Carolina Historical Review* 90 (Apr. 2013): 149–53, 153 n. 12, 158–65, 170; Stevenson, "Indian Reservations in North Carolina," 27–28; Lawrence E. Lee, *Indian Wars of North Carolina, 1663–1763* (1963; reprint, Raleigh: North Carolina Division of Archives and History, 1997), 16; Affidavit of Thos. Miller, Jan. 31, 1679, in *CRNC*, 1:278; Letters to the Virginia Council, June 17, 1707, in *CRNC*, 1:658.

9. Dixon, "'His one Netev ples,'" 45, 58.

10. Council Minutes, Nov. 28, 1694, in *CRNC*, 1:43; Petition of Benjamin Blanchard et al., Mar. 28, 1702, Colonial Court Records (CCR) 192, Indians—Treaties, Petitions, Agreements, and Court Cases, Miscellaneous Papers, State Archives of North Carolina, Raleigh; "Letter from Wm. Duckenfield Relating to Indian Depredations," c. 1696, in *North Carolina Historical and Genealogical Register*, 3 vols., ed. J. R. B. Hathaway (Edenton, NC: n.p., 1900–1903), 3 (Jan. 1903): 64, hereafter cited as *NCHGR*; Adams, "'Sundry Murders,'" 161, 169–71.

11. Stephanie Gamble, "A Community of Convenience: The Saponi Nation, Governor Spotswood, and the Experiment at Fort Christianna, 1670–1740," *Native South* 6 (2013): 74–75; Rice, *Tales from a Revolution*, 47–48; Douglas L. Rights, "The Trading Path to the Indians," *North Carolina Historical Review* 8 (Oct. 1931): 418–19, 420, 422; Miller, *Roanoke*, 259–60; Lawson, *New Voyage to Carolina*, 63; Nowell, "Red, White and Black," 25–26, 30–38; Ethridge, *From Chicaza to Chickasaw*, 103–4; Lesley M. Graybeal, "'Too Light to Be Black, Too Dark to Be White': Redefining Occaneechi Identity through Community Education," *Native South* 5 (2012): 98–99.

12. Gamble, "Community of Convenience," 72–73, 75–76; Rights, "Trading Path," 414, 422; "Treaty between Virginia and the Indians, 1677"; Ethridge, *From Chicaza to Chickasaw*, 103.

13. "Treaty between Virginia and the Indians, 1677."

14. Dawdy, "Meherrin's Secret History," 388–89, 394–96; "The Roanoke-Chowan Story," *Daily Roanoke-Chowan News*, 1960–62, F. Roy Johnson Papers, PC 367.1, oversize, State Archives of North Carolina.

15. Letter to the Virginia Council, June 17, 1703, in *CRNC*, 1:657–60; Minutes of the Council of Virginia, Apr. 28, 1703, in *CRNC*, 1:570; Dawdy, "Meherrin's Secret History," 399–401; Stevenson, "Indian Reservations," 28.

16. Letter to the Virginia Council, June 17, 1707, in *CRNC*, 1:658–59 (quotes); Upon Petition of the Meherrin Indyans, Nov. 2, 1706, in *CRNC2* 7:7; Letter from Thomas Garrett, in *NCHGR* 2 (Jan. 1901): 110–11; Dawdy, "Meherrin's Secret History," 388; Stevenson, "Indian Reservations," 28.

17. Christoph Von Graffenried, *Christoph Von Graffenried's Account of the Founding of New Bern: Edited with an Historical Introduction and an English*

Translation, ed. Vincent H. Todd (Raleigh, NC: Edwards & Broughton for the North Carolina Historical Commission, 1920), 78–79; Virginia: Journal of the Council, Sept. 2, 1707, in *CRNC*, 1:667; McIlvenna, *Very Mutinous People*, 121–26; Louis P. Towles, "Cary's Rebellion and the Emergence of Thomas Pollock," *Journal of the Association of Historians of North Carolina* 4 (Fall 1996): 52.

18. Virginia: Journal of the Council, Sept. 15, 1707, in *CRNC*, 1:670–71.

19. Virginia: Journal of the Council, Feb. 6, 1711, in *CRNC*, 1:754–55; Council Journal, Oct. 27, 1726, in *CRNC*, 2:640; Dawdy, "Meherrin's Secret History," 404.

20. Rountree, with Taukchiray, *Manteo's World*, 122, 131–35.

21. Rountree, with Taukchiray, *Manteo's World*, 122, 126; Lawson, *New Voyage to Carolina*, 242.

22. Garrow, *Mattamuskeet Documents*, 4–5, 14–18; Lawson, *New Voyage to Carolina*, 209, 219; Charles H. Holloman, "Tuscarora Towns in Bath County," *We the People: Official Publication of the North Carolina Citizens Association* 23 (Feb. 1966): 30; Francis La Jau, *The Carolina Chronicle of Dr. Francis La Jau, 1706–1717*, ed. Frank J. Klingberg (Berkeley: Univ. of California Press, 1956), 175–76; Rev. Francis La Jau to Secretary, Society for the Propagation of the Gospel in Foreign Parts (SPG), Mar. 17, 1715–16, in *CRNC2*, 10:216.

23. Petition of Inhabitants of Matchapunga, c. 1703, in *NCHGR* 2 (Apr. 1901): 193.

24. John Lawson to Tobias Knight, Aug. 7, 1705, in *NCHGR* 3 (Apr. 1903): 266.

25. Agreement with the Bay River Indians, Sept. 23, 1699, CCR 192 (quote); Lawson, *New Voyage to Carolina*, 242–43; Address to the Governor and Council, Feb. 29, 1704, in *CRNC2*, 7:401–2.

26. John Powell to Your Honor (quote), Oct. 20, 1704, Miscellaneous Records, 1678–1737, 1:56, Microfilm C. 002 1001, Albemarle County Records, State Archives of North Carolina; John Lawson to Gov. Henderson Walker, June 23, 1701, CCR 192; Petition of Lyonell Reading et al., Feb. 29, 1704, CCR 192.

27. Robert Kingman to William Glover, Feb. 26, 1708, CCR 192 (quote); Lawson, *New Voyage to Carolina*, 233–40, 242–43; "Pamlico," in *Handbook of American Indians North of Mexico*, 2 vols., ed. Frederick Webb Hodge (Washington, DC: US Government Printing Office, 1910), 2:197; Rountree, with Taukchiray, *Manteo's World*, 125–26.

28. Baylus C. Brooks, "John Lawson's Indian Town on Hatteras Island, North Carolina," *North Carolina Historical Review* 91 (Apr. 2014): 181–84, 186; Gary S. Dunbar, "The Hatteras Indians of North Carolina," *Ethnohistory* 7 (Autumn 1960): 410–18; Lawson, *New Voyage to Carolina*, 69, 159, 242–43;

"Hatteras," in *Handbook of American Indians*, ed. Hodge, 1:537; Rountree, with Taukchiray, *Manteo's World*, 123–25.

29. Alonzo Thomas Dill Jr., "Eighteenth Century New Bern: A History of the Town and Craven County, 1700–1800," part 1, *North Carolina Historical Review* 22 (Jan. 1945): 5; "War Declared against the Core & Nynee Indians, 1703," in *NCHGR* 2 (Apr. 1901): 204.

30. William Gale to his Father, Aug. 5, 1703, in *CRNC*, 22:734–35.

31. Lawson, *New Voyage to Carolina*, 242–43.

32. Chancery Court, c. 1697, in *CRNC2*, 3:511–12; Holloman, "Tuscarora Towns," 16, 30; Lawson, *New Voyage to Carolina*, 174.

33. Chancery Court, c. 1697, in *CRNC2*, 3:511–12; Letter of Henderson Walker, Nov. 18, 1699, in *CRNC*, 1:517; "War Declared against the Core & Nynee Indians, 1703," *NCHGR* 2 (Apr. 1901): 204; Lee, *Indian Wars*, 19–20, 23; F. Roy Johnson, *The Tuscaroras: Mythology—Medicine—Culture*, 2 vols. (Murfreesboro, NC: Johnson, 1967), 2:56; Holloman, "Tuscarora Towns," 16, 30; Dill, "Eighteenth Century New Bern," part 1, 12, 14.

34. Lawson, *New Voyage to Carolina*, 242–43; Von Graffenried, *Christoph Von Graffenried's Account*, 374–75; "De Graffenried's Manuscript, Copied for *The Colonial Records of North Carolina* from the Original Mss. in the Public Library at Yverdon, Switzerland, and Translated by M. Du Four," in *CRNC*, 1:981–82.

35. David La Vere, *The Tuscarora War: Indians, Settlers, and the Fight for the Carolina Colony* (Chapel Hill: Univ. of North Carolina Press, 2013), 45.

36. Anthony F. C. Wallace, *Tuscarora: A History* (Albany: State Univ. of New York Press, 2012), 76–78.

37. Lawson, *New Voyage to Carolina*, 242; John E. Byrd and Charles L. Heath, "'The Country here is very thick of Indian Towns and Plantations . . .': Tuscarora Settlement Patterns as Revealed by the Contentnea Creek Survey," in *Indian and European Contact in Context: The Mid-Atlantic Region*, ed. Dennis B. Blanton and Julia A. King (Gainesville: Univ. of Florida Press, 2004), 104–7, 124–25; John E. Byrd and Charles L. Heath, *The Rediscovery of the Tuscarora Homeland: A Final Report of the Archaeological Survey of the Contentnea Creek Drainage, 1995–1997*, David S. Phelps Archaeology Laboratory, East Carolina Univ., Greenville, NC, report submitted to the National Park Service and the North Carolina Division of Archives and History, Raleigh, Greene County Surveys, no. 4153 (Raleigh: North Carolina Office of State Archaeology, 1997), 47–48; Smallwood, "A History of Three Cultures," 63; Wayne E. Lee, "Fortify, Fight or Flee: Tuscarora and Cherokee Defensive Warfare and Military Culture Adaptation," *Journal of Military History* 68 (July 2004): 724–26; La Vere, *Tuscarora War*, 31, 43; J. Bryan Grimes, "Some Notes on Colonial North Carolina, 1700–1750," *North Carolina*

Booklet 5 (Oct. 1905): 101–2; Charles L. Heath, "Woodland Period Mortuary Variability in the Lower Roanoke River Valley: Perspectives from the Jordan's Landing, Sans Souci and Dickerson Sites," research paper presented at the Sixtieth Annual Meeting of the Southeastern Archaeological Conference, Nov. 12–15, 2003, Charlotte, NC.

38. Lawson, *New Voyage to Carolina*, 42–43, 204–6; "De Graffenried's Manuscript," in *CRNC*, 1:978–79; Theda Perdue and Christopher Arris Oakley, *Native Carolinians: The Indians of North Carolina* (Raleigh: North Carolina Department of Cultural Resources, 2010), 22–24; Douglas W. Boyce, "Did a Tuscarora Confederacy Exist?," in *Four Centuries of Southern Indians*, ed. Charles M. Hudson (Athens: Univ. of Georgia Press, 1975), 34–36; Wallace, *Tuscarora*, 64–66; Charles Hudson, *Southeastern Indians* (Knoxville: Univ. of Tennessee Press, 1976), 223–24.

39. Wallace, *Tuscarora*, 66, 69–70, 76–78; Boyce, "Did a Tuscarora Confederacy Exist?," 30.

40. Boyce, "Did a Tuscarora Confederacy Exist?," 30, 34–36; Douglas W. Boyce, "Iroquoian Tribes of the Virginia–North Carolina Coastal Plain," in *Handbook of North American Indians*, vol. 15: *Northeast*, ed. Bruce G. Trigger (Washington, DC: Smithsonian Institution, 1978), 283; Wallace, *Tuscarora*, 66.

41. Lawson, *New Voyage to Carolina*, 217; William Byrd, *William Byrd's Histories of the Dividing Line betwixt Virginia and North Carolina*, ed. William K. Boyd (Raleigh: North Carolina Historical Commission, 1929), 274; Rountree, with Taukchiray, *Manteo's World*, 49; Theda Perdue, *Cherokee Women: Gender and Culture Change, 1700–1835* (Lincoln: Univ. of Nebraska Press, 1998), 70–71.

42. Lawson, *New Voyage to Carolina*, 233–40.

43. Merrell, "The Racial Education of the Catawba Indians"; Nowell, "Red, White and Black," 27; Jordan, *White over Black*, 276–82.

44. Lawson, *New Voyage to Carolina*, 18, 211–12; *Low Administrator v. Solley*, Mar. 27, 1716, in *CRNC2*, 5:92; Byrd, *William Byrd's Histories of the Dividing Line*, 116–18.

45. John Archdale, *A New Description of That Fertile and Pleasant Province of Carolina* (London: John Wyat, 1707), 8; Lawson, *New Voyage to Carolina*, 211–12, 232–33; House Minutes, Mar. 22, 1735, in *CRNC*, 4:45; Christian Feest, "North Carolina Algonquians," in *Handbook of North American Indians*, vol. 15: *Northeast*, ed. Trigger, 279.

46. Peter C. Mancall, *Deadly Medicine: Indians and Alcohol in Early America* (Ithaca, NY: Cornell Univ. Press, 1995), 6–8.

47. Nathaniel Philbrick, *Mayflower: A Story of Courage, Community and War* (New York: Penguin, 2006), 252–53.

48. Shefveland, *Anglo–Native Virginia*, 76.

49. Alan Gallay, *The Indian Slave Trade: The Rise of the English Empire in the American South, 1670–1717* (New Haven, CT: Yale Univ. Press, 2002), 298–305, 311–14; Court Records, Feb. 1694, in *CRNC*, 1:393–94, 613, 650; Lear Estate, Apr.–June 1697, in *CRNC2* 3:62; Lawson, *New Voyage to Carolina*, 240; Paul Kelton, *Epidemics and Enslavement: Biological Catastrophe in the Native Southeast* (Lincoln: Univ. of Nebraska Press, 2007), 126–43; Alan Gallay, ed., *Indian Slavery in Colonial America* (Lincoln: Univ. of Nebraska Press, 2009).

50. La Jau, *Carolina Chronicle*, 116; Gallay, *Indian Slave Trade*, 299, 312.

51. Harriot, "Briefe and True Report," 71–72.

52. Archdale, *New Description*, 29 (quote); Gallay, *Indian Slave Trade*, 213; Silver, *New Face*, 74, 92; Kelton, *Epidemics and Enslavement*, 143–59: Tai S. Edwards, "The 'Virgin' Soil Thesis Cover-Up: Teaching Indigenous Demographic Collapse," in *Understanding and Teaching Native American History*, ed. Kristofer Ray and Brady DeSanti (Madison: Univ. of Wisconsin Press, 2022), 29–40.

53. Robbie Ethridge, "Introduction: Mapping the Mississippian Shatter Zone," in *Mapping the Mississippian Shatter Zone: The Colonial Indian Slave Trade and Regional Instability in the American South*, ed. Robbie Ethridge and Sheri M. Shuck-Hall (Lincoln: Univ. of Nebraska Press, 2008), 2.

54. Wood, "Changing Population of the Colonial South," 44; Silver, *New Face*, 82.

55. Lee, *Indian Wars*, 3–5.

56. Lee, *Indian Wars*, 3–5; Johnson, *Tuscaroras*, 2:41–42; Silver, *New Face*, 82; Ethridge, *From Chicaza to Chickasaw*, 159.

57. Lawson, *New Voyage to Carolina*, 232.

58. Stephen C. Saraydar, "No Longer Shall You Kill: Peace, Power and the Iroquois Great Law," *Anthropology and Humanism Quarterly* 15 (Feb. 1990): 26; Francis Jennings, *The Ambiguous Iroquois Empire: The Covenant Chain Confederation of Indian Tribes with English Colonies from Its Beginning to the Lancaster Treaty of 1744* (New York: Norton, 1984), 23, 93–94; Timothy J. Shannon, *Iroquois Diplomacy on the Early American Frontier* (New York: Viking, 2008), 68–71; Nicholas Spencer to Sir Leoline Jenkins, Nov. 22, 1683, in *Calendar of State Papers, Colonial, America and West Indies, 1574–1739*, 46 vols., ed. Cecil Headlam (London, 1860), 11:1406, British History Online, at https://www.british -history.ac.uk/search/series/cal-state-papers–colonial-america-west-indies.

59. Lawson, *New Voyage to Carolina*, 53, 175, 49–50, 207–8.

60. Report of John French and Henry Worley, July 8, 1710, in *Minutes of the Provincial Council of Pennsylvania*, 10 vols. (Philadelphia: Jo. Severns, 1852), 2:511–12; Shannon, *Iroquois Diplomacy*, 43, 66; Rebecca M. Seaman, "John Lawson, the Outbreak of the Tuscarora Wars, and 'Middle Ground' Theory," *Journal of the Association of North Carolina Historians* 18 (Apr. 2010): 20–21.

61. Joseph W. Barnwell, "The Tuscarora Expedition: Letters of Colonel John Barnwell," *South Carolina Historical and Genealogical Magazine* 9 (Jan. 1908): 35.

62. McIlvenna, *Very Mutinous People*, 127–48; Towles, "Cary's Rebellion," 47–51; Von Graffenried, *Christoph Von Graffenried's Account*, 231–32.

63. Alan Simpson and Mary Simpson, introduction to Benjamin Church, *Diary of King Philip's War, 1675–76* (1716), ed. Alan Simpson and Mary Simpson (Chester, CT: Pequot Press, 1975), 12.

64. Lawson, *New Voyage to Carolina*, 243.

65. La Vere, *Tuscarora War*, 58–60, 69; Stephen Feeley, "Intercolonial Conflict and Cooperation during the Tuscarora War," in *New Voyages to Carolina: Reinterpreting North Carolina History*, ed. Larry E. Tise and Jeffrey J. Crow (Chapel Hill: Univ. of North Carolina Press, 2017), 60–84.

66. La Vere, *Tuscarora War*, 143–45.

67. La Vere, *Tuscarora War*, 122–23.

68. Barnwell, "Tuscarora Expedition," 43, 53–54; La Vere, *Tuscarora War*, 132–33.

69. La Vere, *Tuscarora War*, 146–47, 173.

70. La Vere, *Tuscarora War*, 165–70, 176; David La Vere, "Of Fortifications and Fire: The Tuscarora Response to the Barnwell and Moore Expeditions during North Carolina's Tuscarora War in 1712 and 1713," *North Carolina Historical Review* 94 (Oct. 2017): 363–90.

3. A Tributary King for the Tuscaroras

1. Marvin L. Kay and Lorin Lee Cary, *Slavery in North Carolina, 1748–1775* (Chapel Hill: Univ. of North Carolina Press, 1995), 19.

2. La Vere, *Tuscarora War*, 179–83, 189.

3. Laws of North Carolina, 1715, in *CRNC*, 23:3.

4. Dixon, "'His one Netev ples,'" 44–45.

5. F. Roy Johnson, "Tom Blunt," in *Dictionary of North Carolina Biography*, ed. William Powell, 6 vols. (Chapel Hill: Univ. of North Carolina Press, 1979), 1:186; Lowery, *Lumbee Indians in the Jim Crow South*, 5.

6. Lt. Governor Spotswood to the Council of Trade, June 2, 1713, in *Calendar of State Papers*, ed. Headlam, 27:355.

7. Letter to Pollock, Apr. 1713, in *CRNC*, 2:31–32.

8. Johnson, *Tuscaroras*, 2:162; Johnson, "Tom Blunt," in *Dictionary*, ed. Powell, 1:185; Lawson, *New Voyage to Carolina*, 204.

9. Lawson, *New Voyage to Carolina*, 59.

10. Executive Council Papers, c. June 25, 1705, in *CRNC2*, 7:372.

11. La Vere, *Tuscarora War*, 95.

12. President Pollock to Governor of South Carolina, c. Oct. 1712, in *CRNC*, 1:883; President Pollock to the Governor of Virginia, Oct. 5, 1712, in *CRNC*, 1:880–81; Sent by Lieutenant Woodhouse and Thomas Johnson, Oct. 3, 1712, in *CRNC*, 1:878.

13. President Pollock to Governor of South Carolina, c. Oct. 1712, in *CRNC*, 1:883; Letter to Gov. Pollock on Indian Affairs, Dec. 13, 1712, in *CRNC*, 1:890–91; Pollock to Spotswood, Dec. 28, 1712, in *CRNC*, 1:895–897; Johnson, *Tuscaroras*, 2:133.

14. Gov. Pollock in reply on the Same Subject, Dec. 23, 1712, in *CRNC*, 1:894; William Stanard, ed., "Examination of Indians, 1713," Miscellaneous Colonial Documents, *Virginia Magazine of History and Biography* 19 (July 1911): 272–75; Letter from Tho. Pollock, Feb. 24, 1713, in *CRNC*, 2:21–22; Johnson, *Tuscaroras*, 2:128.

15. Council Minutes, June 25, 1713, in *CRNC*, 7:39.

16. Giles Rainsford to Mr. Chamberlayne, July 18, 1713, in *CRNC*, 2:53–55; Rev. Giles Rainsford to Secretary, SPG, July 13, 1713, in *CRNC2*, 10:160–61, 161 n. 1; Letter of Tho. Pollock, Nov. 16, 1713, in *CRNC*, 2:73–75.

17. Ruth Y. Wetmore, "The Role of the Indian in North Carolina History," *North Carolina Historical Review* 56 (Apr. 1979): 168.

18. Copy to Mr. Hart, Sept. 1, 1713, in *CRNC*, 2:61–62; Letter of Tho. Pollock, Nov. 16, 1713, in *CRNC*, 2:73–75.

19. This idea comes from my own interactions with Indian people of eastern North Carolina in the twentieth and twenty-first centuries. In informal conversation about Blount and the Tuscarora War, many express a certain distaste for King Blount and his actions.

20. Pollock to [Spotswood], Apr. 25, 1713, Pollock Letter-Book, p. 10, Thomas Pollock Papers, 1708–1859, 1711–1842, PC 31.2, State Archives of North Carolina.

21. Pollock to [Spotswood], Apr. 25, 1713, Pollock Papers.

22. Council Minutes, Apr. 14, 1713, in *CRNC*, 2:35 (quote); Council Journal, May 8, 1713, in *CRNC*, 2:44.

23. Pollock to [Spotswood], Apr. 25, 1713, Pollock Papers.

24. Pollock's Letterbook, May 3, 1718, in *CRNC*, 2:304–5; Stephen Feeley, "Reservation, Outpost or Homeland? Indians Woods in the 18th Century," paper presented at the Three Hundred Years of Indian Woods, 1717–2017, Tercentenary Conference, Oct. 7–9, 2017, Hope Plantation, Windsor, NC.

25. Governor Spotswood to Governor Pollock on Indian Policy, May 1713, in *CRNC*, 2:47–48; Journal of the Virginia Council, Aug. 12, 1713, in *CRNC*, 2:57.

26. Pollock Letter, June 8, 1713, Pollock Letter-Book, p. 11, Pollock Papers; Letter of Thomas Pollock, Sept. 1, 1713, in *CRNC*, 2:59–60.

27. Council Minutes, Jan. 23, 1714, in *CRNC*, 2:117 (quote); Johnson, "Tom Blunt," in *Dictionary*, ed. Powell, 1:186.

28. Council Journal, June 5, 1717, in *CRNC*, 2:283.

29. Council Journal, June 5, 1717, in *CRNC*, 2:283.

30. Council Minutes, Mar. 10, 1715, in *CRNC*, 2:171.

31. Hugh Jones, *The Present State of Virginia: From Whence Is Inferred a Short View of Maryland and North Carolina* (Chapel Hill: Univ. of North Carolina Press, 1956), 61 (quotes); Dixon, "'His one Netev ples,'" 65.

32. La Vere, *Tuscarora War*, 57–58, 64–65, 109; Barnwell, "Tuscarora Expedition," 35.

33. Lt. Governor Spotswood to the Council of Trade, Nov. 16, 1713, in *Calendar of State Papers*, ed. Headlam, 27: 502.

34. Wallace, *Tuscarora*, 72–73.

35. Smallwood, "A History of Three Cultures," 97–99.

36. William N. Fenton, *The Great Law and the Longhouse: A Political History of the Iroquois Confederacy* (Norman: Univ. of Oklahoma Press, 1998), 383.

37. Fenton, *Great Law*, 389.

38. Feeley, "Reservation, Outpost, or Homeland?"

39. Smallwood, "A History of Three Cultures," 91–94; Boyce, "Iroquoian Tribes," 287–88.

40. Fenton, *Great Law*, 381.

41. Dixon, "'His one Netev ples,'" 65.

42. Wallace, *Tuscarora*, 69–70, 77–78.

43. Letter of Thomas Pollock, Sept. 1, 1713, *CRNC*, 2:59–60.

44. Pollock's Letterbook, July 8, 1717, in *CRNC*, 2:288–89; Rev. John Urmston to Secretary, SPG, June 12, 1715, in *CRNC2*, 10:200–201.

45. James Mooney, *The Siouan Tribes of the East* (1894; reprint, New York: Johnson Reprint, 1970), 60.

46. Council Minutes, Aug. 3, 1716, in *CRNC2*, 7:64.

47. Lee, *Indian Wars*, 44–45.

48. Council Minutes, Aug. 23, 1716, in *CRNC*, 2:246–47; Journal of Virginia Council, Nov. 3, 1716, in *CRNC*, 2:247; Pollock's Letterbook, Feb. 16, 1718, in *CRNC*, 2:298.

49. Lee, *Indian Wars*, 44–45; Lowery, *Lumbee Indians*, 5–7.

50. Council Journal, June 5, 1717, in *CRNC*, 2:283.

51. Lawson, *New Voyage to Carolina*, 242; Pollock's Letterbook, Nov. 13, 1717, in *CRNC*, 2:295–96; Byrd and Heath, "'The Country here,'" 104; Stevenson, "Indian Reservations," 29.

52. LeMaster, "In the 'Scolding Houses,'" 196–98.

53. Dixon, "'His one Netev ples,'" 52–53.

54. Council Journal, July 31, 1724, in *CRNC*, 2:534; Council Minutes, Oct. 28, 1724, in *CRNC2*, 7:147; Council Minutes, Aug. 3, 1725, in *CRNC2*, 7:159; Council Journal, Apr. 3, 1727, in *CRNC*, 2:674; Petition of Isaac Hill, Apr. 23, 1731, in *CRNC*, 3:218.

55. Council Journal, Oct. 31, 1725, in *CRNC*, 2:573.

56. LeMaster, "In the 'Scolding Houses,'" 207–10.

57. Journal of Mr. Watis' mission to the Indian[s] of North Carolina at Edenton, May 10, 1731, in *Calendar of State Papers*, ed. Headlam, 39:490; Copy of Mr. Wate's Journal to North Carolina, May 10, 1731, in *CRNC*, 11:10–15.

4. New Realities for the Tributaries

1. Francis Paul Prucha, *The Great Father: The United States Government and the American Indians* (Lincoln: Univ. of Nebraska Press, 1984), 463–67.

2. DuVal, *Native Ground*, 5; White, *Middle Ground*, 50–53.

3. Quoted in Dixon, "'His one Netev ples,'" 48, 71.

4. Milteer, "From Indians to Colored People," 30; Fischer, *Suspect Relations*, 86–88; LeMaster, "In the 'Scolding Houses,'" 220; J. K. Dane and B. Eugene Griessman, "The Collective Identity of Marginal Peoples: The North Carolina Experience," *American Anthropologist* 74 (June 1972): 697.

5. Copy of Mr. Wates Journal to North Carolina, May 10, 1731, in *CRNC*, 11:10–16.

6. Council Minutes, Aug. 4, 1723, in *CRNC*, 2:496.

7. Council Minutes, July 20, 1725, in *CRNC2*, 7:157 (quote); Council Minutes, Aug. 24, 1725, in *CRNC2*, 7:160.

8. Gamble, "Community of Convenience," 80–84; Graybeal, "'Too Light to Be Black, Too Dark to Be White,'" 98.

9. Gamble, "Community of Convenience," 87–89.

10. Byrd, *Histories of the Dividing Line*, 220, 300 (quotes); Hugh Meredith, *An Account of the Cape Fear Country, 1731*, ed. Earl Greg Swem (Perth Amboy, NJ: Charles F. Heartman, 1922), 27–28; Council Minutes, Apr. 3, 1727, in *CRNC2*, 7:170; Rights, "Trading Path," 410.

11. Examination of John Cope, Aug. 5, 1722, and Deposition of Cullen Pollock, c. Aug. 8, 1722, CCR 192; General Court, Aug. 14, 1722, in *CRNC2*, 5:320–21.

12. Council Minutes, May 28, 1725, in *CRNC2*, 7:155.

13. Council Records, Aug. 10, 1714, in *CRNC*, 2:140; Laws of North Carolina, 1720, in *CRNC*, 25:164; Feeley, "Reservation, Outpost, or Homeland?"

14. John Brickell, *The Natural History of North-Carolina* (1737; reprint, Murfreesboro, NC: Johnson, 1978), 283–85; Andrea Feeser, *Red, White & Black Make Blue: Indigo in the Fabric of Colonial South Carolina Life* (Athens: Univ. of Georgia Press, 2013), 26, 36.

15. Brickell, *Natural History*, 283–85; Dixon, "'His one Netev ples,'" 40–42.

16. House Minutes, Mar. 22, 1735, in *CRNC*, 4:45.

17. Council Minutes, June 14, 1722, in *CRNC*, 2:458; Michelle LeMaster, *Brothers Born of One Mother: British–Native American Relations in the Colonial Southeast* (Charlottesville: Univ. of Virginia Press, 2012), 144.

18. Order of Chief Justice Christopher Gale, Mar. 13, 1723, CCR 192 (quote); Memorandum of Gyles Shute and Joshua Porter, Mar. 16, 1723, CCR 192.

19. General Court, Aug. 25, 1726, in *CRNC2*, 6:281–82 (quote); Council Minutes, Aug. 25, 1726, in *CRNC2*, 7:165–66.

20. Perdue, *Cherokee Women*, 17–19, 41–44, 52–53; LeMaster, *Brothers Born of One Mother*, 88.

21. Lowery, *Lumbee Indians*, 6–7.

22. Gary Clayton Anderson, *The Indian Southwest 1580–1830: Ethnogenesis and Reinvention* (Norman: Univ. of Oklahoma Press, 1999), 4, 267 n. 2, 3.

23. Alan D. Watson, with Eva C. Latham and Patricia M. Samford, *Bath: The First Town in North Carolina* (Raleigh: North Carolina Office of Archives and History, 2005), 7; Smallwood, "A History of Three Cultures," 129–30, 166–67.

24. Brickell, *Natural History*, 284.

25. Lawson, *New Voyage to Carolina*, 62 (quote), 13, 15, 20–23, 37, 64–65.

26. Examination of William Lees, Examination of John Spellman, Aug. 23, 1697, in *CRNC2*, 3:126–27; Lawson, *New Voyage to Carolina*, 66; Silver, *New Face*, 83; Byrd, *William Byrd's Histories of the Dividing Line*, 160; David S. Cecelski, *The Waterman's Song: Slavery and Freedom in Maritime North Carolina* (Chapel Hill: Univ. of North Carolina Press, 2001), 8; Frank G. Speck, "Remnants of the Machapunga Indians of North Carolina," *American Anthropologist* 18 (Apr.–June 1916): 273.

27. LeMaster, *Brothers Born of One Mother*, 144.

28. Wallace, *Tuscarora*, 66; Lawson, *New Voyage to Carolina*, 92–93; Council Minutes, May 27, 1719, in *CRNC2*, 7:84–86.

29. Council Minutes, Apr. 4, 1720, in *CRNC2*, 7:99; Milteer, "From Indians to Colored People," 41.

30. *Hitaw v. Sale*, Mar. 1723, in *CRNC2*, 5:365.

31. LeMaster, "In the 'Scolding Houses,'" 226–28.

32. Lawson, *New Voyage to Carolina*, 175 (quote), 243; Wallace, *Tuscarora*, 57, 66; LeMaster, "In the 'Scolding Houses,'" 226.

33. Merrell, *Indians' New World*, 210–11.

34. Byrd, *William Byrd's Histories of the Dividing Line*, 312; Smallwood, "A History of Three Cultures," 128–29; Johnson, *Tuscaroras*, 2:162–64; Milteer, "From Indians to Colored People," 38–40.

35. Deposition of Thomas Barcock, Mar. 1703, in *CRNC2*, 4:54; Garrow, *Mattamuskeet Documents*, 57.

36. Harriot, "Briefe and True Report," 67–75; Feest, "North Carolina Algonquians," 15:278–79.

37. Extract from the Journal of George Fox for the Year 1672, in *CRNC*, 1:217.

38. Lawson, *New Voyage to Carolina*, 45.

39. Byrd, *William Byrd's Histories of the Dividing Line*, 198–202.

40. "De Graffenried's Manuscript," in *CRNC*, 1:983–94.

41. Harriot, "Briefe and True Report," 71.

42. A Declaration and Proposals to all that will Plant in Carolina, Aug. 25, 1663, in *CRNC*, 1:43; Extract from the Journal of George Fox for the Year 1672, in *CRNC*, 1:217–18; Archdale, *New Description*, 11–12, 29, 31.

43. Parishioners of St. Andrews Parish to Rev. Gideon Johnston, Oct. 19, 1716, in *CRNC2*, 10:229–30; Affidavit of Rev. John Blacknell, Jan. 27, 1726, in *CRNC2*, 10:305; Rev. Thomas Newnam to Secretary, SPG, June 29, 1722, in *CRNC2*, 10:282–83 (quote); Rev. Thomas Baylye to Bishop of London, May 12, 1726, in *CRNC2*, 10:306; Account of Rev. John Garzia, 1738, in *CRNC2*, 10:378–81.

44. George Whitefield to the Bishop of Oxford, July 28, 1741, in *CRNC2*, 10:424.

45. Letter of Bishop Spangenberg, Sept. 12, 1752, in *CRNC*, 4:1313–14.

46. Alexander Stewart to the Secretary, SPG, Nov. 22, 1765, in *CRNC*, 7:126.

47. Mr. Stewart to the Secretary, SPG, May 22, 1761, in *CRNC*, 6:563; Garrow, *Mattamuskeet Documents*, 28–29.

48. Mr. Stewart to the Secretary, SPG, Nov. 6, 1763, in *CRNC*, 6:995–96.

49. Lawson, *New Voyage to Carolina*, 64–65.

50. Gamble, "Community of Convenience," 85–86; W. Hall to Secretary, SPG, Nov. 24, 1712, in *CRNC2*, 10:154; Bishop of London to Secretary, SPG, Jan. 17, 1713, in *CRNC2*, 10:157; Troy Richardson, "Tuscarora, Saponi and Tutelo at William and Mary College and Fort Christianna, 1690–1715: Rethinking the Cultural Broker Paradigm of the History of Indian Education," paper presented at the Three Hundred Years of Indian Woods, 1717–2017, Tercentenary Conference, Oct. 7–9, 2017, Hope Plantation, Windsor, NC.

51. Rev. Giles Ra[i]nsford to Secretary, SPG, July 25, 1712, in *CRNC2*, 10:143; Mr. Rainsford to the Secretary, SPG, Jan. 19, 1715, in *CRNC*, 2:152.

52. Bishop of London to Secretary, SPG, Oct. 3, 1712, in *CRNC2*, 10:149.

53. Rev. Giles Ra[i]nsford to Secretary, SPG, July 25, 1712, in *CRNC2*, 10:143.

54. James Francis to Alexr. Stewart, Feb. 20, 1764, and James Francis letter, Feb. 22, 1764, in *Native Americans in Early North Carolina: A Documentary History*, ed. Dennis L. Isenbarger (Raleigh: North Carolina Office of Archives and History, 2013), 271–72.

55. Stewart to the Secretary, SPG, Oct. 3, 1767, in *CRNC* 7:522.

56. Byrd, *William Byrd's Histories of the Dividing Line*, 118.

57. Letter of Bishop Spangenberg, Sept. 12, 1752, in *CRNC*, 4:1313–14 (quote); Petition of William Dunbonfort, Jan. 25, 1696, CCR 192; House Minutes, Oct. 2, 1736, in *CRNC*, 4:237; LeMaster, "In the 'Scolding Houses,'" 198.

5. Fade of the Smaller Tributaries

1. Fundamental Constitutions of Carolina, Mar. 1, 1669, in *CRNC*, 1:203–4.

2. Wallace, *Tuscarora*, 66; Land Sale, July 1, 1702, Beaufort County, NC, Land & Deed Records, 15, at http://files.usgwarchives.net/nc/beaufort/deeds/p1-50.txt.

3. Johnson, *Tuscaroras*, 2:41–42; Stevenson, "Indian Reservations," 29–30; Complaint of John Durant, Apr. 27, 1714, in *CRNC2*, 5:481; Adams, "'Sundry Murders and Depredations,'" 152.

4. Stevenson, "Indian Reservations," 29–30; Court of Chancery, Mar. 10, 1715, in *CRNC2*, 5:498.

5. Council Minutes, Mar. 10, 1715, in *CRNC*, 2:172.

6. General Court, July 1725, in *CRNC2*, 6:136–37.

7. Council Minutes, Nov. 23, 1715, in *CRNC*, 2:204–5; Council Minutes, Mar. 28, 1723, in *CRNC2*, 7:118.

8. Dennis Isenbarger, "Reservations," in *Native Americans*, ed. Isenbarger, 287 (quote); John Durant to Edward Tyler, Nov. 29, 1740, 3:27–28, Currituck County Deeds, microfilm, State Archives of North Carolina, Raleigh; Petition of John Durant, Feb. 22, 1739, in *CRNC2*, 8:101; Stevenson, "Indian Reservations," 29–30; Rountree, with Taukchiray, *Manteo's World*, 135.

9. John Hoyter petition, 1704, in *NCHGR* 1 (Oct. 1900): 614 (quote); John Hoyter, petition, n.d., CCR 192.

10. Johnson, *Tuscaroras*, 2:41–42; Stevenson, "Indian Reservations," 27–28.

11. Council Minutes, Aug. 11, 1714, in *CRNC*, 2:140–41.

12. Milteer, "From Indians to Colored People," 32–33; Rountree, with Taukchiray, *Manteo's World*, 139.

13. Council Minutes, Aug. 11, 1714, in *CRNC*, 2:140–41; Council Minutes, Nov. 22, 1717, in *CRNC2*, 7:70; Council Minutes, July 31, 1718, in *CRNC2*, 7:73; Council Journal, Apr. 4, 1720, in *CRNC*, 2:380; Milteer, "From Indians to Colored People," 32; Stevenson, "Indian Reservations," 27–28.

14. Petition of the Chowan Indians, Jan. 30, 1734, in *CRNC2*, 8:8–9 (quote); Chowan Land Sale, Jan. 9, 1733, CCR 192; Rountree, with Taukchiray, *Manteo's World*, 140.

15. Chowan Nation to John Freeman, Aug. 7, 1733, Chowan County Deeds, microfilm, vol. 1, no. 216, State Archives of North Carolina; Chowan Land Sales, Aug. 2–4, 1733, in *NCHGR* 1 (Jan. 1900): 106; Milteer, "From Indians to Colored People," 33; Indenture of James Bennett and the Chowan Indians, Sept. 10, 1733, CCR 192; Thomas Hoyter to John Freeman, Aug. 7, 1733, in *Native Americans*, ed. Isenbarger, 286.

16. Petition of the Chowan Indians, Jan. 30, 1734, in *CRNC2*, 8:8–9; Land Sales, Apr. 7 and May 20, 1734, CCR 192; Council Records, Jan. 30, 1735, in *CRNC*, 4:33–35; Council Records, Dec. 16, 1735, in *CRNC*, 4:74–75; Milteer, "From Indians to Colored People," 35.

17. Hyter and Bennet, Indians to Gabriel Lasseter, Deed, Mar. 22, 1742–43, in *CRNC2*, 8:389, 391; Hyter and Bennet, Indians to Hill, Deed, Mar. 22, 1742–43, in *CRNC2*, 8:390.

18. Petition of the Chowan Indians, Mar. 23, 1743, in *CRNC2*, 8:139.

19. Council Records, Mar. 25, 1743, in *CRNC*, 4:630–31.

20. Council Records, Dec. 4, 1744, in *CRNC*, 4:713–14.

21. Petition of James Bennett, Mar. 12, 1745, in *CRNC2*, 8:199; Milteer, "From Indians to Colored People," 35–36.

22. Council Records, Oct. 10, 1751, in *CRNC*, 4:1254; James Bennett petitions, 1751, in *Native Americans*, ed. Isenbarger, 284–85.

23. *Dom. Rex v. Henry Hill*, July 1747, Chowan County Criminal Action Papers, State Archives of North Carolina.

24. Deposition of Jean Brown, Sept. 4, 1753, Miscellaneous Records, Chowan County Records, CR 024.928.7, State Archives of North Carolina.

25. Deposition of Timothy Walton, *et al*, Sept. 5, 1753, Miscellaneous Records, Chowan County Records, CR 024.928.7; Deposition of Henry Hill, Sept. 5, 1753, in *Native Americans*, ed. Isenbarger, 253–54.

26. Diary of Bishop Spangenberg, Sept. 13, 1752, in *CRNC*, 5:1.

27. Abstracts from returns from the several counties, c. Dec. 1754, in *CRNC*, 5:162.

28. Indians in North Carolina, Jan. 4, 1755, in *CRNC*, 5:320–21.

29. Milteer, "From Indians to Colored People," 36–37.

30. Marilyn Poe Lair, *Gates County, North Carolina, Land Deeds, 1776–1795*, vol. A (Raleigh: Government and Heritage Library, North Carolina State Library, 1977), 65.

31. Milteer, "From Indians to Colored People," 36–37.

32. Dawdy, "Meherrin's Secret History," 408–9.

33. Stevenson, "Indian Reservations," 28–29.

34. Journal of the Virginia Council, Oct. 24, 1723, in *CRNC*, 2:499–500.

35. Council Minutes, Apr. 9, 1724, in *CRNC*, 2:526–27.

36. Council Minutes, Aug. 3, 1726, in *CRNC*, 2:639 (quote); Council Minutes, Oct. 28, 1726, in *CRNC2*, 7:165–69.

37. Council Minutes, Aug. 25, 1726, in *CRNC*, 2:640.

38. Council Minutes, Oct. 27, 1726, in *CRNC*, 2:643.

39. Council Minutes, Oct. 27, 1726, in *CRNC*, 2:644–45 (quotes); Dawdy, "Meherrin's Secret History," 409.

40. Dawdy, "Meherrin's Secret History," 408–9; Stevenson, "Indian Reservations," 28–29.

41. Byrd, *William Byrd's Histories of the Dividing Line*, 106 (quote); Dawdy, "Meherrin's Secret History," 407–10.

42. Laws of North Carolina, 1729, chapter II, in *CRNC*, 25:211 (quote); Council Journal, May 4 and 5, 1742, in *CRNC*, 4:615–17; Dawdy, "Meherrin's Secret History," 410; Stevenson, "Indian Reservations," 28–29.

43. Stevenson, "Indian Reservations," 28–29; Dawdy, "Meherrin's Secret History," 414.

44. Council Journal, May 4 and 5, 1742, in *CRNC*, 4:615–17; Dawdy, "Meherrin's Secret History," 410–13; Stevenson, "Indian Reservations," 29.

45. House Minutes, June 17, 1742, in *CRNC*, 4:820.

46. Dawdy, "Meherrin's Secret History," 412–13.

47. Dawdy, "Meherrin's Secret History," 413.

48. House Minutes, May 26, 1757, in *CRNC*, 5:839.

49. Council Minutes, Nov. 29, 1758, in *CRNC*, 5:995 (quote); Dawdy, "Meherrin's Secret History," 413.

50. Dawdy, "Meherrin's Secret History," 414–15 (quote); Stevenson, "Indian Reservations," 29; "The Roanoke-Chowan Story," *Daily Roanoke-Chowan News*, Johnson Papers.

51. Stevenson, "Indian Reservations," 28; Garrow, *Mattamuskeet Documents*, 22.

52. Garrow, *Mattamuskeet Documents*, 22–25.

53. Petition of Nicholas Dove, *et al*, n.d., CCR 192; General Court, Oct. 28, 1718, in *CRNC2*, 5:188; Council Journal, Nov. 11, 1718, in *CRNC*, 2:315; Gov. Charles Eden to Anthony Hatch, Feb. 18, 1719, CCR 192; Garrow, *Mattamuskeet Documents*, 22–25; Rountree, with Taukchiray, *Manteo's World*, 128–30.

54. Council Journal, Nov. 11, 1718, in *CRNC*, 2:316; Garrow, *Mattamuskeet Documents*, 45.

55. Council Records, Apr. 15, 1724, in *CRNC*, 2:528; Garrow, *Mattamuskeet Documents*, 20–21; Stevenson, "Indian Reservations," 28.

56. Land Grant to Mattamuskeet Indians, Apr. 1, 1727, Secretary of State Records, microfilm, book 2, pp. 149–50, State Archives of North Carolina; Garrow, *Mattamuskeet Documents*, 7–8, 20, 45.

57. Machapunga Nation to Henry Gibbs, Sept. 27, 1731, Hyde County Deeds, microfilm, vol. H, pp. 96–98, State Archives of North Carolina; Garrow, *Mattamuskeet Documents*, 45.

58. Deed Abstract, July 16, 1742, Deed Book 1787–1789, Hyde County Deeds, vol. C, pp. 307–8; Garrow, *Mattamuskeet Documents*, app. 11.

59. Burrington to the Duke of Newcastle, July 2, 1731, in *CRNC*, 3:153.

60. Garrow, *Mattamuskeet Documents*, 25, 27, 157, app. 12; Weynette Parks Haun, *Hyde County North Carolina Court Minutes, 1736–1756*, book 1 (Raleigh: Government and Heritage Library, North Carolina State Library, 1985), no. 70, p. 36.

61. Garrow, *Mattamuskeet Documents*, 22–23, 68, app. 30.

62. Jacob [Joseph] Farrow to Charles Squires, Apr. 2, 1740, Chowan County Deeds, microfilm, vol. 3, no. 40.

63. Garrow, *Mattamuskeet Documents*, 26, 63, app. 22.

64. Garrow, *Mattamuskeet Documents*, 30, 70, app. 33; Machapunga Nation to William Stephenson, Nov. 24, 1752, in *Native Americans*, ed. Isenbarger, 290.

65. Indians in North Carolina, Jan. 4, 1755, in *CRNC*, 5:320–21.

66. "The Colony, Its Climate, Soil, Population, Government, Resources, &c.," c. 1761, in *CRNC*, 6:616.

67. Haun, *Hyde County North Carolina Court Minutes*, no. 219, 1:123.

68. Garrow, *Mattamuskeet Documents*, 22, 28, 70, app. 33; Stevenson, "Indian Reservations," 28.

69. Garrow, *Mattamuskeet Documents*, 22, 27–28, 70, app. 33.

70. Mr. Stewart to the Secretary, SPG, May 22, 1761, in *CRNC*, 6:563; Garrow, *Mattamuskeet Documents*, 28–29.

71. Brooks, "John Lawson's Indian Town," 188, 191–93.

72. Brooks, "John Lawson's Indian Town," 201.

73. Brooks, "John Lawson's Indian Town," 199–201, 203–4; Stevenson, "Indian Reservations," 28; Dunbar, "Hatteras Indians."

74. Council Minutes, July 31, 1712, in *CRNC2*, 7:24.

75. Gamble, "Community of Convenience," 80–84; Graybeal, "'Too Light to Be Black, Too Dark to Be White,'" 98.

76. Byrd, *William Byrd's Histories of the Dividing Line*, 310.

77. Gamble, "Community of Convenience," 80–84; Nowell, "Red, White and Black," 40–43.

78. Council Journal, Apr. 3, 1727, in *CRNC*, 2:674.

79. "The Colony, Its Climate, Soil, Population, Government, Resources, &c.," c. 1761, in *CRNC*, 6:616 (quote); Gamble, "Community of Convenience," 89–94. Lord Granville's tract, which existed from 1729 to 1777, consisted of just about the top third of North Carolina, with the Tuscaroras, Meherrins, Saponis, Yeopim, Chowans, and others falling into the tract.

80. Nowell, "Red, White and Black," 41–48: Graybeal, "'Too Light to Be Black, Too Dark to Be White,'" 99.

81. Rev. Thomas Newnam to Secretary, SPG, June 29, 1722, in *CRNC2*, 10:282–83.

82. Brickell, *Natural History of North Carolina*, 282.

83. Burrington to the Duke of Newcastle, July 2, 1731, in *CRNC*, 3:153.

84. Burrington to the Duke of Newcastle, July 2, 1731, in *CRNC*, 3:153; Smallwood, "A History of Three Cultures," 100.

85. Council Minutes, Apr. 3, 1733, in *CRNC*, 3:537–38; Dane and Griessman, "Collective Identity," 695, 697.

86. A List of Northampton Regiments, c. 1748, in *CRNC*, 22:274.

87. James Craven to Gov. Dobbs, Dec. 7, 1754, in *CRNC*, 22:329.

88. Indians in North Carolina, Jan. 4, 1755, in *CRNC*, 5:320–21; "The Colony, Its Climate, Soil, Population, Government, Resources, &c.," c. 1761, in *CRNC*, 6:616.

6. The Tuscarora Scattering

1. Council Journal, Mar. 30, 1721, in *CRNC*, 2:428–29.

2. Council Minutes, Apr. 4, 1722, in *CRNC*, 2:456; Council Minutes, Apr. 5, 1722, in *CRNC*, 2:456; Council Minutes, June 14, 1722, in *CRNC*, 2:456; Council Records, Apr. 1, 1723, in *CRNC*, 2:485; Stevenson, "Indian Reservations," 27–29.

3. Bertie Precinct, Oct. 1722, in *NCHGR* 2 (July 1901): 412; Smallwood, "A History of Three Cultures," 613.

4. Petition of Humphrey Bates, petitions rejected or not acted on, Colonial Lower House Papers, Nov.–Dec. 1758, box 1, General Assembly Session Records (GASR), State Archives of North Carolina, Raleigh; Petition of Humphrey Bates, Nov. 29, 1758, in *CRNC*, 5:1046; Petition of George Charleton, Dec. 19, 1758, in *CRNC*, 5:1082.

5. Council Minutes, Mar. 5, 1739, in *CRNC*, 4:345.

6. Laws of North Carolina, 1748, in *CRNC*, 23:299.

7. Council Minutes, Jan. 20, 1732, in *CRNC*, 3:404.

8. Council Records, Oct. 14, 1736, in *CRNC*, 4:224; Smallwood, "A History of Three Cultures," 102.

9. Council Minutes, Apr. 2, 1741, in *CRNC*, 4:592.

10. Petition of Humphrey Bates, petitions rejected or not acted on, Colonial Lower House Papers, Nov.–Dec. 1758, box 1, GASR; Petition of Humphrey Bates, Nov. 29, 1758, in *CRNC*, 5:1046; Petition of George Charleton, Dec. 19, 1758, in *CRNC*, 5:1082.

11. Laws of North Carolina, 1748, in *CRNC*, 23:299–301; An Act of Assembly Relating to the Tuskerora [*sic*] Indians, Oct. 15, 1748, in *NCHGR* 2 (July 1901): 426–28; Letter of Bishop Spangenberg, Sept. 12, 1752, in *CRNC*, 4:1313–14.

12. Laws of North Carolina, 1748, in *CRNC*, 23:299–301 (quote); An Act of Assembly Relating to the Tuskerora [*sic*] Indians, Oct. 15, 1748, in *NCHGR* 2 (July 1901): 426–28.

13. Laws of North Carolina, 1749, in *CRNC*, 23:340.

14. Petition of Humphrey Bates, petitions rejected or not acted upon, Colonial Lower House Papers, Nov.–Dec. 1758, box 1, GASR.

15. Letter of Bishop Spangenberg, Sept. 12, 1752, in *CRNC*, 4:1313.

16. Letter of Bishop Spangenberg, Sept. 12, 1752, in *CRNC*, 4:1313.

17. Letter of Bishop Spangenberg, Sept. 12, 1752, in *CRNC*, 4:1314.

18. Diary of Bishop Spangenberg, Sept. 13, 1752, in *CRNC*, 5:1.

19. Petition of the Tuscaroras, Mar. 28 and 29 and May 21, 1753, in *CRNC*, 5:31, 35.

20. Dobbs to Board of Trade, Dec. 19, 1754, in *CRNC*, 5:155 (quotes); Indians in North Carolina, Jan. 4, 1755, in *CRNC*, 5:320–21.

21. Daniel J. Tortora, *Carolina in Crisis: Cherokees, Colonists, and Slaves in the American Southeast, 1756–1763* (Chapel Hill: Univ. of North Carolina Press, 2015), 10–28.

22. Tortora, *Carolina in Crisis*, 44.

23. Buck Woodard, "'Take up the Hatchet . . . and Go to War with Us': The Tuscarora of Indian Woods during the French and Indian War," paper presented at the Three Hundred Years of Indian Woods, 1717–2017, Tercentenary Conference, Oct. 7–9, 2017, Hope Plantation, Windsor, NC.

24. Journal of Council [of Virginia], Apr. 4, 1757, in *Executive Journals of the Council of Colonial Virginia*, 6 vols., ed. Henry R. McIllwaine, Wilmer L. Hall, and Benjamin J. Hillman (Richmond: Virginia State Library, 1925–66), 6:38–39; Dawdy, "Meherrin's Secret History," 413.

25. House Minutes, May 26, 1757, in *CRNC*, 5:839.

26. Gov. Dinwiddie to Gov. Dobbs, June 20, 1757, in *CRNC*, 5:765.

27. Woodard, "'Take Up the Hatchet.'"

28. Tortora, *Carolina in Crisis*, 154, 165.

29. Deposition of John Liscomb, May 24, 1757, CCR 192 (quote); Indictment of James Strawberry, Oct. 1757, CCR 192; Report of the Committee of Public Claims, Nov. 27, 1758, in *CRNC*, 5:977, 981.

30. James Blount to Arthur Dobbs, Sept. 25, 1757, Governor Arthur Dobbs Papers, 1754–1765, CGO.5, Colonial Governor's Papers, State Archives of North Carolina.

31. Council Minutes, Nov. 25, 1758, in *CRNC*, 5:1043 (quote); Council Minutes, May 3, 1758, in *CRNC*, 5:1007–8.

32. Petition of Humphrey Bates, Nov. 29, 1758, in *CRNC*, 5:1046; Complaint of King Blunt, Nov. 29, 1758, in *CRNC2*, 9:57; Petition of George Charlton, Dec. 19, 1758, in *CRNC*, 5:1082.

33. Dobbs to the Speaker, May 11, 1759, in *CRNC*, 6:100; House Minutes, May 16, 1759, in *CRNC*, 6:108.

34. Tortora, *Carolina in Crisis*, 154, 165.

35. House Minutes, Nov. 19 and 20, 1762, in *CRNC*, 6:913–14.

36. Instructions to our Trusty and Well-beloved William Tryon, c. Dec. 1765, in *CRNC*, 7:141–42.

37. Gregory Evans Dowd, *War under Heaven: Pontiac, the Indian Nations & the British Empire* (Baltimore: Johns Hopkins Univ. Press, 2002), 174–77.

38. House Minutes, Nov. 13, 1764, in *CRNC*, 6:1232; William Tryon to Sir William Johnson, June 15, 1766, in William Tryon, *The Correspondence of William Tryon and Other Selected Papers*, 2 vols., ed. William S. Powell (Raleigh: North Carolina Department of Cultural Resources, 1980), 1:310–11; Petition from Tuscarora headmen to Governor William Tryon, July 12, 1766, in *Native Americans*, ed. Isenbarger, 292–94.

39. Gov. Tryon to Sir William Johnson, June 15, 1766, in *CRNC*, 7:218–19; William Tryon to Sir William Johnston, June 15, 1766, in Tryon, *Correspondence*, 1:310–11; Fenton, *Great Law*, 383.

40. Petition from the chiefs of the Tuscarora Indians, July 12, 1766, in Tryon, *Correspondence*, 1:321–23.

41. Tuscarora Indians to Robert Jones, *et al*, July 12, 1766, Miscellaneous Papers, 1697–1823, PC 21.1, p. 35, State Archives of North Carolina; Smallwood, "A History of Three Cultures," 109–10.

42. Gov. Tryon to Board of Trade, Aug. 2, 1766, in *CRNC*, 7:248–49; William Tryon to the Board of Trade, Aug. 2, 1766, in Tryon, *Correspondence*, 1:341; Land Indenture, July 12, 1766, Lewis Thompson Papers, Collection No. 716, series 1.1, folder 1, 1723–98, Southern Historical Collection, Wilson Library, Univ. of North Carolina, Chapel Hill.

43. House Minutes, Nov. 4, 1766, in *CRNC*, 7:293–94; Council to Gov. Tryon, Nov. 5, 1766, in *CRNC*, 7:298; House Minutes, Nov. 10, 1766, in *CRNC*, 7:300; Order in Council, Jan. 11, 1769, in *CRNC2*, 9:617–20; Bill for conforming a lease made by the Tuscarora Indians to Robert Jones, William Williams, and Thomas Pugh, Esquires, Nov. 10, 1766, Nov.–Dec. 1766, oversize box,

GASR; William Tryon to John Stuart, June 17, 1766 in Tryon, *Correspondence*, 1:312–13.

44. Rev. William Smith to Secretary, SPG, Sept. 22, 1766, in *Native Americans*, ed. Isenbarger, 294; William Tryon to the Earl of Shelburne, Jan. 31, 1767, in Tryon, *Correspondence*, 1:412.

45. Journal of Indian Affairs, Dec. 18, 1766, in *Native Americans*, ed. Isenbarger, 295.

46. Journal of Indian Affairs, Feb. 25, 1767, in *Native Americans*, ed. Isenbarger, 296.

47. Speech of Thomas Baskett, Nov. 11, 1766, in *CRNC*, 7:361 (quotes); William Tryon to the Earl of Shelburne, Jan. 31, 1767, in Tryon, *Correspondence*, 1:412; Gov. Tryon to Earl of Shelburne, Jan. 31, 1767, in *CRNC*, 7:431.

48. Speech of Thomas Baskett, Nov. 11, 1766, in *CRNC*, 7:361 (quotes); Thomas Baskett and Others to William Tryon, Nov. 7, 1766, in Tryon, *Correspondence*, 1:363; William Tryon to the Assembly, Nov. 11, 1766, in Tryon, *Correspondence*, 1:365, William Tryon to the Earl of Shelburne, Jan. 31, 1767, in Tryon, *Correspondence*, 1:412; Laws of North Carolina, 1766, in *CRNC*, 23:687.

49. Proclamation by the King, July 16, 1767, in *CRNC2*, 9:182–83.

50. LeMaster, "In the 'Scolding Houses,'" 228–30, 232.

51. Motion, Apr. 1769, 1691–1758 folder, CCR 192; *Dominus Rex vs. Sarah Bates*, 1770, in *Native Americans*, ed. Isenbarger, 298.

52. Council Minutes, Dec. 18, 1773, in *CRNC*, 9:790.

53. Tuscarora Indians to Thomas Pugh, *et al*, Dec. 2, 1775, PC 21.1, p. 44, Miscellaneous Papers, 1697–1823; Indians to Pugh & Others, Dec. 2, 1775, Real Estate Conveyances, vol. M, nos. 316–17, microfilm: C.010.4005, Bertie County Records, State Archives of North Carolina; Tuscarora Nation to William King, Dec. 13, 1775, in *Native Americans*, ed. Isenbarger, 299–300.

54. Tuscarora Nation to William King, Dec. 13, 1775, Real Estate Conveyances, vol. M., nos. 317–18, microfilm: C.010.4005, Bertie County Records; Tuscarora Nation to William King, Dec. 13, 1775, in *Native Americans*, ed. Isenbarger, 301–2.

55. Indians to Stone, Feb. 10, 1777, Real Estate Conveyances, vol. M, nos. 314–15, microfilm: C.010.4005, Bertie County Records.

56. Indians to Pugh, Mar. 28, 1777, Real Estate Conveyances, vol. M, nos. 315–16, microfilm: C.010.4005, Bertie County Records; Tuscarora Indians to Thomas Pugh, Mar. 28, 1777, PC 21.1, p. 46, Miscellaneous Papers, 1697–1823.

57. Titus Edward Lease, Sept. 7, 1777, PC 21.1, p. 46, Miscellaneous Papers, 1697–1823.

58. Gerald W. Thomas, "Indian Woods: A Lost Reservation," paper presented at the Three Hundred Years of Indian Woods, 1717–2017, Tercentenary

Conference, Feb. 7–9, 2017, Hope Plantation, Windsor, NC; Joshua Irvin, "Ties to Home: Tuscarora Autonomy and the Sale of Indian Woods, 1801–1831," paper presented at the Three Hundred Years of Indian Woods, 1717–2017, Tercentenary Conference, Feb. 7–9, 2017, Hope Plantation, Windsor, NC.

59. House Minutes, Dec. 22, 1777, in *CRNC*, 12:427, 431 (quotes); Senate Minutes, Dec. 22, 1777, in *CRNC*, 12:246; Smallwood, "A History of Three Cultures," 112–13.

60. Laws of North Carolina, 1778, in *CRNC*, 24:171.

61. Laws of North Carolina, 1778, in *CRNC*, 24:173.

62. Laws of North Carolina, 1762, in *CRNC*, 23:559.

63. Laws of North Carolina, 1762, in *CRNC*, 23:559.

64. Laws of North Carolina, 1778, in *CRNC*, 24:173.

65. Laws of North Carolina, 1778, in *CRNC*, 24:173.

66. Petition of the Tuscarora Indians in Bertie County, Apr.–May 1780, Joint Papers, Miscellaneous Petitions, GASR; Laws of North Carolina, 1780, in *CRNC*, 24:335.

67. Court of Indian Commission, Feb. 24, 1781, in *Native Americans*, ed. Isenbarger, 303. The twelve settler jurors included William Freeman, John Walston, Peter Clifton, Hugh Hyman, Samuel Milburn, James House, Henry Averit, Elisha Rhodes, Andrew Oliver, James Bentley, William Watson, and Henry Smit.

68. Zedekiah Stone indenture, Feb. 11, 1782, PC 21.1, p. 51, Miscellaneous Papers, 1697–1823.

69. Article of Agreement, July 20, 1787, PC 21.1, p. 54, Miscellaneous Papers, 1697–1823.

70. Zedekiah Stone payment, Jan. 5, 1789, PC 21.1, p. 57, Miscellaneous Papers, 1697–1823.

71. Map of North Carolina, 1783, in *CRNC*, 18:496–97; Smallwood, "A History of Three Cultures," 103–4; LeMaster, "In the 'Scolding Houses,'" 228–29.

72. David Stone letter, Dec. 4, 1801, Bertie County Folder (Tuscarora Lands), 1801–6, PC 82, David Stone Papers, State Archives of North Carolina.

73. Thomas Parramore, "The Great Slave Conspiracy: 'The Colerain Letter' and Other Plots—Real or Imagined—Which in 1802 Launched the Worst Insurrection Panic in North Carolina History," *The State* 39 (Aug. 15, 1971): 7–10; Examination of Several Negro Slaves Respecting a Rebellion, June 9 and 11, 1802, folder 23, PC 1629, Slave Collection, State Archives of North Carolina; Smallwood, "A History of Three Cultures," 117–18.

74. Parramore, "Great Slave Conspiracy," 7–10; Examination of Several Negro Slaves Respecting a Rebellion, June 9 and 11, 1802, folder 23, PC 1629, Slave Collection.

75. A Letter Concerning the Lands Held by the Tuscarora Indians in Bertie County, North Carolina, North Carolina Secretary of State, Apr. 5, 1911, Cp970.03. N87s, North Carolina Collection, Wilson Library, Univ. of North Carolina.

76. Smallwood, "A History of Three Cultures," 117.

77. A Letter Concerning the Lands Formerly Held by the Tuscarora Indians in Bertie County, North Carolina, North Carolina Secretary of State, Apr. 5, 1911, North Carolina Collection; "The Roanoke–Chowan Story," Johnson Papers; Letter of John Binford and William Hawkins, May 23, 1803, Bertie County Folder (Tuscarora Lands), 1801–6, Stone Papers.

78. Smallwood, "A History of Three Cultures," 34, 121–22; Wallace, *Tuscarora*, 74–76; LeMaster, "In the 'Scolding Houses,'" 232 n. 102.

79. Smallwood, "A History of Three Cultures," 120.

80. *Sacarusa & Longboard v. King Heirs* (1815), Case 754, 1800–1909, nos. 746–72, box 17, Supreme Court Original Cases, State Archives of North Carolina.

81. Smallwood, "A History of Three Cultures," 124–25 (quote); Letter Concerning the Lands Formerly Held by the Tuscarora Indians in Bertie County, North Carolina, North Carolina Secretary of State, Apr. 5, 1911, North Carolina Collection; "The Roanoke–Chowan Story," Johnson Papers.

7. From Native People to People of Color and Back

1. William Strachey, *The History of Travel into Virginia Britannia: The First Book of the First Decade*, in *Jamestown Narratives: Eyewitness Accounts of the Virginia Colony, the First Decade: 1607–1617*, ed. Edward Wright Haile (Champlain, VA: Roundhouse, 1998), 629. See also Fullam, *Manteo*, 13–14, and Gordon M. Sayre, *Les Sauvages Américains: Representations of Native Americans in French and English Colonial Literature* (Chapel Hill: Univ. of North Carolina Press, 1997), 156–58.

2. Fischer, *Suspect Relations*, 1–2; Saunt, *Black, White, and Indian*, 55–56.

3. Fischer, *Suspect Relations*, 2; Saunt, *Black, White, and Indian*, 57–58.

4. Nowell, "Red, White, and Black," 6–10, 18; Kupperman, "English Perception of Treachery"; Pulsipher, *Subjects unto the Same King*, 15; Nash, "Image of the Indian," 223–27, 230.

5. Thomas Jefferson, *Notes on the State of Virginia* (1785; reprint, Boston: Lilly & Wait, 1832), quotes on 151, 61–67, 98, 106–10, 144–50; Coleman, *That the Blood Stay Pure*, 44–48, 54–55, 61–62.

6. Saunt, *Black, White, and Indian*, 16.

7. Gallay, *Indian Slave Trade*, 311–14.

8. General Court, Apr.–June 1697, in *CRNC2*, 3:40.

9. Complaint, May 26, 1698, in *CRNC2*, 3:528.

10. Land deed, July 1702, Beaufort County, NC, Land & Deed Records, 15.

11. Warren Eugene Milteer Jr., *Beyond Slavery's Shadow: Free People of Color in the South* (Chapel Hill: Univ. of North Carolina Press, 2021), 9; Wright, *The Only Land They Knew*, 149–50, 255–56; Saunt, *Black, White, and Indian*, 58.

12. Theda Perdue, *Slavery and the Evolution of Cherokee Society, 1540–1866* (Knoxville: Univ. of Tennessee Press, 1979), 4–9, 23; Ethridge, "Introduction," in *Mississippian Shatter Zone*, ed. Ethridge and Shuck-Hall, 14; Forbes, *Black Africans and Native Americans*, 192–93; Jack D. Forbes, "Mustees, Half-Breeds and Zambos in Anglo North America: Aspects of Black–Indian Relations," *American Indian Quarterly* 7 (1983): 58–59, 61, 63; Milteer, *Beyond Slavery's Shadow*, 9.

13. Theda Perdue, *"Mixed Blood" Indians: Racial Construction in the Early South* (Athens: Univ. of Georgia Press, 2003), 4.

14. Crow, Escott, and Hatley, *History of African Americans in North Carolina*, 25; Perdue, *"Mixed Blood" Indians*, 5–6.

15. Feeley, "Reservation, Outpost, or Homeland?"; Snyder, *Slavery in Indian Country*, 195–96; Perdue, *"Mixed Blood" Indians*.

16. Smallwood, "A History of Three Cultures," 107, 117.

17. Council Journal, July 31, 1724, in *CRNC*, 2:534; Council Minutes, Oct. 28, 1724, in *CRNC2*, 7:147; Council Minutes, Aug. 3, 1725, in *CRNC2*, 7:159; Council Journal, Apr. 3, 1727, in *CRNC*, 2:674; Petition of Isaac Hill, Apr. 23, 1731, in *CRNC*, 3:218.

18. Garrow, *Mattamuskeet Documents*, 45; Brooks, "John Lawson's Indian Town," 200.

19. Council Minutes, Apr. 3, 1733, in *CRNC*, 3:537–38.

20. Lowery, *Lumbee Indians in the Jim Crow South*, 5; C. D. Brewington, *The Five Civilized Indian Tribes of Eastern North Carolina* (Newton Grove, NC: Sampson County Historical Society, 1959), 17–25; Lowery, *Lumbee Indians*, 31–33; Smallwood, "A History of Three Cultures," 127; Peter H. Wood, *Tuscarora Roots: An Historical Report regarding the Relation of the Hatteras Tuscarora Tribe of Robeson County, North Carolina, to the Original Tuscarora Indian Tribe*, University Libraries, Digital Collections Repository, Univ. of North Carolina, Durham, 1992, 42–43.

21. Kianga Lucas, "The Granville County–Lumbee Connections," 1–10, Native American Roots: Genealogy and History of Native Americans of Granville County and Northeast North Carolina, website, at https://nativeamericanroots. wordpress.com.

22. Brooks, "John Lawson's Indian Town," 201–3; Lawson, *New Voyage to Carolina*, 41, 69.

23. Lowery, *Lumbee Indians*, 33.

24. Garrow, *Mattamuskeet Documents*, 28.

25. Lowery, *Lumbee Indians in the Jim Crow South*, 14.

26. Byrd, *William Byrd's Histories of the Dividing Line*, 4.

27. Fischer, *Suspect Relations*, 57.

28. Laws of North Carolina, 1715, in *CRNC*, 23:12–13.

29. Petition of Sundry Inhabitants of the Counties of Northampton, Edge-combe and Granville, c. 1763, in *CRNC*, 6:982–83.

30. Laws of North Carolina, 1715, in *CRNC*, 23:12–13.

31. Laws of North Carolina, 1741, in *CRNC*, 23:160, 195 (quote); Fischer, *Suspect Relations*, 85–87; Crow, Escott, and Hatley, *History of African Americans in North Carolina*, 5; Oscar Reiss, *Blacks in Colonial America* (Jefferson, NC: McFarland, 1997), 117–18.

32. William Powell, *North Carolina through Four Centuries* (Chapel Hill: Univ. of North Carolina Press, 1989), 105; Harry Roy Merrens, *Colonial North Carolina in the Eighteenth Century: A Study in Historical Geography* (Chapel Hill: Univ. of North Carolina Press, 1964), 74–81; Crow, Escott, and Hatley, *History of African Americans in North Carolina*, 3; Kay and Cary, *Slavery in North Carolina*, 19.

33. Perdue, *"Mixed Blood" Indians*, 4.

34. Wright, *The Only Land They Knew*, 258; Adams, "'Sundry Murders and Depredations,'" 171–72; Kay and Cary, *Slavery in North Carolina*, 25; Ablavsky, "Making Indians 'White,'" 1520.

35. Lowery, *Lumbee Indians in the Jim Crow South*, 14; Miles, "Native Americans and African Americans," 116; Graybeal, "'Too Light to Be Black, Too Dark to Be White,'" 102–4,

36. Mr. Taylor to the Secretary, SPG, Apr. 23, 1719, in *CRNC*, 2:332.

37. Quoted in Wesley H. Wallace, "Property and Trade: Main Themes of Early North Carolina Newspaper Advertisements," *North Carolina Historical Review* 32 (Oct. 1955): 453.

38. Richard Blackledge's Will, Feb. 20, 1776, in *North Carolina Wills and Inventories Copied from the Original and Recorded Wills and Inventories in the Office of the Secretary of State*, ed. J. Bryan Grimes (Raleigh, NC: Edwards & Broughton, 1912), 41–49.

39. Indentures of Joshua & Jordan Longtom, May 19 and Sept. 18, 1804, Apprentice Bonds and Records, 1771–1892 N.D., C.R. 053.101.1, folder 1771–1811, Hyde County Records, State Archives of North Carolina, Raleigh.

40. Milteer, "From Indians to Colored People," 41–42; LeMaster, "In the 'Scolding Houses,'" 208–10, 222–23.

41. LeMaster, "In the 'Scolding Houses,'" 222–23.

42. Garrow, *Mattamuskeet Documents*, 33–40.

43. Karin L. Zipf, *Labor of Innocents: Forced Apprenticeship in North Carolina, 1715–1919* (Baton Rouge: Louisiana State Univ. Press, 2005), 14–15, 22.

44. Marilyn Poe Lair, *Gates County, North Carolina, Court Minutes, 1779–1787, North Carolina County Courts*, vol. 1 (Raleigh: Government and Heritage Library, North Carolina State Library, n.d.), 24, 26.

45. Benjamin Robbins indenture, Nov. 1, 1779, Apprentice Bonds and Records, 1779–1824, C.R. 041.101.3, folder 1779, Gates County Records, State Archives of North Carolina.

46. James Robbins indenture, Feb. 23, 1792, Apprentice Bonds and Records, 1779–1824, C.R. 041.101.3, folder 1779, Gates County Records.

47. Samuel Robbins indenture, Nov. 18, 1783, and Jethro Robbins indenture, 1798, Apprentice Bonds and Records, 1779–1824, C.R. 041.101.3, folder 1779, Gates County Records.

48. Lewis Robbins indenture, 1800, Apprentice Bonds and Records, 1779–1824, C.R. 041.101.3, folder 1779, Gates County Records; Milteer, "From Indians to Colored People," 42–43 (quote); Raymond Parker Fouts, *Minutes of County Court of Pleas and Quarter Sessions. Gates County, North Carolina, 1779–1796*, vol. 00 (Cocoa, FL: GenRec Books, 1994), 29.

49. Indentures of Joshua & Jordan Longtom, May 19 and Sept. 18, 1804, Apprentice Bonds and Records, Hyde County Records.

50. Garrow, *Mattamuskeet Documents*, 32–33, 72–73, app. 36 and 37.

51. Garrow, *Mattamuskeet Documents*, 32–40, 75–76, app. 40 and 41.

52. Milteer, "From Indians to Colored People," 30.

53. Garrow, *Mattamuskeet Documents*, 30–31, 71, app. 34.

54. Garrow, *Mattamuskeet Documents*, 31–40, 45–46, 75–76, app. 40 and 41; Stevenson, "Indian Reservations," 28, 30.

55. Milteer, "From Indians to Colored People," 44; Hazel, "Looking for Indian Town," 38–39.

56. Lair, *Gates County, North Carolina, Land Deeds*, 71, 83.

57. Report on Petition of William Lewis and Samuel Harrell (with petition, rejected), Nov. 13, 1790, Committee of Propositions & Grievances, Nov. 6–20, 1790, Joint Standing Committee, box 2, GASR; Hazel, "Looking for Indian Town," 37–39.

58. Milteer, "From Indians to Colored People," 37–38, 44; Adams, "'Sundry Murders and Depredations,'" 172; Stevenson, "Indian Reservations," 28.

59. Milteer, "From Indians to Colored People," 53.

60. Milteer, "From Indians to Colored People," 44–45; Hazel, "Looking for Indian Town," 44–46.

61. Milteer, "From Indians to Colored People," 38, 43, 47; Adams, "'Sundry Murders and Depredations,'" 172; Marvin T. Jones, "A Rebirth on the Chowan,"

in *We Will Always Be Here: Native Peoples on Living and Thriving in the South*, ed. Denise E. Bates (Gainesville: Univ. of Florida Press, 2016), 57–58; Doug Patterson, "The Chowanoke Indian Resurgence," in *We Will Always Be Here*, ed. Bates, 72–78.

62. Milteer, "From Indians to Colored People," 30 (quote); Warren Eugene Milteer Jr., *North Carolina's Free People of Color, 1715–1885* (Baton Rouge: Louisiana State Univ. Press, 2020), 20.

63. Lowery, "On the Antebellum Fringe," 43.

64. Milteer, *North Carolina's Free People of Color*, 17, 20.

65. Milteer, *North Carolina's Free People of Color*, 15.

66. Milteer, *North Carolina's Free People of Color*, 19.

67. Brooks, "John Lawson's Indian Town," 203.

68. Milteer, *North Carolina's Free People of Color*, 8, 2.

69. Christopher Arris Oakley, *Keeping the Circle: American Indian Identity in Eastern North Carolina, 1885–2004* (Lincoln: Univ. of Nebraska Press, 2005), 11, 69–72; Lars Adams, "From Cherokee to Chowanoke: Discovering the North Carolina Algonquians," in *We Will Always Be Here*, ed. Bates, 67–69; Graybeal, "'Too Light to Be Black, Too Dark to Be White,'" 99, 104–5; Nowell, "Red, White and Black," 52; Brewington, *The Five Civilized Tribes of Eastern North Carolina*, 15–28; Dane and Griessman, "Collective Identity," 695, 697.

70. Smallwood, "A History of Three Cultures," 126.

71. Wood, *Tuscarora Roots*, 38–39; Karen I. Blu, *The Lumbee Problem: The Making of an American Indian People* (London: Cambridge Univ. Press, 1980), 43–44.

72. Wood, *Tuscarora Roots*, 36–47; Blu, *Lumbee Problem*, 56.

73. Smallwood, "A History of Three Cultures," 127; Oakley, *Keeping the Circle*, 72.

74. Lowery, *Lumbee Indians in the Jim Crow South*, 243, 246–48; Lowery, *Lumbee Indians*, 18; Oakley, *Keeping the Circle*, 70, 89–92, 131; Fullam, *Manteo*, 67–74.

75. Abstract of Returns for Several Counties, 1754, in *CRNC*, 5:161.

76. Patricia Barker Lerch, *Waccamaw Legacy: Contemporary Indians Fight for Survival* (Tuscaloosa: Univ. of Alabama Press, 2004), 3–4.

77. David S. Cecelski, *The Fire of Freedom: Abraham Galloway & the Slaves' Civil War* (Chapel Hill: Univ. of North Carolina Press, 2012), xv, 1.

78. Lowery, *Lumbee Indians*, 70.

79. *Journal of the Convention, Called by the Freemen of North-Carolina, to Amend the Constitution of the State, Which Assembled in the City of Raleigh, on the 4th of June, 1835, and Continued in Session until the 11th Day of July Thereafter*, elec. ed., Documenting the American South: A Primary Resource for the Study

of Southern History, Literature, and Culture, Univ. of North Carolina, Chapel Hill, at https://docsouth.unc.edu/nc/conv1835/conv1835.html.

80. John Hope Franklin, *The Free Negro in North Carolina, 1790–1860* (1943; reprint, New York: Norton, 1971), 109–16.

81. Hazel, "Looking for Indian Town," 43.

82. Lowery, *Lumbee Indians*, 65–88.

83. Oakley, *Keeping the Circle*, 18–35; Lowery, *Lumbee Indians*, 10, 17–18, 135–36; "Indian Tribes," North Carolina Commission of Indian Affairs, website, at https://ncadmin.nc.gov/citizens/american-indians/nc-tribal-communities.

84. "Indian Tribes."

85. Lowery, *Lumbee Indians*, 92, 117–21, 215.

Conclusion

1. *Journal of the Convention Called by the Freemen of North-Carolina . . . 4th of June, 1835.*

2. Franklin, *Free Negro in North Carolina*, 52–53.

Bibliography

Archives

Beaufort County, NC, Land & Deed Records. At http://files.usgwarchives
.net/nc/beaufort/deeds/p1-50.txt.

Calendar of State Papers, Colonial, America and West Indies, 1574–1739.
46 vols. Edited by Cecil Headlam. London, 1860. British History Online, at https://www.british-history.ac.uk/search/series/cal-state-papers
–colonial–america-west-indies.

Documenting the American South: A Primary Resource for the Study of
Southern History, Literature, and Culture. Univ. of North Carolina,
Chapel Hill. At https://docsouth.unc.edu.

Minutes of the Provincial Council of Pennsylvania. 10 vols. Philadelphia:
Jo. Severns, 1852.

State Archives of North Carolina, Raleigh.
    Albemarle County Records. Microfilm C. 002 1001.
    Batts, Nathaniel, Papers. PC 1293.1.
    Bertie County Records. Microfilm.
    Chowan County Criminal Action Papers.
    Chowan County Deeds.
    Chowan County Records.
    Colonial Governor's Papers.
    Dobbs, Gov. Arthur, Papers, 1754–65. CGO.5.
    Currituck County Deeds.
    Gates County Records.
    General Assembly Session Records.
    Hyde County Deeds.
    Hyde County Records. CR 053.101.1.
    Johnson, F. Roy, Papers. PC 367.1, oversize.

Miscellaneous Papers, 1697–1823. PC 21.1.
  Colonial Court Records. Indians—Treaties, Petitions, Agreements, and Court Cases. CCR 192.
Pollock, Thomas, Papers, 1708–1859, 1711–1842. PC 31.2.
Secretary of State Records.
Slave Collection. PC 1629.
Stone, David, Papers. PC 82.
Supreme Court Original Cases.
Wilson Library, Univ. of North Carolina, Chapel Hill.
North Carolina Collection.
Southern Historical Collection.
  Thompson, Lewis, Papers.

Primary Sources

Archdale, John. *A New Description of That Fertile and Pleasant Province of Carolina*. London: John Wyat, 1707.
Barlowe, Arthur. "Arthur Barlowe's Narrative of the 1584 Voyage." In *The First Colonists: Documents on the Planting of the First English Settlements in North America, 1584–1590*, edited by David B. Quinn and Alison M. Quinn, 1–12. Raleigh: North Carolina Department of Cultural Resources, 1982.
Barnwell, Joseph W. "The Tuscarora Expedition: Letters of Colonel John Barnwell." *South Carolina Historical and Genealogical Magazine* 9 (Jan. 1908): 28–54.
Brickell, John. *The Natural History of North-Carolina*. 1737. Reprint. Murfreesboro, NC: Johnson, 1978.
Byrd, William. *William Byrd's Histories of the Dividing Line betwixt Virginia and North Carolina*. Edited by William K. Boyd. Raleigh: North Carolina Historical Commission, 1929.
Church, Benjamin. *Diary of King Philip's War, 1675–76* (1716). Edited by Alan Simpson and Mary Simpson. Chester, CT: Pequot Press, 1975.
Colonial Records of North Carolina. 26 vols. Edited by William L. Saunders. 1886. Reprint. Wilmington, NC: Broadfoot, 1993.
Colonial Records of North Carolina. Second Series, 10 vols. Edited by Mattie Erma Edwards Parker and Robert J. Cain. 1968. Reprint.

Raleigh: North Carolina Department of Cultural Resources, Division of Archives, 1999.

"De Graffenried's Manuscript, Copied for *The Colonial Records of North Carolina* from the Original Mss. in the Public Library at Yverdon, Switzerland, and Translated by M. Du Four." In *Colonial Records of North Carolina*, 26 vols., edited by William L. Saunders, 1:905–85. 1886. Reprint. Wilmington, NC: Broadfoot, 1993.

Fouts, Raymond Parker. *Minutes of County Court of Pleas and Quarter Sessions. Gates County, North Carolina, 1779–1796.* Vol. 00. Cocoa, FL: GenRec Books, 1994.

Grimes, J. Bryan, ed. *North Carolina Wills and Inventories Copied from the Original and Recorded Wills and Inventories in the Office of the Secretary of State.* Raleigh, NC: Edwards & Broughton, 1912.

Hakluyt, Richard. *Discourse of Western Planting, 1584.* In *The Original Writings & Correspondence of the Two Richard Hakluyts*, edited by E. G. R. Taylor, 211–326. London: Hakluyt Society, 1933.

———. "The Letters Patents granted by her Majestie to Sir Humfrey Gilbert knight, for the inhabiting and planting of our people in America. June 11, 1578." In *Hakluyt's Voyages: The Principal Voyages, Traffiques & Discoveries of the English Nation*, edited by Irwin R. Blacker, 210–15. New York: Viking Press, 1965.

———. "Letters Patents of King Henry the Seventh granted unto John Cabot and his three sonnes, Lewis, Sebastian, and Sancius for the discoverie of new and unknowen lands. March 1496." In *Hakluyt's Voyages: The Principal Voyages, Trafffiques & Discoveries of the English Nation*, edited by Irwin R. Blacker, 17–18. New York: Viking Press, 1965.

———. "Second Voyage of Master Martin Frobisher, made to the West and Northwest Regions in the yeere 1577, with a description of the country and people. Written by Master Dionise Settle." In *Hakluyt's Voyages: The Principal Voyages, Trafffiques & Discoveries of the English Nation*, edited by Irwin R. Blacker, 182–98. New York: Viking Press, 1965.

Harriot, Thomas. "A Briefe and True Report of the New Found Land of Virginia (1588)." In *The First Colonists: Documents on the Planting of the First English Settlements in North America, 1584–1590*, edited by David B. Quinn and Alison M. Quinn, 46–76. Raleigh: North Carolina Department of Cultural Resources, 1982.

Hathaway, J. R. B., ed. *North Carolina Historical and Genealogical Register.* 3 vols. Edenton, NC: n.p., 1900–1903.

Haun, Weynette Parks. *Hyde County North Carolina Court Minutes, 1736–1756.* Book 1. Raleigh: Government and Heritage Library, North Carolina State Library, 1985.

"Indian Tribes." North Carolina Commission of Indian Affairs, website. At https://ncadmin.nc.gov/citizens/american-indians/nc-tribal-communities.

Isenbarger, Dennis L., ed. *Native Americans in Early North Carolina: A Documentary History.* Raleigh: North Carolina Office of Archives and History, 2013.

Jane, Cecil, and E. G. R. Taylor. "Third Voyage of Columbus Carta." In *Select Documents Illustrating the Four Voyages of Columbus,* 2 vols., 2:48–71. London: Hakluyt Society, 1929–32.

Jefferson, Thomas. *Notes on the State of Virginia.* 1785. Reprint. Boston: Lilly & Wait, 1832.

Jones, Hugh. *The Present State of Virginia: From Whence Is Inferred a Short View of Maryland and North Carolina.* Edited and with an introduction by Richard L. Morton. Chapel Hill: Univ. of North Carolina Press, 1956.

"Journal of the 1585 Virginia Voyage." In *The First Colonists: Documents on the Planting of the First English Settlements in North America, 1584–1590,* edited by David B. Quinn and Alison M. Quinn, 13–19. Raleigh: North Carolina Department of Cultural Resources, 1982.

Journal of the Convention, Called by the Freemen of North-Carolina, to Amend the Constitution of the State, Which Assembled in the City of Raleigh, on the 4th of June, 1835, and Continued in Session until the 11th Day of July Thereafter. Elec. ed. Documenting the American South: A Primary Resource for the Study of Southern History, Literature, and Culture, Univ. of North Carolina, Chapel Hill. At https://docsouth.unc.edu/nc/conv1835/conv1835.html.

Lair, Marilyn Poe. *Gates County, North Carolina, Court Minutes, 1779–1787, North Carolina County Courts.* Vol. 1. Raleigh: Government and Heritage Library, North Carolina State Library, n.d.

———. *Gates County, North Carolina, Land Deeds, 1776–1795.* Vol. A. Raleigh: Government and Heritage Library, North Carolina State Library, 1977.

La Jau, Francis. *The Carolina Chronicle of Dr. Francis La Jau, 1706–1717.* Edited by Frank J. Klingberg. Berkeley: Univ. of California Press, 1956.

Lane, Ralph. "Narrative of the Settlement of Roanoke Island, 1585–1586." In *The First Colonists: Documents on the Planting of the First English Settlements in North America, 1584–1590*, edited by David B. Quinn and Alison M. Quinn, 24–45. Raleigh: North Carolina Department of Cultural Resources, 1982.

Lawson, John. *A New Voyage to Carolina* (1709). Edited by Hugh Talmage Lefler. Chapel Hill: Univ. of North Carolina, 1967.

McIllwaine, Henry R., Wilmer L. Hall, and Benjamin J. Hillman, eds. *Executive Journals of the Council of Colonial Virginia.* 6 vols. Richmond: Virginia State Library, 1925–66.

Meredith, Hugh. *An Account of the Cape Fear Country, 1731.* Edited by Earl Greg Swem. Perth Amboy, NJ: Charles F. Heartman, 1922.

Quinn, David B., and Alison M. Quinn, eds. *The First Colonists: Documents on the Planting of the First English Settlements in North America, 1584–1590.* Raleigh: North Carolina Department of Cultural Resources, 1982.

Return of the Whole Number of Persons with the Several Districts of the United States. US Census, 1800. Dec. 8, 1801. At www2.census.gov /library/publications/decennial/1800/1800-returns.pdf.

Smith, John. *The Generall History of Virginia, the Somer Iles, and New England, with the Names of the Adventurers and Their Adventures.* Vol. 2 of *The Complete Works of John Smith*, 3 vols. Edited by Philip L. Barbour. Chapel Hill: Univ. of North Carolina Press, 1986.

Stanard, William, ed. "Examination of Indians, 1713." Miscellaneous Colonial Documents. *Virginia Magazine of History and Biography* 19 (July 1911): 272–75.

Strachey, William. *The History of Travel into Virginia Britannia: The First Book of the First Decade.* In *Jamestown Narratives: Eyewitness Accounts of the Virginia Colony, the First Decade: 1607–1617*, edited by Edward Wright Haile, 563–689. Champlain, VA: Roundhouse, 1998.

"Treaty between Virginia and the Indians, 1677, in the Virginia Colonial Records." *Virginia Magazine of History and Biography* 14 (Jan. 1907): 289–96.

Tryon, William. *The Correspondence of William Tryon and Other Selected Papers*. 2 vols. Edited by William S. Powell. Raleigh: North Carolina Department of Cultural Resources, 1980.

Von Graffenried, Christoph. *Christoph Von Graffenried's Account of the Founding of New Bern: Edited with an Historical Introduction and an English Translation*. Raleigh, NC: Edwards & Broughton for the North Carolina Historical Commission, 1920.

White, John. "John White's Narrative of the 1587 Virginia Voyage." In *The First Colonists: Documents on the Planting of the First English Settlements in North America, 1584–1590*, edited by David B. Quinn and Alison M. Quinn, 93–106. Raleigh: North Carolina Department of Cultural Resources, 1982.

———. "John White's Narrative of the 1590 Virginia Voyage." In *The First Colonists: Documents on the Planting of the First English Settlements in North America, 1584–1590*, edited by David B. Quinn and Alison M. Quinn, 117–30. Raleigh: North Carolina Department of Cultural Resources, 1982.

Wroth, Lawrence C. *The Voyages of Giovanni da Verrazzano, 1524–1528*. New Haven, CT: Yale Univ. Press, 1970.

Secondary Sources

Ablavsky, Gregory. "Making Indians 'White': The Judicial Abolition of Native Slavery in Revolutionary Virginia and Its Racial Legacy." *University of Pennsylvania Law Review* 159 (Apr. 2011): 1457–531.

Adams, Lars C. "From Cherokee to Chowanoke: Discovering the North Carolina Algonquians." In *We Will Always Be Here: Native Peoples on Living and Thriving in the South*, edited by Denise E. Bates, 65–71. Gainesville: Univ. of Florida Press, 2016.

———. "'Sundry Murders and Depredations': A Closer Look at the Chowan River War, 1676–1677." *North Carolina Historical Review* 90 (Apr. 2013): 149–72.

Anderson, Gary Clayton. *The Indian Southwest 1580–1830: Ethnogenesis and Reinvention*. Norman: Univ. of Oklahoma Press, 1999.

Barth, Jonathan Edward. "'The Sinke of America': Society in the Albemarle Borderlands of North Carolina, 1663–1729." *North Carolina Historical Review* 87 (Jan. 2010): 1–27.

Bates, Denise E., ed. *We Will Always Be Here: Native Peoples on Living and Thriving in the South*. Gainesville: Univ. of Florida Press, 2016.

Blu, Karen I. *The Lumbee Problem: The Making of an American Indian People*. London: Cambridge Univ. Press, 1980.

Boyce, Douglas W. "Did a Tuscarora Confederacy Exist?" In *Four Centuries of Southern Indians*, edited by Charles M. Hudson, 28–45. Athens: Univ. of Georgia Press, 1975.

———. "Iroquoian Tribes of the Virginia–North Carolina Coastal Plain." In *Handbook of North American Indians*, vol. 15: *Northeast*, edited by Bruce G. Trigger, 282–89. Washington DC: Smithsonian Institution, 1978.

Brewington, C. D. *The Five Civilized Indian Tribes of Eastern North Carolina*. Newton Grove, NC: Sampson County Historical Society, 1959.

Brooks, Baylus C. "John Lawson's Indian Town on Hatteras Island, North Carolina." *North Carolina Historical Review* 91 (Apr. 2014): 171–207.

Byrd, John E., and Charles L. Heath. "'The Country here is very thick of Indian Towns and Plantations . . .': Tuscarora Settlement Patterns as Revealed by the Contentnea Creek Survey." In *Indian and European Contact in Context: The Mid-Atlantic Region*, edited by Dennis B. Blanton and Julia A. King, 98–125. Gainesville: Univ. of Florida Press, 2004.

———. *The Rediscovery of the Tuscarora Homeland: A Final Report of the Archaeological Survey of the Contentnea Creek Drainage, 1995–1997*. David S. Phelps Archaeology Laboratory, East Carolina Univ., Greenville, NC. Report submitted to the National Park Service and the North Carolina Division of Archives and History, Raleigh. Greene County Surveys, no. 4153. Raleigh: North Carolina Office of State Archaeology, 1997.

Cecelski, David S. *The Fire of Freedom: Abraham Galloway & the Slaves' Civil War*. Chapel Hill: Univ. of North Carolina Press, 2012.

———. *The Waterman's Song: Slavery and Freedom in Maritime North Carolina*. Chapel Hill: Univ. of North Carolina Press, 2001.

Coleman, Arica L. *That the Blood Stay Pure: African Americans, Native Americans, and the Predicament of Race and Identity in Virginia*. Bloomington: Indiana Univ. Press, 2013.

Crane, Verner W. *The Southern Frontier, 1670–1732*. New York: Norton, 1981.

Craven, Wesley Frank. *The Southern Colonies in the Seventeenth Century, 1607–1689.* Baton Rouge: Louisiana State Univ. Press, 1949.

Crow, Jeffrey J., Paul D. Escott, and Flora J. Hatley. *A History of African Americans in North Carolina.* Raleigh: North Carolina Department of Cultural Resources, 1992.

Cumming, W. P. "The Earliest Permanent Settlement in Carolina: Nathaniel Batts and the Comberford Map." *American Historical Review* 45 (Oct. 1939): 82–89.

Dane, J. K., and B. Eugene Griessman. "The Collective Identity of Marginal Peoples: The North Carolina Experience." *American Anthropologist* 74 (June 1972): 694–704.

Darby, Melissa. *Thunder Go North: The Hunt for Sir Francis Drake's Fair & Good Bay.* Salt Lake City: Univ. of Utah Press, 2019.

Dawdy, Shannon Lee. "The Meherrin's Secret History of the Dividing Line." *North Carolina Historical Review* 72 (Oct. 1995): 387–415.

Dill, Alonzo Thomas, Jr. "Eighteenth Century New Bern: A History of the Town and Craven County, 1700–1800." Part 1. *North Carolina Historical Review* 22 (Jan. 1945): 1–21. Part 2, 22 (Apr. 1945): 152–75. Part 3, 22 (July 1945): 293–319.

Dixon, Bradley J. "'His one Netev ples': The Chowans and the Politics of Native Petitions in the Colonial South." *William and Mary Quarterly,* 3rd Series, 76 (Jan. 2019): 41–74.

Dobyns, Henry F. *Their Number Become Thinned: Native American Population Dynamics in Eastern North America.* Knoxville: Univ. of Tennessee Press, 1983.

"Doctrine of Discovery, 1493." Gilder Lehrman Institute of American History. At https://www.gilderlehrman.org/history-by-era/imperial-rivalries/resources/doctrine-discovery-1493.

Dowd, Gregory Evans. *War under Heaven: Pontiac, the Indian Nations & the British Empire.* Baltimore: Johns Hopkins Univ. Press, 2002.

Dunbar, Gary S. "The Hatteras Indians of North Carolina." *Ethnohistory* 7 (Autumn 1960): 410–18.

DuVal, Kathleen. *The Native Ground: Indians and Colonists in the Heart of the Continent.* Philadelphia: Univ. of Pennsylvania Press, 2006.

Edwards, Tai S. "The 'Virgin' Soil Thesis Cover-Up: Teaching Indigenous Demographic Collapse." In *Understanding and Teaching Native*

American History, edited by Kristofer Ray and Brady DeSanti, 29–43. Madison: Univ. of Wisconsin Press, 2022.

Elliott, John H. "The Seizure of Overseas Territories by European Powers." In *Theories of Empire, 1450–1800*, edited by David Armitage, 139–57. Aldershot, UK: Ashgate, 1998.

Ellis, Steven G. *Ireland in the Age of the Tudors 1447–1603: English Expansion and the End of Gaelic Rule*. London: Addison Wesley Longman, 1998.

Ethridge, Robbie. *From Chicaza to Chickasaw: The European Invasion and the Transformation of the Mississippian World, 1540–1715*. Chapel Hill: Univ. of North Carolina Press, 2010.

———. "Introduction: Mapping the Mississippian Shatter Zone." In *Mapping the Mississippian Shatter Zone: The Colonial Indian Slave Trade and Regional Instability in the American South*, edited by Robbie Ethridge and Sheri M. Shuck-Hall, 1–62. Lincoln: Univ. of Nebraska Press, 2008.

Feeley, Stephen. "Intercolonial Conflict and Cooperation during the Tuscarora War." In *New Voyages to Carolina: Reinterpreting North Carolina History*, edited by Larry E. Tise and Jeffrey J. Crow, 60–84. Chapel Hill: Univ. of North Carolina Press, 2017.

———. "Reservation, Outpost or Homeland? Indian Woods in the 18th Century." Paper presented at the Three Hundred Years of Indian Woods, 1717–2017, Tercentenary Conference, Oct. 7–9, 2017, Hope Plantation, Windsor, NC.

Feeser, Andrea. *Red, White & Black Make Blue: Indigo in the Fabric of Colonial South Carolina Life*. Athens: Univ. of Georgia Press, 2013.

Feest, Christian, "North Carolina Algonquians." In *Handbook of North American Indians*, vol. 15: *Northeast*, edited by Bruce G. Trigger, 271–81. Washington, DC: Smithsonian Institution, 1978.

Fenton, William N. *The Great Law and the Longhouse: A Political History of the Iroquois Confederacy*. Norman: Univ. of Oklahoma Press, 1998.

Fischer, Kirsten. *Suspect Relations: Sex, Race, and Resistance in Colonial North Carolina*. Ithaca, NY: Cornell Univ. Press, 2002.

Forbes, Jack D. *Black Africans and Native Americans: Color, Race, and Caste in the Evolution of Red–Black Peoples*. New York: Blackwell, 1988.

———. "Mustees, Half-Breeds and Zambos in Anglo North America: Aspects of Black–Indian Relations." *American Indian Quarterly* 7 (1983): 57–83.

Foster, R. F. *The Oxford History of Ireland.* Oxford: Oxford Univ. Press, 1989.

Franklin, John Hope. *The Free Negro in North Carolina, 1790–1860.* 1943. Reprint. New York: Norton, 1971.

Fullam, Brandon. *Manteo and the Algonquians of the Roanoke Voyages.* Jefferson, NC: McFarland, 2020.

Gallay, Alan, ed. *Indian Slavery in Colonial America.* Lincoln: Univ. of Nebraska Press, 2009.

———. *The Indian Slave Trade: The Rise of the English Empire in the American South, 1670–1717.* New Haven, CT: Yale Univ. Press, 2002.

Gamble, Stephanie. "A Community of Convenience: The Saponi Nation, Governor Spotswood, and the Experiment at Fort Christanna, 1670–1740." *Native South* 6 (2013): 70–109.

Garrow, Patrick H. *The Mattamuskeet Documents: A Study in Social History.* Raleigh: North Carolina Department of Cultural Resources, 1975.

Gleach, Frederic W. *Powhatan's World and Colonial Virginia: A Conflict of Cultures.* Lincoln: Univ. of Nebraska Press, 1997.

Graybeal, Lesley M. "'Too Light to Be Black, Too Dark to Be White': Redefining Occaneechi Identity through Community Education." *Native South* 5 (2012): 95–122.

Greenblatt, Stephen. *Marvelous Possessions: The Wonder of the New World.* Chicago: Univ. of Chicago Press, 1991.

Grimes, J. Bryan. "Some Notes on Colonial North Carolina, 1700–1750." *North Carolina Booklet* 5 (Oct. 1905): 90–149.

Hazel, Forest. "Looking for Indian Town: The Dispersal of the Chowan Indian Tribe in Eastern North Carolina, 1780–1915." *North Carolina Archaeology* 63 (Oct. 2014): 34–64.

Heath, Charles L. "Woodland Period Mortuary Variability in the Lower Roanoke River Valley: Perspectives from the Jordan's Landing, Sans Souci and Dickerson Sites." Research paper presented at the Sixtieth Annual Meeting of the Southeastern Archaeological Conference, Nov. 12–15, 2003, Charlotte, NC.

Hodge, Frederick Webb, ed. *Handbook of American Indians North of Mexico.* 2 vols. Washington, DC: US Government Printing Office, 1910.

Holloman, Charles R. "Tuscarora Towns in Bath County." *We the People: Official Publication of the North Carolina Citizens Association* 23 (Feb. 1966): 16–30.

Hudson, Charles. *Southeastern Indians.* Knoxville: Univ. of Tennessee Press, 1976.

Irvin, Joshua. "Ties to Home: Tuscarora Autonomy and the Sale of Indian Woods, 1801–1831." Paper presented at the Three Hundred Years of Indian Woods, 1717–2017, Tecentenary Conference, Feb. 7–9, 2017, Hope Plantation, Windsor, NC.

Jennings, Francis. *The Ambiguous Iroquois Empire: The Covenant Chain Confederation of Indian Tribes with English Colonies from Its Beginning to the Lancaster Treaty of 1744.* New York: Norton, 1984.

———. *The Invasion of America: Indians, Colonialism, and the Cant of Conquest.* New York: Norton, 1975.

Johnson, F. Roy. *The Tuscaroras: Mythology—Medicine—Culture.* 2 vols. Murfreesboro, NC: Johnson, 1967.

Jones, Marvin T. "A Rebirth on the Chowan." In *We Will Always Be Here: Native Peoples on Living and Thriving in the South*, edited by Denise E. Bates, 56–61. Gainesville: Univ. of Florida Press, 2016.

Jordan, Winthrop D. *White over Black: American Attitudes toward the Negro, 1550–1812.* Chapel Hill: Univ. of North Carolina Press, 1968.

Kawashima, Yasu. "Legal Origins of the Indian Reservation in Colonial Massachusetts." *American Journal of Legal History* 13 (Jan. 1969): 42–56.

Kay, Marvin L., and Lorin Lee Cary. *Slavery in North Carolina, 1748–1775.* Chapel Hill: Univ. of North Carolina Press, 1995.

Kelton, Paul. *Epidemics and Enslavement: Biological Catastrophe in the Native Southeast.* Lincoln: Univ. of Nebraska Press, 2007.

Kupperman, Karen Ordahl. "English Perception of Treachery, 1583–1640: The Case of the American Savages." *Historical Journal* 20 (June 1977): 263–87.

———. *Roanoke: The Abandoned Colony.* Lanham, MD: Rowman & Littlefield, 1984.

La Vere, David. "Of Fortifications and Fire: The Tuscarora Response to the Barnwell and Moore Expeditions during North Carolina's Tuscarora War in 1712 and 1713." *North Carolina Historical Review* 94 (Oct. 2017): 363–90.

———. *The Tuscarora War: Indians, Settlers, and the Fight for the Carolina Colony.* Chapel Hill: Univ. of North Carolina Press, 2013.

Lee, Lawrence E. *Indian Wars of North Carolina, 1663–1763.* 1963. Reprint. Raleigh: North Carolina Division of Archives and History, 1997.

Lee, Wayne E. "Fortify, Fight or Flee: Tuscarora and Cherokee Defensive Warfare and Military Culture Adaptation." *Journal of Military History* 68 (July 2004): 713–70.

Lefler, Hugh T., and William S. Powell. *Colonial North Carolina: A History.* New York: Scribner's, 1973.

LeMaster, Michelle. *Brothers Born of One Mother: British–Native American Relations in the Colonial Southeast.* Charlottesville: Univ. of Virginia Press, 2012.

———. "In the 'Scolding Houses': Indians and the Law in Eastern North Carolina, 1684–1760." *North Carolina Historical Review* 83 (Apr. 2006): 193–232.

Lerch, Patricia Barker. *Waccamaw Legacy: Contemporary Indians Fight for Survival.* Tuscaloosa: Univ. of Alabama Press, 2004.

Lowery, Malinda Maynor. *The Lumbee Indians: An American Struggle.* Chapel Hill: Univ. of North Carolina Press, 2018.

———. *Lumbee Indians in the Jim Crow South: Race, Identity, & the Making of a Nation.* Chapel Hill: Univ. of North Carolina Press, 2010.

———. "On the Antebellum Fringe: Lumbee Indians, Slavery, and Removal." *Native South* 10 (2017): 40–59.

Lucas, Kianga. "The Granville County–Lumbee Connections." Native American Roots: Genealogy and History of Native Americans of Granville County and Northeast North Carolina, website. At https://nativeamericanroots.wordpress.com.

Mallios, Seth. *The Deadly Politics of Giving: Exchange and Violence at Ajacan, Roanoke, and Jamestown.* Tuscaloosa: Univ. of Alabama Press, 2006.

Mancall, Peter C. *Deadly Medicine: Indians and Alcohol in Early America.* Ithaca, NY: Cornell Univ. Press, 1995.

Mandell, Daniel R. *Behind the Frontier: Indians in Eighteenth-Century Eastern Massachusetts.* Lincoln: Univ. of Nebraska Press, 1996.

McCartney, Martha W. "Cockacoeske, Queen of Pamunkey: Diplomat and Suzeraine." In *Powhatan's Mantle: Indians in the Colonial Southeast,* edited by Peter H. Wood, Gregory A. Waselkov, and M. Thomas Hatley, 173–95. Lincoln: Univ. of Nebraska Press, 1989.

McIlvenna, Noeleen. *A Very Mutinous People: The Struggle for North Carolina, 1660–1713.* Chapel Hill, NC: Univ. of Chapel Hill Press, 2009.

McLoughlin, William G. "Red Indians, Black Slavery and White Racism: America's Slaveholding Indians." *American Quarterly* 26 (Oct. 1974): 367–85.

Merrell, James. *Indians' New World: Catawbas and Their Neighbors from European Contact through the Era of Removal.* New York: Norton, 1989.

———. "The Racial Education of the Catawba Indians." *Journal of Southern History* 50 (Aug. 1984): 363–84.

Merrens, Harry Roy. *Colonial North Carolina in the Eighteenth Century: A Study in Historical Geography.* Chapel Hill: Univ. of North Carolina Press, 1964.

Miles, Tiya. "Native Americans and African Americans." In *The New Encyclopedia of Southern Culture*, vol. 24: *Race*, edited by Thomas C. Holt, Laurie C. Green, and Charles Reagan Wilson, 114–20. Chapel Hill: Univ. of North Carolina Press, 2013.

Miller, Lee. *Roanoke: Solving the Mystery of the Lost Colony.* New York: Penguin, 2000.

Milling, Chapman J. *Red Carolinians.* 1940. Reprint. Columbia: Univ. of South Carolina Press, 1969.

Milteer, Warren Eugene, Jr. *Beyond Slavery's Shadow: Free People of Color in the South.* Chapel Hill: Univ. of North Carolina Press, 2021.

———. "From Indians to Colored People: The Problem of Racial Categories and the Persistence of the Chowans in North Carolina." *North Carolina Historical Review* 93 (Jan. 2016): 28–57.

———. *North Carolina's Free People of Color, 1715–1885.* Baton Rouge: Louisiana State Univ. Press, 2020.

Moody, Robert Earle. "Massachusetts Trade with Carolina, 1686–1709." *North Carolina Historical Review* 20 (Jan.–Oct. 1943): 43–53.

Mooney, James. *The Siouan Tribes of the East.* 1894. Reprint. New York: Johnson Reprint, 1970.

Nash, Gary B. "The Image of the Indian in the Southern Colonial Mind." *William and Mary Quarterly* 29 (Apr. 1972): 197–230.

———. *Red, White and Black: The Peoples of Early America*. Englewood Cliffs, NJ: Prentice-Hall, 1974.

Nowell, Jeremiah James, Jr. "Red, White, and Black: Race Formation and the Politics of American Indian Recognition in North Carolina." PhD diss., Univ. of North Carolina, Chapel Hill, 2000.

Oakley, Christopher Arris. *Keeping the Circle: American Indian Identity in Eastern North Carolina, 1885–2004*. Lincoln: Univ. of Nebraska Press, 2005.

Oberg, Michael Leroy. *Dominion & Civility: English Imperialism & Native America, 1585–1685*. Ithaca, NY: Cornell Univ. Press, 1999.

———. "Gods and Men: The Meeting of Indian and White Worlds on the Carolina Outer Banks, 1584–1586." *North Carolina Historical Review* 77 (Oct. 1999): 367–90.

———. *The Head in Edward Nugent's Hand: Roanoke's Forgotten Indians*. Philadelphia: Univ. of Pennsylvania Press, 2008.

Pagden, Anthony. "Dispossessing the Barbarian: The Language of Spanish Thomism and the Debate over the Property Rights of American Indians." In *Theories of Empire, 1450–1800*, edited by David Armitage, 159–78. Aldershot, UK: Ashgate, 1998.

Parramore, Thomas. "The Great Slave Conspiracy: 'The Colerain Letter' and Other Plots—Real or Imagined—Which in 1802 Launched the Worst Insurrection Panic in North Carolina History." *The State* 39 (Aug. 15, 1971): 7–10, 19.

———. "The 'Lost Colony' Found: A Documentary Perspective." *North Carolina Historical Review* 78 (Jan. 2001): 67–83.

Patterson, Doug. "The Chowanoke Indian Resurgence." In *We Will Always Be Here: Native Peoples on Living and Thriving in the South*, edited by Denise E. Bates, 72–78. Gainesville: Univ. of Florida Press, 2016.

Perdue, Theda. *Cherokee Women: Gender and Culture Change, 1700–1835*. Lincoln: Univ. of Nebraska Press, 1998.

———. *"Mixed Blood" Indians: Racial Construction in the Early South*. Athens: Univ. of Georgia Press, 2003.

———. *Slavery and the Evolution of Cherokee Society, 1540–1866*. Knoxville: Univ. of Tennessee Press, 1979.

Perdue, Theda, and Christopher Arris Oakley. *Native Carolinians: The Indians of North Carolina*. Raleigh: North Carolina Department of Cultural Resources, 2010.

Philbrick, Nathaniel. *Mayflower: A Story of Courage, Community and War.* New York: Penguin, 2006.

Potter, Stephen R. *Commoners, Tribute, and Chiefs: The Development of Algonquian Culture in the Potomac Valley.* Charlottesville: Univ. Press of Virginia, 1993.

Powell, William, ed. *Dictionary of North Carolina Biography.* 6 vols. Chapel Hill: Univ. of North Carolina Press, 1979.

———. *North Carolina through Four Centuries.* Chapel Hill: Univ. of North Carolina Press, 1989.

———. *The Proprietors of Carolina.* 1963. Reprint. Raleigh: North Carolina Department of Archives and History, 1968.

Prucha, Francis Paul. *The Great Father: The United States Government and the American Indians.* Lincoln: Univ. of Nebraska Press, 1984.

Puglisi, Michael J. "'Whether They Be Friends or Foes': The Roles and Reactions of Tributary Native Groups Caught in Colonial Conflicts." *International Social Science Review* 70 (1995): 76–86.

Pulsipher, Jenny Hale. *Subjects unto the Same King: Indians, English, and the Contest for Authority in Colonial New England.* Philadelphia: Univ. of Pennsylvania Press, 2005.

Quinn, David Beers. *Set Fair for Roanoke: Voyages and Colonies, 1584–1606.* Chapel Hill: Univ. of North Carolina Press, 1985.

Rana, Aziz. *The Two Faces of American Freedom.* Cambridge, MA: Harvard Univ. Press, 2010.

Ray, Kristofer. "Constructing a Discourse of Indigenous Slavery, Freedom and Sovereignty in Anglo-Virginia, 1600–1750." *Native South* 10 (2017): 19–39.

Reiss, Oscar. *Blacks in Colonial America.* Jefferson, NC: McFarland, 1997.

Rice, James D. *Tales from a Revolution: Bacon's Rebellion and the Transformation of Early America.* Oxford: Oxford Univ. Press, 2012.

Richardson, Troy. "Tuscarora, Saponi and Tutelo at William and Mary College and Fort Christianna, 1690–1715: Rethinking the Cultural Broker Paradigm of the History of Indian Education." Paper presented at the Three Hundred Years of Indian Woods, 1717–2017, Tercentenary Conference, Oct. 7–9, 2017, Hope Plantation, Windsor, NC.

Rights, Douglas L. "The Trading Path to the Indians." *North Carolina Historical Review* 8 (Oct. 1931): 403–26.

Robinson, W. Stitt. "Tributary Indians in Colonial Virginia." *Virginia Magazine of History and Biography* 67 (Jan. 1959): 49–64.

Rountree, Helen C. *Pocahontas's People: The Powhatan Indians of Virginia through Four Centuries*. Norman: Univ. of Oklahoma Press, 1990.

Rountree, Helen C., with Wesley D. Taukchiray. *Manteo's World: Native American Life in Carolina's Sound Country before and after the Lost Colony*. Chapel Hill: Univ. of North Carolina Press, 2021.

Saraydar, Stephen C. "No Longer Shall You Kill: Peace, Power and the Iroquois Great Law." *Anthropology and Humanism Quarterly* 15 (Feb. 1990): 20–28.

Saunt, Claudio. *Black, White, and Indian: Race and the Unmaking of an American Family*. Oxford: Oxford Univ. Press, 2005.

Sayre, Gordon M. *Les Sauvages Américains: Representations of Native Americans in French and English Colonial Literature*. Chapel Hill: Univ. of North Carolina Press, 1997.

Seaman, Rebecca M. "John Lawson, the Outbreak of the Tuscarora Wars, and 'Middle Ground' Theory." *Journal of the Association of North Carolina Historians* 18 (Apr. 2010): 9–33.

Shannon, Timothy J. *Iroquois Diplomacy on the Early American Frontier*. New York: Viking, 2008.

Shefveland, Kristalyn Marie. *Anglo–Native Virginia: Trade, Conversion, and Indian Slavery in the Old Dominion, 1646–1722*. Athens: Univ. of Georgia Press, 2016.

Sider, Gerald M. *Lumbee Indian Histories: Race, Ethnicity, and Indian Identity in the Southern United States*. Cambridge: Cambridge Univ. Press, 1993.

Silver, Timothy. *A New Face on the Countryside: Indians, Colonists, and Slaves in South Atlantic Forests, 1500–1800*. New York: Cambridge Univ. Press, 1990.

Sloan, Kim. *A New World: England's First View of America*. Chapel Hill: Univ. of North Carolina Press, 2007.

Smallwood, Arwin D. "A History of Native American and African Relations from 1502 to 1900." *Negro History Bulletin* 62 (Apr.–Sept. 1999): 18–31.

———. "A History of Three Cultures: Indian Woods, North Carolina, 1585 to 1995." PhD diss., Ohio State Univ., 1997.

Snyder, Christina. *Slavery in Indian Country: The Changing Face of Captivity in Early America*. Cambridge, MA: Harvard Univ. Press, 2012.

Speck, Frank G. "Remnants of the Machapunga Indians of North Carolina." *American Anthropologist* 18 (Apr.–June 1916): 271–76.

Stevenson, George, Jr. "Indian Reservations in North Carolina." *Carolina Comments* 57 (Jan. 2009): 26–31.

Thomas, Gerald W. "Indian Woods: A Lost Reservation." Paper presented at the Three Hundred Years of Indian Woods, 1717–2017, Tercentenary Conference, Feb. 7–9, 2017, Hope Plantation, Windsor, NC.

Tortora, Daniel J. *Carolina in Crisis: Cherokees, Colonists, and Slaves in the American Southeast, 1756–1763*. Chapel Hill: Univ. of North Carolina Press, 2015.

Towles, Louis P. "Cary's Rebellion and the Emergence of Thomas Pollock." *Journal of the Association of Historians of North Carolina* 4 (Fall 1996): 36–58.

Usner, Daniel H., Jr. *Indians, Settlers, & Slaves in a Frontier Exchange Economy: The Lower Mississippi Valley before 1783*. Chapel Hill: Univ. of North Carolina Press, 1992.

Wallace, Anthony F. C. *Tuscarora: A History*. Albany: State Univ. of New York Press, 2012.

Wallace, Wesley H. "Property and Trade: Main Themes of Early North Carolina Newspaper Advertisements." *North Carolina Historical Review* 32 (Oct. 1955): 451–82.

Watson, Alan D. *Society in Colonial North Carolina*. Raleigh: North Carolina Department of Cultural Resources, 1996.

Watson, Alan D., with Eva C. Latham and Patricia M. Samford. *Bath: The First Town in North Carolina*. Raleigh: North Carolina Office of Archives and History, 2005.

Wetmore, Ruth Y. "The Role of the Indian in North Carolina History." *North Carolina Historical Review* 56 (Apr. 1979): 162–76.

White, Richard. *The Middle Ground: Indians, Empires, and Republics in the Great Lakes Region, 1650–1815*. New York: Cambridge Univ. Press, 1991.

Wood, Peter H. "The Changing Population of the Colonial South: An Overview by Race and Region, 1685–1790." In *Powhatan's Mantle: Indians in the Colonial Southeast*, edited by Peter H. Wood, Gregory

A. Waselkov, and M. Thomas Hatley, 35–103. Lincoln: Univ. of Nebraska Press, 1989.

————. *Tuscarora Roots: An Historical Report regarding the Relation of the Hatteras Tuscarora Tribe of Robeson County, North Carolina, to the Original Tuscarora Indian Tribe*. University Libraries, Digital Collections Repository, Univ. of North Carolina, Durham, 1992.

Wood, Peter H., Gregory A. Waselkov, and M. Thomas Hatley, eds., *Powhatan's Mantle: Indians in the Colonial Southeast*. Lincoln: Univ. of Nebraska Press, 1989.

Woodard, Buck. "'Take Up the Hatchet . . . and Go to War with Us': The Tuscarora of Indian Woods during the French and Indian War." Paper presented at the Three Hundred Years of Indian Woods, 1717–2017, Tercentenary Conference, Oct. 7–9, 2017, Hope Plantation, Windsor, NC.

Wright, J. Leitch. *The Only Land They Knew: The Tragic Story of the American Indians in the Old South*. New York: Free Press, 1981.

Zipf, Karin L. *Labor of Innocents: Forced Apprenticeship in North Carolina, 1715–1919*. Baton Rouge: Louisiana State Univ. Press, 2005.

Index

David La Vere is professor of Native American history at the University of North Carolina Wilmington and author of *The Tuscarora War: Indians, Settlers, and the Fight for the Carolina Colonies* (2013), among other books.

Milton Keynes UK
Ingram Content Group UK Ltd.
UKHW010900070424
440652UK00003B/24

9 780815 638360